Christian Education
and the Emerging Church

Christian Education and the Emerging Church

Postmodern Faith Formation

WENDI SARGEANT

PICKWICK *Publications* · Eugene, Oregon

CHRISTIAN EDUCATION AND THE EMERGING CHURCH
Postmodern Faith Formation

Pickwick Publications
An Imprint of Wipf and Stock Publishers
199 W. 8th Ave., Suite 3
Eugene, OR 97401

www.wipfandstock.com

ISBN 13: 978–1-4982–0430-9

Cataloging-in-Publication data:

Sargeant, Wendi

Christian education and the emerging church : postmodern faith formation / Wendi Sargeant.

xiv + 222 p. ; 23 cm. —Includes bibliographical references and index(es).

ISBN 13: 978–1-4982–0430-9

1. Christian education. 2. Spiritual formation. 3. Emerging church movement. I. Title.

BV1464 S37 2015

Manufactured in the U.S.A.   07/24/2015

Contents

List of Tables | vi

Acknowledgments | vii

Introduction | xi

Chapter 1
A Note on the Practical Theology Approach | 1

Chapter 2
The Western Christian Church in a Postmodern Context | 6

Chapter 3
Insights from the Emerging Church | 29

Chapter 4
Key Influences on the Development of Christian Education | 66

Chapter 5
The Current Crisis of Christian Education | 95

Chapter 6
An Interpretive Framework | 125

Chapter 7
The Appropriate Place of Christian Education in the Life of the Church:
At the Intersection of Doxa and Dogma | 138

Chapter 8
Transformed Action in Christian Education:
A Teaching and Learning Matrix | 171

Conclusion | 203

Bibliography | 207

Index | 221

Tables

Table 1   Gathering, with Key Questions for Reflection—In Liturgy and In Life | 179

Table 2   Praise and Thanksgiving, with Key Questions for Reflection—In Liturgy and In Life | 180

Table 3   Prayer of Confession and Declaration of Forgiveness and Assurance, with Key Questions for Reflection—In Liturgy and In Life | 182

Table 4   Hearing God's Word, with Key Questions for Reflection—In Liturgy and In Life | 184

Table 5   Eucharist and Baptism, with Key Questions for Reflection—In Liturgy and In Life | 186

Table 6   Responding, with Key Questions for Reflection—In Liturgy and In Life | 187

Table 7   Benediction, Blessing, Being Sent Out to Worship in the World, with Key Questions for Reflection—In Liturgy and In Life | 187

Table 8A   Key Question—What Is the Practice of Worship? | 188

Table 8B   Key Question—What Is the Worship Environment? | 190

Table 8C   Key Question—How Do We Enter into Worship? | 191

Table 8D   Key Question—What Do We Bring to Worship? 1. Our Culture of Consumerism | 193

Table 8E   Key Question—What Is Hospitality and Why Is It So Important? | 195

Table 8F   Key Question—What Is Forgiveness? | 196

Table 8G   Key Question—What Is Hermeneutics? | 198

Acknowledgments

MY GRATEFUL THANKS GOES to Shirley Sargeant for editorial advice and proof reading, to the Librarians at Trinity College Queensland for their patience and skill, and to my constant inspiration, Murray Fysh.

Introduction

THIS BOOK EXPLORES THE potential for Christian education to find (or in
fact, re-find) its essential place in the life of the Christian community. By
observing the rise and evolution of the Emerging Church movement as both
a response to its context in postmodernity, and an expression of contemporary Christian faith, we will challenge Christian education to emerge as a
postmodern reality.

The field of Christian education is concerned with the formation, nurture and development of Christian faith in individuals and communities.
Definitions for Christian education will be discussed in further depth later,
but as a starting point it will be sufficient to say that Christian education
involves intentional guidance of the growth of people in Christian faith and
ethos.

The Emerging Church describes a movement that represents a variety
of attempts by the Christian church to express its faith in current, predominantly Western, culture. The term Emerging Church has been used variously to depict a wide assortment of expressions of the Christian practice.
In this book, the Emerging Church refers to the specifically new forms of
church life arising from the Modern church of the twentieth and twenty-
first centuries.

This so-called "New Paradigm," known as the Emerging Church, has
some insights to share with the Western mainline church about how to
continue to form and pass on Christian faith to present and future generations. This diverse, international and growing movement represents a
postmodern Christian response to the issues around being the church in
a world that is *past-Modern* but may not have arrived yet at the next fully
fledged era. It is often observed that contemporary Western society is in a
transitional time in human history. In chapter 2 the term "transmodern"
is borrowed, to describe this current phase of Western human existence. It
seems that many in the Western mainline church continue to respond to

the world in ways that have been born out of Modernist aligned thinking and worldviews. These worldviews sometimes do not seem to connect with the current ever-changing context. In part, this has happened because the ways of relating to the world around us have altered so dramatically, and so very quickly over the last century, that many people have not been able to respond appropriately or adequately, other than by way of lamenting what is past and clinging to the old ways.

The situation the Western church finds itself in today reflects this lamenting. The disquiet surrounds news of declining church attendances, an aging church membership, the closing down of some church congregations and buildings, fewer candidates for ministry training, and a growing cynicism about church leadership and the church as an institution generally. It is easy to be pessimistic about the future of the church.

A number of societal commentators (both formal and living-room!) advocate the termination of the entire Christian project. They would say that the church has run its course and should be abandoned. To someone who values God's faithfulness and what the church still has to offer, however, this transition time of cultural shift could be an opportunity rather than a time of despairing demise. As an ordained Minister of a mainline Protestant Christian denomination, it seems futile, either to continue rearranging the deck chairs on a sinking ship, or to sit down happily on the deckchairs, relax and go down with the vessel! But where to from here?

The Emerging Church, with creative enthusiasm and vigour, brashness, and at times, blatant arrogance, appears to be somewhat of a sign of hope on the ecclesiastical horizon. Of course, the one holy catholic and apostolic church of God is, in many senses, always emerging. As the church follows the leading of Jesus Christ by God's life-giving Holy Spirit, it continues to evolve as communities of people who tell the story of Jesus. The Emerging Church is not separate from the one holy catholic and apostolic church. This international emerging movement is "a fresh understanding of what the church can be in the midst of this tension between the old and the new."[1] To continue the nautical imagery, the surfacing of the Emerging Church movement at the end of the twentieth century seems like something tangible to keep hope afloat, to swim towards, or at least a speck of light on the horizon of the ecclesial sea.

In examining the postmodern response that the Emerging Church movement represents, the aim is to use these insights to assist the whole church, especially in the area of Christian education. To this end, this book has been structured using a practical theology methodology, which is more

---

1. Taylor, *Out Of Bounds Church?* 11.

fully outlined in the first chapter, *A Note on the Practical Theology Approach*. This process begins with some analysis of the current situation, which occurs in chapter 2, *The Western Christian Church In A Postmodern Context*. Here, relevant aspects of the current situation in contemporary Western society are described, along with the Christian church's place within this context. These aspects of contemporary culture will be examined historically, and analysed from philosophical, sociological and theological perspectives.

This historical and contemporary study helps to engender the pivotal question for the current context. The pivotal question, flowing from a concern about the place of the Christian church in Western society and its ability to regenerate, continue and pass on its faith becomes, *What is an adequate theological understanding of the nature of the church?* A theological discussion on this matter follows, offering a modicum of balance to the present understanding of the church and its relationship with Jesus Christ. At this point, we will briefly look at pertinent parts of the doctrine of the Uniting Church in Australia, as a postmodern ecclesiastical attempt to construct and become a mainline church in a postmodern context. Some other international Christian responses to postmodernity will also be addressed. These considerations will be undertaken in order to clarify what we mean by "Emerging Church."

Chapter 3 discusses the Emerging Church as it presents itself in its literature and other forms of communication. The works of major Emerging Church writers and practitioners will be referred to and considered under several headings, namely, *What is the Emerging Church?*, *How Did the Emerging Church Begin?*, *Emerging Themes*, *Links to Established Mainstream Denominations*, *Blogs and Other Net-based Approaches and Virtual Communities*; *Models of Congregational/Community Life*; *Developing Emerging Theology*; *Critiques of the Emerging Church*; and *Christian Education in the Emerging Church*.

In chapter 4 we begin to clarify what is meant by Christian education, as a further step in analysing the current context. The concept of Christian education as it *has* been understood will be outlined. The discussion will take place around descriptive topics, including *The Earliest Emergence of Christian Education*; *The Influence of Ancient Greek Educational Philosophy*; *The Hebrew Heritage*; *The Catechumenate*; *Monasticism*; and *A Postmodern Parallel: the New Monasticism of the Emerging Church*. The issue of the Sunday School movement as a key Modernist approach to Christian education will also be raised and addressed. This will form the foundation for the argument that Christian education most appropriately occurs within the context of the worshipping Christian community, and not separated from its doxological life. This contention is at the heart of the ensuing discussion.

This then leads into chapter 5, where we examine the current crisis of Christian education and its loss of theological place in the life of the church. In this chapter I will briefly analyse the findings of two research studies into Christian education, one in the United States of America, and a similar study conducted in Australia. Both these studies indicate that Christian education in Western protestant congregations is generally suffering from biblical and liturgical illiteracy, a lack of organising frameworks and models, and un-skilled leadership. I contend that this stems from using outdated, modernist educational approaches that no longer engage postmodern learners, or pre-pare them for their world. These approaches have also separated Christian worship from Christian formation. The outcome of all of this has been a serious loss of capacity, in both individuals and the Christian community as a whole, to pass on the Christian faith, to compellingly tell and genuinely embody the Christian Story.

The styles and outcomes for Christian education that I will be propos-ing will then be clarified, as a result of the examination of insights from the Emerging Church. This will focus on the context, with an analysis that the Christian worshipping community is the most appropriate context for Christian formation and discipleship. A discussion of the nature of Chris-tian knowledge and epistemology will help to introduce my interpretive framework for Christian education, in chapter 6. A fresh interpretive frame-work is central to any consideration of Christian education in a cultural context that has moved beyond Modernity. Christian education, in this interpretive framework, is understood as an ongoing process of action and reflection on teaching, learning and living the Christian story in order to grasp Christian ethos. The framework is designed to be set in the context of the worshipping community, which means identifying of the significance of the members of the worshipping community as key teachers and learners in forming Christian ethos.

In chapter 7 Christian education is posited theologically, as an inter-section of doxology and doctrine. This will entail a theological study of the natures and purposes of doctrine and doxology, where their inseparability will become clear. They are intersected in and by Christian education, as interpreted above. I assert that this is the rightful place of Christian edu-cation for the life of the church and especially for the Emerging Church movement. In a methodological sense, this chapter represents the dialogue with Scripture and theological Tradition advocated in the mutual critical correlational method.

Opportunities for transformed action are offered in chapter 8. Here, you will find the genesis of a matrix of worship-based *processes of action and reflection on teaching, learning and living the Christian story in order to grasp*

Christian ethos. Following insights gained from the Emerging Church, the particular elements of Christian ethos that are focussed upon are practices that nurture, develop and teach worship of God as theologically informing all the activities of everyday life.

Chapter 1

A Note on the Practical Theology Approach

THE PARADIGM OF PRACTICAL theology provides the structure and methodological considerations for this book.[1] Practical theology involves theological reflection on a contemporary issue or practice in dialogue with contemporary experience and understanding, to produce a transformed action or practice. This is known as a hermeneutical spiral.[2] The departure point of this hermeneutical spiral is an issue which is raised in practice. This leads to theology's mutual critical correlation[3] with human sciences such as educational theory, sociology and psychology, which in turn gives birth to transformed action and fresh theologies. David Tracy's work on method has been important in this regard for practical theologians. According to Tracy:

> There is only one demand—the properly theological demand— that wherever and whoever the practical theologian is, he or she is bound by the very nature of the enterprise as theological to show how one interprets the present situation and how these

---

1. These considerations are variously described by Browning, *Practical Theology*; Browning, *Fundamental Practical Theology*; Swinton and Mowat, *Practical Theology*; Ballard and Pritchard, *Practical Theology in Action*; Forrester, *Truthful Action*; Volf and Bass, *Practicing Theology*; Veling, *Practical Theology*; Anderson *The Shape of Practical Theology*; Graham, et al., *Theological Reflection*; and Darragh, "Practice of Practical Theology."

2. Browning, *Fundamental Practical Theology*; Darragh, "Practice of Practical Theology."

3. Tracy, *Blessed Rage*; Tracy, "Foundations of Practical Theology"; Browning, *Religious Ethics and Pastoral Care*.

1

two interpretations correlate: either as identities of meaning, analogies, or radical non-identities.[4]

This dialectical movement offers the possibility of challenge and critique to and from theology by the world of human action and experience.[5] This movement flows in both directions, in a dialogue which is mutually confronting, clarifying and has as its aim, genuinely authentic making of meaning.

The hermeneutic approach invites a "merging of horizons"[6] as an ongoing process of construction, deconstruction and reconstruction of data, creating transformed theology for new contexts. This merging of horizons happens as conversation between various texts or data sources enables further interpretation. Practical theological process invites not merely the application of a body of propositional theory,[7] but the ongoing ability for Christians to choose and create authentic practice.

In this book, two critical dialogues will be outlined. The first dialogue that is detailed occurs between the ideas and practices of the Emerging Church, and the field of Christian education. This discussion is set out in order to establish the actual practice of the Emerging Church, through its literature, with regard to Christian education. The second dialogue that is outlined occurs between both Christian education and Western protestant ecclesial practice on the one hand, and secular philosophy on the other. The mutual critical correlation method will be used only in this second dialogue, as this discussion represents an ongoing opportunity to create and develop authentic practice.

The resources for these dialogues will include a review and analysis of literature concerning the Emerging Church. The amount of literature has grown considerably in recent years, with contributions developing greater theological rigor over time. This will be discussed further in later chapters. Most Emerging Church authors are also practitioners. Practical theology methodology thus engages well with much of their work.

Following a practical theology research framework, an analysis of the current context and its antecedents will be the departure point, taking the form of a survey of social, historical and philosophical factors that have been influential in the development of occidental postmodern understandings in society. This will provide a context and foundation for examining the attitudes, theology and practices evident in the Emerging Church.

4. Tracy, *Blessed Rage*, 20.

5. Swinton and Mowat, *Practical Theology*, 136.

6. Ibid. Also Browning, *Fundamental Practical Theology*, 52.

7. Graham, "Practical Theology," 106.

These insights will be examined further as possible directions for the field of Christian education. The way in which Christian education will be interpreted here, is framed as an ongoing process involving the whole Christian worshipping community of teaching, learning, and living the Christian story in order to grasp Christian ethos. The development of the Christian worshiping community as the Christian teaching and learning community will then be considered, based on some of the insights gained by the research into the priorities and practices of the Emerging Church. This will then lead to the creation of several concrete strategies and resources adding "flesh to the bones" of the interpretive framework. My aim is to use and adapt certain theological perspectives and concrete practices developed by leaders in the Emerging Church movement to bring fresh insights to the task of implementing effective Christian education in a postmodern Western Protestant context.

Various questions about the Emerging Church and Christian education will be explored. These questions grow out of critical reflection on Western culture, the Church, past, present and future, and on Christian education as part of it. Consideration and critical reflection on these questions will form a platform from which to discover and construct new understandings, through mutually critical dialogue between what Don Browning calls "interpretations of the Christian message and interpretations of contemporary cultural experiences and practices."[8] Some of these questions include: What are some prominent ways in which Western Protestantism has related to contemporary society? What is the Emerging Church? How has Christian education developed in recent times, and what are its tasks into the future?

In order that these questions and other issues that arise are reflected upon systematically, theologically and critically, Don Browning's three "movements of fundamental practical theology"[9] will be used. These movements are firstly *descriptive theology*, where relevant contemporary religious and cultural practices are described in order to clarify and hone the practical questions. An exploration of Emerging Church literature will offer perspectives, historically, theologically, sociologically, politically and ecclesiastically, for the growing enthusiasm for finding new ways of being Church. These insights will speak into a regenerated understanding of Christian education. This step in the process will utilize a mutually critical

8. Browning, *Fundamental Practical Theology*, 46.
9. Ibid., 47–54.

correlation approach based on the work of Tracy,[10] Browning,[11] Mudge and Poling,[12] and Ballard and Pritchard.[13]

The second of Browning's three movements is *historical theology*, which confronts the "scene" set in the first movement with the central normative texts of Christianity. Browning asks, "What do the normative texts that are already part of our effective history *really* imply for our *praxis* when they are confronted as honestly as possible?"[14] This is intended to create a hermeneutical dialogue within this research. This dialogue will generate a flow into the third of Browning's movements—namely *systematic theology*. Here, a vision for future action can begin to be formed by fusing the vision of contemporary practices with the insights offered by normative Christian texts. Systematic theology provides an orderly, coherent outline of general themes, values, and principles that undergird the gospel. Systematic theology's practical task is to show how these general gospel themes correlate with the questions generated by the practice under consideration.

This movement seeks to answer two key questions. The first is: What new set of meanings emerges through this process of bringing the fundamental values and principles of the gospel to bear on the questions generated by the practice under investigation? The second question is: What rational justification can be offered for this set of meanings? That is, systematic theology has the responsibility of testing philosophically the practical claims of the Christian faith.

A systematic approach will structure the practical theological reflection design.[15] This will also guide ethical considerations by addressing basic theological questions in the light of contemporary understandings and practice. Essentially, this is the analysis phase of the research, centred on theological reflection, and leading to the final phase which is transformed *praxis*—value-committed action.[16] This comes in the form of a matrix which includes stimulus questions and other activities to facilitate transformed action. As we have already noted, practical theology is not a kind of applied theology in which "systematic and historical theology provide norms for

---

10. Tracy, *Blessed Rage*.

11. Browning, *Practical Theology*.

12. Mudge and Poling, *Formation and Reflection*.

13. Ballard and Pritchard, *Practical Theology in Action*.

14. Browning, *Practical Theology*, 49.

15. Killen and de Beer, *Art of Theological Reflection*, 29.

16. Groome, *Christian Religious Education*; Groome, *Sharing Faith*; Graham, et al., *Theological Reflection*.

pastoral care or ethics. Rather, here, practice is both the origin and the end of theological reflection."[17]

Analysis of the gathered data will attempt to isolate patterns of present *praxis* which should be addressed as part of the development of future value-committed action. The use of the questions of systematic theology, located within a practical theology paradigm, is an attempt to "search the Christian tradition for the common themes that will address these broadly practical and existential questions."[18]

In this type of methodology, local contextual issues are bound to arise at this stage. These will be taken into consideration as they pertain to more universally applicable themes and patterns. In a practical theology style of research, this becomes the task of systematic theology.

Next, the research will seek a contemporary application[19] that could transform future planning by Emerging churches, especially in the realm of Christian education—our original context. In this way, the hermeneutical spiral, implicit in practical theological methodology, continues—emerging and evolving new possibilities for the life of the Church. In this book, the reconstruction phase will see the development of a systematic matrix of teaching and learning experience options designed to offer a new approach for future practice in Christian education. This provides the reader with opportunities to be involved in and interact with this transformed practice.

---

17. Graham, et al., *Theological Reflection*, 170.

18. Browning, *Fundamental Practical Theology*, 53.

19. Darragh, "Decisions and Hazards," 127.

Chapter 2

The Western Christian Church in a Postmodern Context

THE CONTEXT OF THE Western Christian church at the beginning of the third millennium is varied to say the least. Occidental culture of the late twentieth century and the early twenty-first century has often been described as "postmodern." The definitions of postmodern are also many and varied, which aligns with postmodern understanding itself. In a general sense, postmodernism is concerned with a post World War II reaction against the structures, mass consumption and universal truths of modernity.

In order to critically examine some of the defining characteristics of postmodernity, the influence it has had on the church generally, and on the Emerging Church in particular, it is essential to look at some historical antecedents. The Enlightenment, which sparked the birth of modernity, was itself ignited by a Renaissance re-emergence of classical philosophical and artistic enquiry. Philosopher Immanuel Kant (1724–1804) gives a deceptively simple answer to the question of enlightenment, which in many ways sums up the entire Enlightenment project:

> *Enlightenment is man's emergence from his self-incurred immaturity. Immaturity* is the inability to use one's own understanding without the guidance of another. This immaturity is *self-incurred* if its cause is not lack of understanding, but lack of resolution and courage to use it without the guidance of another. The motto of enlightenment is therefore: Sapere aude! [Dare to be wise!] Have courage to use your *own* understanding![1]

1. Kant, *An Answer*, 1 (italics original).

6

Here Kant is critiquing the elitist, socially regimented society (and particularly the church) of his time. Kant criticized this social order for often rigidly opposing freedom of individual thought, and thus restricting intellectual growth and development. He described enlightenment as humanity's "emergence from . . . self-incurred immaturity,"[2] and focussed on critiquing religious naïvety above all, describing this as "the most pernicious and dishonourable variety [of immaturity] of all."[3] Kant saw his philosophical quest as searching for the principles of the physical universe and the "moral universe within," with the objective of drawing together scientific rationalism and the romantic concern for "the self."

The theme of the creative thinking "self" began to be pervasive in romanticism. The church had just experienced a period of great revival starting in Europe and rapidly moving beyond. Reflected in the romantic thinking of the time, there was growing interest in the notion of personal piety. The religious revival, known as "the Great Awakening," had also called for major social and moral reforms. The Great Awakening which encompassed, among other developments, the founding of the Methodist Church in Britain and North America, was to have lasting implications socially, geopolitically and ecclesiastically.

The seventeenth- and eighteenth-century Enlightenment was an era of progress in science and philosophy, where earlier beliefs and methods were questioned and discarded in line with the new developments of an increasingly industrial age. Philosophical questions about God, humanity, knowledge and reality had come to the fore in the thinking of French philosopher and mathematician, René Descartes (1596–1650). Descartes sought to show that the human ability to question, doubt and reason proves its independent existence, hence the deductive reasoning surrounding his renowned formula, *cogito ergo sum*: "I think therefore I am." Cartesian thought underpinned the later development of the philosophical and epistemological movements of empiricism, positivism and foundationalism, which we will discuss later. The "notion" of the existence of God, that cannot be proved or scientifically verified, could thus be disputed, questioned and certainly doubted.

The Enlightenment's newborn scientific sagacity regarding the power of the human mind was further reinforced by the technological advances of nineteenth- and twentieth-century modernity. The modernist belief in humankind's ability to understand and dominate all things endowed a demigod-like status on human achievement. It was believed that scientific

2. Ibid., 9.
3. Ibid., 10.

progress would lead to humanity gaining control over virtually every area of life.

Modernity heralded new technologies on a mass scale for mass consumption.[4] Mass transport, mass media, and mass production were major hallmarks of modernity. In real terms this meant innovations such as automobiles, aeroplanes and fast trains which led to new thinking in terms of movement, time and space. This then generated the need for the exploration of new sources of power and energy, which in turn facilitated advances in the production of oil and petroleum, electricity and nuclear power.

After the Great Depression, the Holocaust, the desolation of the Second World War and the fear of global annihilation rife during the Cold War, there was growing disillusionment with the promise of modernity. This was evidenced in the rise of anti-war and anti-establishment movements into the 1960s and 1970s. A new post-modern era was emerging.

The term "postmodern" is commonly used to describe the nature of many aspects of society since the 1950s[5] and (especially since the 1980s) including philosophy, theology, literature, economics, architecture and the arts. The term actually originated as far back as 1870 with the period of art history given the title, "Post-Impressionism." As an art movement, Post-Impressionism was seen in some senses as attempting to counter and critique Modern forms of technology such as photography, which produced mass identical images relatively easily and quickly. Subsequent art schools more fully embraced Modernism and then subsequently caricatured it, until well after World War II. By the 1970s, however, postmodern art was recognised as a discrete movement within the art world. A distinguishing feature of postmodernism, that an examination of the arts illustrates, is its constant disillusionment with and subsequent attack on the ideals of post-Enlightenment Modernism.

In his *The Postmodern Condition: A Report on Knowledge*, French philosopher, Jean-François Lyotard discusses postmodernism as a critique of the mechanistic nature of modernism. He argues that scientific, technological and artistic knowledge has undergone a momentous change of status since the nineteenth century, and even more so from the first half of the twentieth century.

Using the avant-garde art world as a means for criticism of Modernity, Lyotard scathingly disparages modern art, describing it as devoting "its little technical expertise . . . to present the fact that the unpresentable exists. To make visible that there is something which can be conceived and which

---

4. Rodrigues and Garratt, *Introducing Modernism*, 16.

5. Inbody, "Postmodernism," 524.

can neither be seen nor made visible: this is what is at stake in modern painting."[6] Lyotard discusses Modern art's attempts to portray "the sublime" as that which is able to be conceived of, but not in our power to represent. A pertinent example of the sublime is the infinite or divine. In Modern thinking, the way to present the sublime is by abstraction. Lyotard suggests that the attempt by Russian artist, Kasimir Malevitch to do this in 1915, by painting a white square onto a white background, "will enable us to see only by making it impossible to see; it will please only by causing pain."

The concept of *abstraction* gives an insight into modernity's relationship with the notion of God, also illustrating something of a Kantian phenomenology, synthesising empiricism and rationalism. Enlightenment philosophy had been dominated by two main epistemological positions: empiricism, which views knowledge as the product of sensory perception, and rationalism, which views knowledge as the product of reasoned thought. According to Kant, knowledge results from the organisation of perceptual information by means of instinctive cognitive structures, which he calls "categories."[7] Categories include space, time, objects, and causality. Kant's epistemology acknowledges the subjectivity of basic concepts, like space and time, drawing these *phenomena* together with the impossibility of reaching genuinely objective representations of the *noumenon* or essence of things. The *a priori* categories however, remain static or given. Thus, Kant is arguing that reason is the means by which the phenomena of experience are translated into understanding.

As we have seen, this view formed the basis of a wider philosophy of Modernity. To the Modernist rational mind, if God could be understood and for that matter portrayed, it would be by means of *abstraction*. Through a process of abstraction, which is a rational "seeing into" or insight, it is possible to achieve fundamental insights into reality. In this conception, these insights in turn can lead to further truths.[8] Following this logic, the power of reason to penetrate the transcendent realm of God could thus be called into question.

The art movements which embodied the idea of abstract art, Abstraction and later Cubism, Bauhaus, Futurism, and Constructivism, also embraced an optimistic belief in abstraction's role for all of life. These movements advocated the ability of artists to reproduce a mechanistic aesthetic that was universally modern, transcending any cultural style.[9] This

6. Lyotard, *Postmodern Condition*, 78.

7. Heylighen, "Epistemology."

8. Alfino, "First Phenomenologist."

9. Appignanesi, et al., *Introducing Postmodernism*, 27.

International style (which still architecturally dominates many contemporary cityscapes) is distinguished by buildings which are machine-like, with undecorated flat surfaces and mass-produced, repetitive concrete veneers. One protagonist of this movement, Walter Gropius, in his 1919 *Bauhaus Manifesto*, enthuses:

> Together let us desire, conceive and create the new building of the future. It will combine architecture, sculpture and painting in one unity, a single form, and which will one day rise towards heaven from the hands of a million workers like the crystalline symbol of a new and coming faith.[10]

There are clear overtones here of the typical modern utopian promises of mechanistic and political progress, universality and human achievement. The First World War had devastatingly influenced Gropius and the Bauhaus movement, which had originated in the Weimar Republic, and the movement was banned by the Nazis in 1933.[11]

The Latin origin of the word "modern" (*modo*) literally means "just now." So "postmodern" indicates "after just now." Lyotard discusses this curious logic, again using references to art movements:

> What, then, is the postmodern? What place does it or does it not occupy in the vertiginous work of the questions hurled at the rules of image and narration? It is undoubtedly a part of the modern. All that has been received, if only yesterday. . .must be suspected. What space does Cézanne challenge? The Impressionists.' What object do Picasso and Braque attack? Cézanne's. What presupposition does Duchamp break with in 1912? That which says one must make a painting, be it cubist. And Buren questions the other presupposition which he believes had survived untouched by the work of Duchamp: the place of presentation of the work. In an amazing acceleration, the generations precipitate themselves. A work can become modern only if it is first postmodern. Postmodernism thus understood is not modernism at its end but in the nascent state, and this state is constant.[12]

Postmodernism, it seems, is not merely the philosophical era following modernity or a continuation of the aggrieved promises of modernity. As a critical corrective to modernity, postmodernism, according to practical

10. Gropius, "Bauhaus Manifesto," 124.

11. Ibid.

12. Lyotard, *Postmodern Condition*, 79.

theologian, Elaine Graham, "exposes the hubris of Enlightenment optimism, tempers the excesses of literalism, objectivism and humanism, and retrieves from the margins the repressed and hidden 'Others' of Western modernity."[13] There is a political and social intentionality about the tasks of postmodernism. With the demise of grand narratives, the voice of local narratives may be liberated and more fully heard. The insights of those who have been sidelined by traditional Western capitalism, for example, may be more fully respected.[14]

It is evident that postmodernism eludes a single, concrete definition. There are, however, a number of characteristics of this era and the world-view that it generates that can be quite clearly identified. These include the decline of Western cultural dominance, the collapse of universally accepted truths or grand meta-narratives, the emergence of the intellectual market place with its emphasis on information rather than knowledge, and the concept and action of deconstruction.[15] Monumental advances in information technology have led to a delegitimizing of knowledge, the equating of information with knowledge, and the granting of pre-eminence to information over knowledge.[16]

The implications of all of this for the church and Christian education are indeed challenging. The concept of Christian knowledge logically lies close to the heart of Christian education. Philosophically, we have briefly touched on how the rationalism of the Kantian approach to knowledge influenced the Enlightenment world-view as it grew into modernity. Derivatives of this overarching Kantian understanding also ensued as scientific advances proliferated. Positivism further extended and refined the thought of Descartes, Kant and that of British Empiricism. Broadly speaking, Positivism argues that the scientific method is the only ultimate means of obtaining knowledge.[17] In other words, sense-experience is the foundational element and only source of knowledge. All metaphysical speculation and abstract theorising are rejected in this approach. The epistemological methodology of Foundationalism[18] followed on from this, giving rise to and enhancing an acceptance of and even belief in the absolute truth claims and the verifiability of science, technology and human progress, generally. Emerging Church proponent Tony Jones, comments on the developments

---

13. Graham, "Practical Theology," 107.

14. For more analysis on this topic see Rieger, *God and the Excluded*.

15. Adams, "Toward a Theological Understanding," 418.

16. Sajjadi, "Religious Education," 185.

17. Vesey and Foulkes, *Collins Dictionary of Philosophy*, 229.

18. Pence, *Dictionary of Common Philosophical Terms*, 23.

of the Modern era: "The universe was quantified into laws of physics (*laws*, not theories), the celestial realm was figured out, and it no longer needed a God turning a crank to keep it moving."[19]

Friedrich Nietzsche (1844–1900) made the well-known statement, "God is dead," which reflected Western society's reliance on Modern science and increasing secularization at this time. For Nietzsche, this assertion ultimately led to perspectivism, nihilism and Deconstructionism—a movement central to postmodernism. Patently anti-Christian, he described the "modern spirit" thus: "One lives for today, one lives very fast—one lives very irresponsibly: it is precisely this which one calls 'freedom.'"[20] Later German philosopher Martin Heidegger, commenting on Nietzsche's proposition, noted, "If God as the suprasensory ground and goal of all reality is dead, if the suprasensory world of the Ideas has suffered the loss of its obligatory and above all its vitalizing and upbuilding power, then nothing more remains to which man can cling and by which he can orient himself."[21]

Following the course of Nietzsche's perspectivism resulted in the loss of any universal perspective, and along with it any coherent form of objective truth, including even scientific truth.[22] He contended that an unending variety of diverse and fluid perspectives would be all that would remain. Ultimately this thinking rebounded on itself in truly postmodern fashion, with the realisation that this too is just one perspective. Contemporary philosopher, John Caputo, aptly concludes:

> Enlightenment secularism, the objectivist reduction of religion to something other than itself—say, to a distorted desire for one's mommy, or a way to keep the ruling authorities in power—is one more story told by people with historically limited imaginations, with contingent conceptions of reason and history, of economics and labor, of nature and human nature, of desire, sexuality, and women, and of God, religion, and faith.[23]

Postmodernism, then, embraces diversity, difference, local stories as opposed to global uniformity. The designer of the popular *Timeation* running shoe for the Reebok company in the United States, John Maeda, has also created a best-selling shoe that individuals design themselves, for their own needs and tastes, and is then manufactured for them.[24] Alongside that,

19. Jones, *Postmodern Youth Ministry*, 19.
20. Nietzsche, *Twilight of the Idols*, 105.
21. Heidegger, "Word of Nietzsche," 61.
22. Caputo, *On Religion*, 59.
23. Ibid., 60.
24. Maeda, *Art Is Everything*.

George Ritzer's *McDonaldization of Society*[25] is more relevant now than when it was written in 1993. Ritzer critiques the imperialism of the American fast food chain McDonald's, known all over the world for its standard appearance, work practices and menu. The company strives to replicate the same experience of US culture wherever one may be, including the military bases in Iraq and Afghanistan. This kind of homogenous branding is as vital to many global corporations as it is to image-conscious postmoderns. At the same time, the Japanese originated art design franchise, Muji, only produces cutting-edge articles which display no trademark, signature or brand at all. The focus is on the product.[26] In a culture where there are no universal truths, every perspective holds equal value and status.

What becomes predominantly clear is that postmodernism is a way of recognizing that the Western world is in a period of transition. The church, of course, has not been immune to this shift. The movement is principally a progression from relative stability and uniformity to a sense of rapid change and marked uncertainty. Robert Webber, in his *Ancient-Future Faith: Rethinking Evangelicalism for a Postmodern World*, states poetically:

> Indications of a postmodern worldview suggest that mystery, with its emphasis on complexity and ambiguity, community, with its emphasis on the interrelation of all things, and symbolic forms of communication, with an emphasis on the visual, are all central to the new way of thinking.[27]

Clearly this understanding has influenced the church and in many ways has encouraged the development of the Emerging Church movement, as we shall investigate more fully in the next chapter.

THE PIVOTAL QUESTION FOR THE CONTEXT: WHAT IS THE PRESENT CRISIS?

A story will begin to illustrate what is at stake here:

A busload of unruly nine-year-olds pulled up in the centre of Brisbane city—King George Square. I was the teacher in charge of the Year 4 school excursion. We all tumbled out and made our way down to examine the variety of architectural styles of Brisbane buildings. Two types of building were to be viewed at this stop. The first was the City Hall, an icon of postcards and tourist literature. The second, across the Square, was the Albert Street Uniting

25. Ritzer, *McDonaldization of Society*.

26. Maeda, *Art is Everything*.

27. Webber, *Ancient-Future Faith*, 35.

Church, centre for weddings and typically "church-like" with its post-Gothic arches and steeple. I explained about City Hall and then asked the children to turn around and look at the next building.

"Wow! What's that?" one voice cried.

"That's a church," I remained focussed, suspecting a smart-alec.

"What's a church?" the same voice responded.

Of course there were churches in this child's outer-western suburb. They do not resemble the opulent Christmas card picture of ecclesiastical architecture that Albert Street represents, but they do exist. The question, *What is a church?* also exists.

The *physical* architecture of churches is not our concern here. Our real area of interest is the *spiritual* architecture of the contemporary church, and how the church is perceived in Western postmodern culture.

Contemporary Australian society, as part of a wider movement across the Western world, is experiencing change at a perplexingly rapid and phenomenal rate. Australian sociologist Hugh Mackay stated over twenty years ago that Australians were living "through an age of re-definition."[28] Every area of life has been affected by the post World War II growth in technology and the subsequent ongoing social and structural changes this has brought about.

Monash University's Gary Bouma labels current Australian society as "post-family, . . . post-patriarchal . . . and characterized by different forms of social cohesion and social capital."[29] Peter Corney, Director of the Institute for Contemporary Christian Leadership in Victoria, notes that "at every level of life major change is taking place. The way we eat, bank, shop, work, communicate, the roles of men and women, are all being reshaped."[30] These changes in social structure shift the context for the expression of spirituality and the religious activities of its people.

Even a cursory glance at family life, media, education systems and information dissemination gives huge scope for discussion and the raising of issues for the institution that is the church. Rapid change often gives rise to a sense of uncertainty. What was once "the done thing" may no longer be accepted practice. People look for security, stillness and tranquillity. The search for something that remains the same often brings about a conservative clutching to the solidity of the past, whilst everything else in life is in perpetual motion.

28. Mackay, *Re-inventing Australia*, 1.

29. Bouma, *Australian Soul*, 122.

30. Corney, *Change and the Church*, 1.

In a spiritual sense, in recent years, this has led to a growth in religious fundamentalism, with attendance numbers in Pentecostal and some fundamentalist denominations on the increase.[31] As Hugh Mackay muses in his 2007 commentary, *Advance Australia . . . Where?*:

> Many mystics, theologians and psychologists would argue that *doubt* is both the engine and the essence of faith, since it's the doubts that cause you to take the initial leap of faith, and continuing doubts that sustain your faith. That helps explain the current re-emergence of interest in religion and other aspects of the inward journey: when a society is destabilised by change and gripped by uncertainty, religious consolations can be both appealing and comforting.[32]

According to Australian Bureau of Statistics reports, however, the mainstream Protestant denominations are generally in decline.[33] It would follow, then, that the question, *What is a church?* may not be being adequately answered by the so-called "Old Church."

Canadian Anglican priest and TV presenter Tom Harpur dramatically decries the decline of churches in the West in *The Emerging Christian Way*:

> Christianity today is in the grip of a crisis of monumental proportions. Nothing that has happened in the previous 2000 years of church history has come close to the present convulsion and increasing chaos that is shaking the church's deepest foundations, a predicament that will almost certainly only worsen to the point of threatening the very existence of the hundreds of kinds of churches around the globe. The future—if you project on a graph the current decline of the church in Europe and in North America—looks worse than bleak.[34]

It is this fear which has given rise to the recent rash of Christian book titles such as: *Making Sense of Church*,[35] *In the Ruins of the Church*,[36] *The*

---

31. Frame, *Losing My Religion*, 92, 93, 94.
32. Mackay, *Advance Australia*, 275.
33. Bouma, *Australian Soul*, 53.
34. Harpur, "New Creeds," 51–64.
35. Burke and Pepper, *Making Sense of Church*.
36. Reno, *In the Ruins*.

Church on the Other Side,[37] *Church Re-Imagined,*[38] and the confrontingly pointed *They Like Jesus But Not the Church.*[39]

In *Losing My Religion: Unbelief in Australia,*[40] author and Anglican Bishop Tom Frame discusses the characteristics of those who declare some form of religious affiliation as reported in the 2006 Australian Bureau of Statistics Census. Frame observes that the number of those who declare some form of religious affiliation is 69.46 percent in 2006, which represents a decrease from previous census figures. This number is comprised of 63.89 percent Christian and 5.57 percent other religions. "Christianity not further defined" was the largest growing Christian category, according to this census.[41] Frame quotes researcher Philip Hughes's conclusion that "there are increasingly numbers of people in Australian society who want to identify themselves as Christian but do not want to identify with a particular denomination. A significant part of the movement is a rejection of Christian institutions rather than a rejection of Christianity itself."[42] All these writers and many others are essentially asking the same question: *What is Church, past, present and future?*

WHAT IS CHURCH?

In the context of the scope of this book, this question cannot be given the treatment it requires or deserves, and will be covered summarily at best. However, some exploration is essential to forming an understanding of the current context of Western Christianity.

In considering the essential question, *What is church?* from a practical theology paradigm, the aim is new theologically informed *phronesis* or practical wisdom, and informed action. The progression of reflection on this question starts with an examination of the current context and the church's place within it, asking questions like, *What is happening now, in society and in the church?* This should offer a glimpse into the present situation, raising the issue of a postmodern understanding about the nature of the church and its relationship with Jesus Christ. We then move to the questions: *What is church according to Scripture and Christian tradition?* and, *What insights from current secular thought can be creatively brought into dialogue with this*

37. McLaren, *Church on the Other Side.*
38. Pagitt, *Church Re-imagined.*
39. Kimball, *They Like Jesus.*
40. Frame, *Losing My Religion.*
41. Ibid., 92.
42. Quoted in ibid., 93.

theology of the church? This review sets the stage for dialogue between the rich learnings of the past and the grounded reality of the present. In practical theology terms, we are undertaking a mutually critical dialogue between interpretations of the Christian story and interpretations of contemporary cultural experiences and practices.[43] This mutually critical correlation is designed to lead to a chosen response and informed action into the future.

What, theoretically, is church supposed to be? What has church become, and why? Why is it that, while the whole arena of spirituality is experiencing resurgence in the Western world, church attendance there is falling and the attendees are aging? What insights does the Emerging Church have to contribute? A brief consideration of these issues necessarily precedes any deliberation on Christian education and its place within the church. In any case, the *a priori* question for our current inquiry and one that we must consider as foundational to the rest of the argument becomes: *What is church?* Before we can begin to discuss the shape of the church in a postmodern context, we need to reflect—albeit only very briefly here—on the shape of the church that is presented in the Scriptures and in the writings of some of the great leaders and thinkers in the tradition.

The Scriptures reveal God as desiring community with humankind from the time of its creation onwards. Humans were created in God's image (Gen 1:26, 27). Since God has communion within Godself as Trinity, it follows that we were also made for communion or relationship. Theologian Catherine LaCugna expresses it very well:

> Trinitarian theology is *par excellence* a theology of relationship: God to us, we to God, we to each other. The doctrine of the Trinity affirms that the "essence" of God is relational, other-ward, that God exists as diverse persons united in a communion of freedom, love and knowledge. . . . The correspondence between *theologia* (the eternal being of God) and *oikonomia* (the pattern of salvation history) means that the focus of the doctrine of the Trinity is the communion between God and ourselves.[44]

God institutes and maintains a covenant relationship with humanity, despite our consistent dalliances with rebellion and sin. The Old Covenant established with Abraham declared that God had set aside a people to relate with—particularly Abraham, Sarah and their offspring, later known as Israel (Gen 17:7). This covenant was signified in God's rescue of the Hebrew people from Egypt by the institution of the Passover (Exod 12), and the rite of male circumcision (Gen 17). Thomas Torrance calls these signs:

43. Browning, *Fundamental Practical Theology*, 46.
44. LaCugna, *God for Us*, 243.

> . . . major "sacraments": circumcision, which inscribed the promise of God's blessing in the flesh and seed of his people and covenanted them to a life of obedience and faith; and the passover, in which God renewed his covenant, promising redemption from the bondage of sin and the tyranny of the powers of evil into fellowship with himself through a sacrifice God himself would provide.[45]

This chosen people, Israel, was blessed by God to be a blessing to the rest of the world (Gen 12:2, 3). Through their witness, God would be revealed, and salvation assured (Isa 2:3; John 4:22). The Apostle Paul confirms this in his letter to the Romans:

> They are Israelites, and to them belongs the adoption, the glory, the covenants, the giving of the law, the worship and the promises; to them belong the patriarchs, and from them according to the flesh, comes the Messiah, who is over all, God blessed forever. (Rom 9:4, 5).

All this was God's work throughout salvation history to make the path for the New Covenant in Christ Jesus, and to be the foundations for the Christian church. Jesus himself consecrated the fledgling church by breathing the Holy Spirit into the disciples as they cowered in a locked room after his death (John 20:22). Prior to his crucifixion, Jesus had instituted the sacrament of Holy Communion within the context of sharing the Passover meal together (recorded in Luke 22:14–20; Mark 14:22–25 and Matt 26:26–30). His teaching about God's Reign or Kingdom, his baptism for our sake, and his choosing of the Apostles to participate with him in his ministry, all indicate Jesus' inseparable, gracious connection to and creation of the Christian church. In continuity, the *ecclesia* develops from the People of God—the *congregation* of Israelites as described in Deut 23:3—into God's new covenant people. This organic, incarnational community is the inheritor of God's promises to Israel. But more than that, the church becomes the "growing medium" for God's Reign on earth. Empowered by God's own Spirit made available to all at Pentecost (Acts 2), the church's life and mission come directly from Christ. Torrance points out, however, that:

> The Church did not come into being with the Resurrection or with the pouring out of the Spirit at Pentecost. That was not its birth but its new birth, not its beginning but its transformation into the Body of the risen Lord quickened and filled with his Spirit. Jesus Christ had already gathered and built up the

---

45. Torrance in *Theological Foundations*, 201.

nucleus of the Church round himself, but because he loved it he gave himself for it that he might cleanse it and change it through the mystery of union with himself in death and resurrection. The form he had given it through his ministry was necessarily of a provisional character before the crucifixion and resurrection. He had prepared it for this hour, and therefore far from reject-ing it he reaffirmed it, reconstituted it, and recommissioned it, giving it to participate in him now on the ground of his atoning work in a depth and fullness which was not possible before.[46]

The Apostle Paul gives rich images of the church as the Body of Christ (Col 1:24; Rom 12; 1 Cor 12), Jesus' Bride (2 Cor 11:2; Eph 5:32), and his Temple (1 Cor 3:16; 2 Cor 6:16; Eph 2:20–22). The writers of 1 Peter and Hebrews describe the church's priestly nature. Paul also writes to the early faith communities, encouraging them with practical theological teaching about ethical living as children of God.

The early church underwent and withstood persecution, was exiled, outlawed and thrown to lions for the entertainment of Roman citizens. Early Apologist, Justin Martyr, was converted to Christianity around AD 130. He was later denounced as a Christian, and when he and his company refused to make sacrifices to the Roman Emperor, they were whipped and then beheaded. In his *Dialogue with Trypho the Jew,* Justin Martyr makes some ironic statements:

> Because of our faith we are crucified, beheaded, fed to wild beasts or burned in the flames. By these means some hope to wipe out the Church. But in fact their persecution has had the opposite effect. Think of the vine. When you "behead" it, it does not die, but bursts out in other, fruit-bearing branches. This is what happens with us. What others intend for destruction is turned to growth. Unbelievers see this invincible faith and be-come believers in the Name of Jesus. After all, he once spoke of this Vine, planted by his Father, rooted in him: it is his people.[47]

The church had its fair share of internal conflicts as well, but was drawn together by shared belief in Jesus Christ. In a society stratified by rigid kinship, gender and class restrictions, the church became a new kin-ship group—a clan with Christ as its head. This new family of God overcame many barriers between wealthy and impoverished, honoured and shamed, slave and free, Jew and Gentile. In AD 251 Cyprian of Carthage wrote on the unity of the church:

46. Ibid., 211.

47. Martyr in *After the Gospels,* 73.

> The Church is one, and by her fertility she has extended by degree into many. . . . Yet there is but one head, one source, one mother, abounding in the increase of her fruitfulness. We are born of her womb, we are nourished by her milk, and we are given life from her breath.[48]

This was not mere altruism. It was a unique attempt at creating a community with genuine social unity. Being part of Christ meant being part of his flawed human Body. This Body strove to serve the needy with radical commitment to its head, Jesus. There were problems, divisions and conflicts, but the sense of unity in the midst of diversity fuelled passionate witness to Christ.

With the conversion of Emperor Constantine in AD 313, and the subsequent endorsement of Christianity as the official religion of the Roman Empire, the church became an institution and Christendom was born. This substantially tamed the religious ardour, and in many ways degraded the need for great mission or radical counterculturalism.

By the sixteenth century, the Reformers attempted to recapture some of the church's original understandings of itself, the gospel and the world. *Sola scriptura, sola gratia,* and notions like "the priesthood of all believers," became Reformation catchcries. Martin Luther set out seven distinguishing marks of the true Christian church, including proclamation and listening to the Word of God, Baptism, and Eucharist as the true Christian sacraments, apostolic ministry, proper public worship and the bearing of the cross.[49] In his *Institutes,* Calvin hones these distinguishing marks down to two essential features—namely, the preaching of God's Word and the orderly administration of the sacraments. He stresses:

> When we say that the pure ministry of the Word and pure mode of celebrating the sacraments are a sufficient pledge and guarantee by which we may recognise as a church any society, we mean where both these marks exist, it is not to be rejected, even if it is riddled with faults in other respects.[50]

As we have already discussed, the Enlightenment of the seventeenth and eighteenth centuries gave rise to questioning of the faith as never before. Science now held "the answers" to life and the universe, where the church had once been the source of wisdom. Christendom was showing cracks in the wake of this modern, rational emphasis.

---

48. McGrath, *Christian Theology Reader,* 261.

49. Ibid., 265.

50. Calvin, *Institutes of the Christian Religion,* 289, 290.

Marcus Borg notes: "Significantly, modernity has not only affected the forms of Christianity that have accepted it and sought to integrate it, but also the forms of Christianity that have strongly rejected it."[51] Borg points out that much of what is understood as "traditional" Christianity is actually a product of post-Enlightenment modernity. He cites the concept of the inerrancy of Scripture as one example. Borg states that this notion first developed in the 1600s, but was not considered a crucial feature of some strands in Protestantism until the last two centuries. The "traditional" or Old Church is not the Christian tradition, but one relatively recent view of tradition.[52]

A return to the form of church going back to the earliest times has often been simplistically mooted as the way to solve the current issues for the Christian Church. It must be remembered that context, function and purpose create form. The contemporary postmodern church must understand its function and purpose *within* the context of postmodern culture and *for* postmodern society. It is not enough to reinstate practices emulating those of another time and place, without first investigating the questions, issues and priorities of the context. To neglect this would be to be involved in another form of modern colonialism. The solutions will be, in true postmodern fashion, numerous, multifaceted and diverse.

Postmodern philosopher Jean-François Lyotard discusses postmodernity's "incredulity towards metanarratives."[53] He argues that this is a key element of Western culture today, and yet people are still interested in their own story and how "something bigger" interacts with that story. The analogy of the Body of Christ is important here. There is a danger that Lyotard's conclusion leads to a preoccupation with an individualistic spirituality, often unapologetically self-seeking and egocentric. This is offset by the notion of the Body as an interactive, interconnected organism—something that is essential to Christian life. The concept of community is central to the Trinity in *perichoresis*. The three persons of God *in se*—Father, Son, and Holy Spirit—are mutually loving, moving in perfect harmony one with another. This is what is offered by God, in the sharing of the Eucharist. This is God sharing Godself with humanity in the life of the Body of Christ, the church. What needs to be recaptured within the church is a new kind of enlightenment that fully grasps the implications of the inexorable connectedness of Christ with his church, as his Body.

51. Borg, *Heart of Christianity*, 11.
52. Ibid., 12.
53. Lyotard, "It's Not About the Old Ways," 27.

When people say they like Jesus but not the church, they are displaying a lack of knowledge about the ontology and *telos* of the church as the context for learning and teaching the ethos of Jesus Christ and the story of God's relationship with humanity. In the next chapter we will examine in more detail some of the Emerging Church literature dealing with these concepts. The ways in which this new movement, along with other Christian initiatives, can reflect a rigorous yet grounded knowledge and understanding of what the church really is as the Body of Christ, will be as crucial for the life of the contemporary world as it was in Paul's time.

Helping the church understand and focus on its essential being and purpose in Christ is the crux of the matter. The church is not merely a group of people who follow the teachings of an ancient religious leader. The Emerging Church has a great opportunity at this time to be the "new" old way of being church. This will demand transformed action in our own context. Transformed action requires the kind of reflection, learning and consequent choices that practical theology offers. Now, more than ever, we need to educate people to reflect theologically about the Christian story, about the true theological and doxological nature of the church, and what this transformed theological understanding has to offer their stories.

AN EXAMPLE OF A POSTMODERN EMERGING ATTEMPT

One example of an attempt at transformed action in the current context is the formation, evolution, and practice of the Uniting Church in Australia. Professor Marc Luyckx Ghisi's view of contemporary life, described as *transmodernity*, in opposition to a fully-fledged postmodernity, corresponds closely with one Christian denomination's attempt to address some of modernity's issues for the church. Luyckx Ghisi argues that we should not use the term postmodern, but rather "transmodern."[54] He claims that *transmodern* implies that the best of modernity should be maintained, but there is a need to go beyond it.

The rhetoric of The Uniting Church in Australia—a mainstream denominational movement established in postmodern 1977—lines up with Luyckx Ghisi's proposition of transmodernism. Ghisi argues that a transmodern way of thinking is a more accurate view of the transitional nature of Western life than a completely postmodern outlook. His marks of transmodernism include creative ways of thinking that combine rational and intuitive brainwork; an enthusiastic embrace of new information technologies; a

54. Ghisi, "WCC Champion."

celebration of diversity; an openness to spirituality and spiritual guidance as a basis for both private and public ethics; a conviction that the responsibility for the protection of the environment must be of utmost concern, scientifically and technologically, individually, and corporately; and a move away from vertical authority towards "flatter" more "horizontal" organizations with more consensual decision making.[55]

At least in its doctrinal understandings, structure and governance, the Uniting Church in Australia can be viewed as an attempt at such transmodernism. As part of the ecumenical movement, the beginnings of the Uniting Church were conceived as far back as 1901. At this time dialogue took place between the Methodist Church, the Baptists and the Presbyterian Church. Over many years discussions ebbed and flowed until the Uniting Church in Australia was officially constituted in 1977 as a joining of Australian Methodists, Presbyterians and Congregationalists. A major component of the Uniting Church's governance is its non-hierarchical, "horizontal" polity and governance structure.[56]

Can all similar Christian ecclesiastical or even generally missional initiatives of the late twentieth century be classified as Emerging Churches? This question regarding what is emerging in the light of postmodernity arises because of the postmodern perception of divergent paradigms developing within the life of the Western church. Marcus Borg describes this in his book, *The Heart of Christianity*:

> Christians in North America are living in a time of paradigm change and conflict. The conflict is not about a few items of Christian theology or behavior, but between two comprehensive ways of seeing Christianity as a whole . . . the Earlier and the Emerging Paradigm.[57]

Borg goes on to describe these two paradigms in terms of their vision of the Christian tradition and of the Christian life. He views the earlier paradigm as stemming from modernism, whilst the emerging paradigm is a reaction to that conception, and as such, is postmodern in its vision and interpretation of the meaning of church. The Emerging Church, as we shall explore later, embraces this perspective as its predominant *raison d'être*.

In their book, *Emerging Churches: Creating Christian Community in Postmodern Cultures*, Eddie Gibbs and Ryan Bolger quote a number of

---

55. Ibid.
56. Joint Commission, *Basis of Union*.
57. Borg, *Heart of Christianity*, 5.

authors and discuss many definitions of Emerging Church. They settle on this rather broad understanding:

> The church universal is an emerging church, for as the body of Christ here on earth, it awaits with eager anticipation the return of its Lord. As such, it is a church always in the process of becoming. It has never arrived in any final way. It is a pilgrim church, living the present reality of the reign of God in its provisional form until its consummation. It "emerges" as it engages the complex mosaic of cultures represented by the peoples of the earth. In so doing, it is morphed in those cultures and exerts a redemptive influence within them.[58]

The Uniting Church in Australia has these words as part of its major doctrinal statement, *The Basis of Union*:

> The Church lives between the time of Christ's death and resurrection and the final consummation of all things which he will bring; she is a pilgrim people, always on the way towards a promised goal; here she does not have a continuing city but seeks one to come.[59]

and

> The Uniting Church affirms that she belongs to the people of God on the way to a promised end. She prays God that, through the gift of the Spirit, he will constantly correct that which is erroneous in her life, will bring her into deeper unity with other Churches and will use her worship, witness and service to his eternal glory through Jesus Christ the Lord. Amen.[60]

It seems uncannily similar in many respects. And yet, would the mainline Uniting Church be considered *emerging*? The vision for the Uniting Church as laid out in its confessional documents would suggest so. The life of the church as it is actually lived might suggest otherwise. In its thirty or so years of existence, the Uniting Church has not had time to fully emerge as a postmodern ecclesial entity. In many ways, the Uniting Church is more transmodern than postmodern. My last congregations were made up of people mostly over sixty years old, and we conducted funerals with unfortunate regularity. Like other Australian denominations with traditional roots, in many areas Uniting Church congregations are predominantly aging and

---

58. Gibbs and Bolger, *Emerging Churches*, 43. Other, more comprehensive definitions and discussion will follow in later chapters.

59. Joint Commission, *Basis of Union*, para. 3.

60. Ibid., para. 18.

declining.[61] By this definition, however, there seems little to distinguish my structured, organised, mainstream denomination from an emerging faith community. The doctrinal statements of the Basis of Union appear to encapsulate the emerging vision. This is because, theologically, the one holy catholic and apostolic church should always be emerging in its knowledge of God and of itself. So, what is this New emerging paradigm, and how distinctive is it from the Earlier Paradigm Church?[62]

The question of whether the postmodern experiment of the Uniting Church can be considered an Emerging Church is of interest in this argument because of its self-description as "a church *on the way*, seeking new forms, expressions and out-workings of the Holy Spirit in both our individual and corporate lives."[63] In many ways the formation of the Uniting Church over most of the twentieth century reflects a movement generated out of a desire to travel with cultural change, along with dissatisfaction concerning outdated, duplicated, imperialistic ways of being. The whole church has an obligation to be "on the way," changing and evolving, if it takes seriously the call to follow the way of Christ in the power of God's Holy Spirit.

By Borg's and others' descriptions,[64] my experience of growing up and being in ministry within the Uniting Church could be described as being part of the Earlier Paradigm of the church. However, there are striking similarities between what Gibbs and Bolger describe, and Borg terms the Emerging Paradigm, and the stated rhetoric[65] and empirical experience of my own tradition.

Culturally and empirically the Emerging Church movement seems to be fairly recent, although Marcus Borg says, "the emerging paradigm has been visible for well over a hundred years."[66] He goes on to report, however, that "in the last twenty to thirty years, it has become a major grass roots movement among laity and clergy in 'mainline' or 'old mainline' Protestant denominations. . . .The emerging paradigm is also present in the Catholic church."[67]

61. Frame, *Losing My Religion*, 92ff.

62. Borg, *Heart of Christianity*, 6–21.

63. Joint Commission, *Basis of Union*.

64. Most prominently, Corney, *Change and the Church*; Gibbs and Bolger, *Emerging Churches*; Taylor, *Out of Bounds Church*; and other authors.

65. Joint Commission, *Basis of Union*.

66. Borg, *Heart of Christianity*, 6.

67. Ibid.

OTHER POSTMODERN EMERGING ATTEMPTS

Borg is correct in this assertion regarding new paradigms arising from the established church. Mainline Christian denominations across the Western church promote their various attempts at addressing postmodern culture on their websites and in their literature.[68] One of the most comprehensive of these attempts, called "Fresh Expressions," was originally a joint venture between the Church of England and the Methodist Church in Great Britain. Now it includes other mainline denominations including The United Reformed Church and The Congregational Federation, as well as other para-church organizations.[69] "Fresh expressions of church" is a term coined by the authors of the Church of England report *Mission-Shaped Church*, and used in the Church of England and the Methodist Church in Great Britain since 2005.

It is a way of describing the planting of new congregations or churches which are different in ethos and style from the church which planted them. These new faith communities are designed to reach a different group of people from those already attending the original church. There is no single model for reproduction but a wide variety of approaches for the different contexts and constituencies. The emphasis is on planting or introducing a worshipping community which is appropriate to its context, rather than cloning something which works elsewhere. The "Fresh Expressions" website includes in the introduction by its leader, Bishop Graham Cray, this description of its role within the whole church:

> Christians who want to share good news need first to be good news, to show genuine concern for others. This is the start of "incarnational mission." . . . These are fledgling churches and congregations. They have not had the time to become mature. But they have the potential to grow into a mature expression of church. Traditionally the marks of the church have been listed as one, holy, catholic and apostolic. But maturity will not mean they become like the churches which planted them. They must remain relevant to their cultural context.
>
> This language assumes that all local churches are "expressions of church." No one local church can fully express Christ and his gospel. Each needs to be related to others, which have different gifts or contexts. In particular the fresh expressions of

68. Examples include The Australian Catholic Bishops Conference website: http://www.catholic.org.au/index.php?option=com_content&view=article&id=1121:introduction&catid=78:about-us&Itemid=294.

69. "Fresh Expressions," http://www.freshexpressions.org.uk/.

church are not meant to replace existing forms of church, and they are certainly not in competition with them. We use the expression "the mixed economy church" as a way of saying that the one economy of God's church needs both our inherited approaches and fresh ones.

These are challenging and exciting times. Most denominations are finding that their old ways do not reach some parts of our culture. We need the new and the old and then we can work together to reach our nation.[70]

The principle behind the establishment of this initiative is that the differences in ethnography, composition, priorities and culture of "Old Church" and "New Church" are so great that they are not able to physically co-exist in many contexts. Therefore, fresh expressions or different ways of being church are introduced and developed alongside existing "Old Churches." These are designed to be more culturally attuned or "user-friendly" without departing from a basic theological understanding of the nature of the church.

This raises a new question that we will explore in greater depth in the next chapter: Is "emerging" a new paradigm, or merely a continuation of the leading of Christ? There are some related questions that will also be addressed, for example: Is "emerging" a movement or a state of being? Where is theological integrity, for our time and place, to be found?

In our quest to discover whether the Emerging Church is distinct from, or a continuation of the church as we know it, it will be important for mainline churches to carefully consider the theologies and practices being offered and not to passively accept or reject them out of hand. The danger for mainline Christianity is that the Emerging Church will become "the next big thing," a "silver bullet" that will transform the future of religion, faith and spirituality. Unless we examine our heritage as modern and postmodern followers of Christ, potentially we could blindly but gleefully imbibe these new expressions, until something else comes along. What, within our Emerging Church paradigms, will enhance and enrich Western Christianity? What is flimsy or uninformed, driven by market forces and a continuation of consumerism? Theological examination is timely and necessary for deliberation on the more important issue, at least for its constituents, as to where God is leading the church. As the Psalmist cries, "Teach me your way, O Lord, that I may walk in your truth; give me an undivided heart to revere your name."[71]

---

70. Graham Cray, "Fresh Expressions."

71. Ps 86:11.

In order to research an aspect of change within a structure or organisation, one needs to define what one is actually studying. Is this self-description—New Church—actually *new*? When you read on the front of a breakfast cereal box, "New and Improved Flavor," do you really believe that this box contains something you have never tasted before? Is this "New" combination of grains, fruits and nuts actually unique, or can it ever be?—what would we think about a breakfast cereal that claimed to have an "emerging" flavor? What is new about "New Church"? What is emerging? We will consider these and other issues in fuller detail in the next chapter.

Chapter 3

Insights from the Emerging Church

IN THIS CHAPTER, THE Emerging Church will be described in greater depth. I will attempt to define the Emerging Church movement for the purposes of this book, and outline some of its historical context, major themes and practices, theological development and critique.

The "Emerging Church" describes a movement that represents a variety of attempts by the Christian church to express its faith in contemporary, postmodern culture. The term *Emerging Church* has been used variously to depict a wide assortment of expressions of the Christian faith. There is considerable debate over a variety of terms that have evolved throughout this conversation. What is an emerging church as opposed to an emergent Christianity, emergents, Emergent Village, missional churches and so on? Tony Jones attempts to clarify some of this, offering the following definitions:

> **Emergent Christianity**: The new forms of Christian faith arising from the old; Christianity believed and practiced by the emergents.
>
> **The emergent church**: The specifically new forms of church life rising from the modern American church of the twentieth century.
>
> **The emergents**: The adherents of emergent Christianity.
>
> **Emergent**: Specifically referring to the relational network which formed first in 1997; also known as Emergent Village.[1]

---

1. Jones, *New Christians*, xix, xx.

Mark Driscoll adds:

> Because of this confusion and ambiguity (of definitions), some
> have moved away from using the terms *emerging* or *emergent*. I
> prefer to use the term *missional* to describe those who want the
> church to be a missionary in culture. Some people use the term
> *emerging church* as synonymous with *missional church*, but for
> others, *emerging church* is synonymous with *emergent*.[2]

For the purposes of his book, Driscoll clarifies this statement by defining anyone in the *emergent* stream as liberal, and all the rest as evangelical.[3]
This is far too simplistic. Here, I have determined to use the term *Emerging
Church* as an umbrella term for the movement as I understand it. *Emergent*
as described above implies an American-sourced movement, which is clearly limiting. *Emerging* describes a "global reshaping of how to 'do church' in
postmodern culture."[4] Various writers have their own specificities, but what
has been outlined above is the most common terminology in the literature.

Many from within the Emerging Church movement have utilised the
current interest in and research into postmodernism, and have framed (albeit loose) boundaries for the amorphous entity that is referred to as the
Emerging Church. The Emerging Church movement is unified in its belief
that the Western Christian church needs to change.[5] As we have already
noted, a number of proponents make strong, reactive statements against
the "old church" model, which is seen to be rooted in post-Enlightenment
modernist thought and subsequent practice. In a comprehensive example,
Marcus Borg talks about the "earlier paradigm," comparing it to the "emerging paradigm":

> Significantly, modernity has not only affected the forms of
> Christianity that have accepted it and sought to integrate it, but
> also the forms of Christianity that have strongly rejected it. In
> particular, the earlier paradigm is very much a product of mo-
> dernity. Though it sounds like traditional Christianity to many
> people, including those who embrace it as well as those who
> reject it, it is important to realize that its central features are the
> product of the last few hundred years . . . the earlier paradigm
> is not "the Christian tradition," but a particular and relatively
> recent way of seeing the tradition, shaped by the conflict with

2. Driscoll, *Religion Saves*, 210.
3. Ibid., 214ff.
4. McKnight, "Five Streams."
5. Ibid.

modernity over the past few hundred years. No less than the emerging paradigm, it is a modern product.[6]

Borg goes on to describe, compare and contrast the features of both the earlier and emerging paradigms. Focussing particularly on scriptural interpretation, Borg asserts that the two paradigms are so different that they could almost be thought of as two distinct religions.[7] He discusses the Earlier Paradigm as encompassing the Bible as literally or factually based and sourced as "a divine product with divine authority." The Old church, Borg observes, emphasised life after death and belief-based salvation whereas the Emerging Paradigm sees the Bible as largely a human response to God, historical and metaphorical in interpretation, and Christian living as emphasizing "transformation in this life through relationship with God."

Borg is harshly critical of the Old Paradigm, noting that there is a level of suspicion and even hostility on both sides. He seeks magnanimously, however, to make an attempt in *The Heart of Christianity* at "bridging the gap." Many of the Emerging Church authors cite Borg as one of the first to systematically outline the differences between the modernist and postmodern ways of being and doing church. His views on biblical interpretation, especially, are considered to be quite radical in the eyes of conservative Evangelicals in the United States.

From a more cyclically historical perspective, Phyllis Tickle describes the entrance of a fresh review of modernist church practices as "The Great Emergence." Tickle compares the emerging movement in terms of one huge church spring-clean. She says that "about every five hundred years the church feels compelled to hold a giant rummage sale. . . . We are living in and through one of those five-hundred-year sales."[8] Tickle explains further:

> About every five hundred years the empowered structures of institutionalized Christianity, whatever they may be at the time, become an intolerable carapace that must be shattered in order that renewal and new growth may occur.[9]

Tickle's assessment of the outcomes of these upheavals includes the emergence of a fresher, more vital form of Christianity, a major "refurbishment" of the older forms, and a spreading of the "range and depth of Christianity's reach" through the pain of utter disruption.[10]

---

6. Borg, *Heart of Christianity*, 11, 12.

7. Ibid., 15.

8. Tickle, *Great Emergence*, 16.

9. Ibid.

10. Ibid., 17.

In attempting to track the chronological development of the Emerging Church, Tickle draws together historical trends emerging from before the time of the Reformation until the last decades of the twentieth century. She notes some major historical events and characteristics which she considers formational for what she describes as "The Great Emergence." Some of these early influences include the Reformational re-negotiation of ecclesial authority, the advent of the printing press, and the rise of Protestantism. Later, Tickle points to Enlightenment developments in the sciences, particularly (what would become) physics, chemistry, biology, and psychology, as begetting a hitherto unheard of sense of freedom to debate philosophical, theological, political and social questions, whilst venerating progress and the momentous rise of technology.

Mechanistic progress, a foundational project of modernity, has, however, left many people struggling to find certainty and purpose for their lives individually and corporately. In the United Kingdom, one of the best known Alternative Worship[11] leaders and an Emerging Church spokesperson, Jonny Baker, is quoted in Tom Sine's *The New Conspirators*:

> . . . the old certainties of "Modernity" and the "Enlightenment Project" have been replaced with a huge level of uncertainty and questioning. "Reality isn't what it used to be."[12]

Baker and others in the emerging movement are attempting to challenge modernist conceptions of church and to develop Christian community and worship in ways more compatible with postmodern tastes and worldviews. Sine himself describes the Emerging Church movement in these terms:

> . . . a new generation of leaders in Britain is engaging postmodern culture. They are relational and experiential, involve the arts, are more into narrative than propositional theology. They are more tribal and local. . . . In the UK they tend to display more global awareness than their US counterparts.[13]

Emerging Church leader Doug Pagitt notes that some in the movement will minister *to* postmoderns, others will minister *with* postmoderns and still others will minister *as* postmoderns.[14] This distinction is important for those predominantly Evangelical Christians who view postmodernism as an extension of cynical, subjective relativism that has to be avoided and in

---

11. See Riddell, et al., *Prodigal Project*; and Roberts, *Alternative Worship*.

12. Baker, "Emerging, Missional," 34.

13. Sine, "Brave New Worldview," 53.

14. Pagitt, quoted in McKnight, "Five Streams."

fact rejected at all costs. Those who see postmodern culture as morally and epistemologically bankrupt, proclaim Christ as pejoratively against culture.[15] We will discuss the matter of culture further a little later in this chapter.

Tom Sine summarises the development of the Emerging Church movement most succinctly in the early chapters of *The New Conspirators*. He compares the Emerging Church movement to its predecessors, the various movements within the Western church post World War II, from the Jesus People of the 1960s to the Radical Christian movement, the Christian Community Movement, church planting, house churches, and to the Alternative Worship movement which was the real spark for the Emerging Church.[16] The most prolific author in this discourse, Brian McLaren, similarly notes the changes in Western Christianity in just thirty years since the 1980s:

> . . . the rediscovered, seeker-driven church (Bill Hybels), the purpose-driven church (Rick Warren), the permission-giving church (William Easum), the resurrected church (Mike Regele), the twenty-first century church (Leith Anderson), the metamorphosed church (Carl George), the new apostolic church (George Hunter), the missional church (Alan Roxburgh and others), and more.[17]

Emergent Village proponent, Tony Jones, agrees, noting that many of the Emerging Church leaders were brought up in, or came to faith in, "seeker-sensitive environments."[18] By this he means mega-churches and refers to Rick Warren's Saddleback and Robert Schuller's Crystal Cathedral. Jones continues:

> But as the complexities of a globalized world have encroached on their psyches, the emergents have pursued a faith that spurns easy answers. If the seeker-sensitive movement can be seen as a reaction to the failures of liberal theology or a safe haven for people in a world awash with change, the emergent church movement is a counterreaction, a retrieval of the deep theological tradition of wrestling with the intellectual and spiritual difficulties inherent in the Christian faith.[19]

15. Wells, in De Young and Kluck, *Why We're Not Emergent*, 11.

16. Sine, *New Conspirators*, 33–40.

17. McLaren, *Church on the Other Side*, 20.

18. Jones, *New Christians*, 109.

19. Ibid.

Much of this serves to paint a clearer picture of the turbulence being experienced by Christianity in the West today and over the last half century. It also displays a side of the Emerging Church which thoroughly and actively rejects many aspects incumbent in these forerunners. Of course, in true postmodern fashion, the Emerging Church is also sometimes willing to accept a number of the elements of its predecessors, usually using them in more creative or innovative ways.[20]

The descriptive literature on the Emerging Church has burgeoned since the turn of the twenty-first century, and yet the notion of the Emerging Church and the movement actively encouraging the emergence of "new" forms of ecclesiology are difficult to define as they encompass a wide and diverse range of models and attitudes. An insightful, and yet concomitantly typically vague example comes from Lutheran Pastor, Karen Ward, a leader within the emerging conversation:

> The emerging church is being willing to take the red pill, going down the rabbit hole, and enjoying the ride. It is Dorothy not in Kansas anymore yet finding her way home. It is Superman braving kryptonite to embrace Krypton. It is sight seeking wider vision, relationships seeking expanded embrace, and spirituality seeking holistic practice. It is a "road of destination" where Christ followers, formerly of divergent pasts, are meeting up in the missional present and moving together toward God's future.[21]

The diversity of models is further exemplified by numerous and various writer-practitioners, like Eddie Gibbs and Ryan Bolger,[22] who discuss the movement on both sides of the Atlantic in detail. Gibbs and Bolger define Emerging Churches descriptively and analytically as:

> communities that practice the way of Jesus . . . encompass(ing) nine practices. Emerging Churches (1) identify with the life of Jesus, (2) transform the secular realm, and (3) live highly communal lives. Because of these three activities, they (4) welcome the stranger, (5) serve with generosity, (6) participate as producers, (7) create as created beings, (8) lead as a body, and (9) take part in spiritual activities.[23]

---

20. Bessey, "Walk Like an Emergent"; Sweet, et al., *A Is for Abductive*; and McLaren, *A Generous Orthodoxy*.

21. Ward, "What Is the Emerging Church," 27.

22. Gibbs and Bolger, *Emerging Churches*.

23. Ibid., 44–45.

This, in many senses, is no more nor less than what the church, at its best, has always understood its role to be. In his 2008 work, *The New Conspirators: Creating the Future One Mustard Seed at a Time,* Tom Sine offers a particularly comprehensive set of characteristics "common to many different emerging expressions, though certainly not to all."[24] His list of traits overlaps in parts with that of Gibbs and Bolger. Sine identifies at least eight characteristics of Emerging Churches, including the following: viewing the gospel as story, narrative or metaphor rather than using a propositional approach to theology; emphasising multi-layered, creatively artistic and experiential worship; drawing on ancient symbols and rituals; outwardly focussed in mission; and embracing communal, relational and non-hierarchical governance. We will discuss these characteristics later in this chapter, but now let us briefly examine how the Emerging Church has developed.

SOME BACKGROUND TO THE EMERGING CHURCH

In agreement with Phyllis Tickle, Marcus Borg discusses the Emerging Church as not a particularly recent occurrence, being visible for "well over a century."[25] Borg defines it over and against the contemporary mainstream church paradigm. His criticisms of this "earlier paradigm"[26] are based primarily around the Bible and biblical interpretation. In a pointed critique of Fundamentalism and conservative Evangelicalism, Borg argues for a metaphorical reading of the Scriptures and a return to a more justice-centred approach to Christian living.[27] Borg's criticisms underpin much of the literature describing the reason for the development of the Emerging Church. In many ways, the evolution of the Emerging Church as a reaction against modernism has strong earlier parallels.

Marcus Borg was not the first to critique conservative, modernist theology, or for that matter, over-rationalized liberal theology. Borg stands in a long line of modern reformers. Historically, theology's contexts have markedly affected its concerns and emphases. The theological pendulum has swung back and forth with the social, economic and political times. From the sixteenth century onwards, with the development of Enlightenment thought, with its heavy emphasis on rationality, Protestantism attempted to make its faith acceptable and cogent with the new prominence of science and reason. In the seventeenth and early eighteenth centuries, Deism, with

24. Sine, *New Conspirators,* 39.
25. Borg, *Heart of Christianity,* 13.
26. Ibid., 15.
27. Ibid., 49–57.

its emphasis on reason, natural religion and free thinking came to the fore. In 1794 Deist author, Thomas Paine wrote as a man of his time in his *The Age of Reason*,

> The circumstance that has now taken place in France of the total abolition of the whole national order of priesthood, and of everything appertaining to compulsive systems of religion, and compulsive articles of faith, has not only precipitated my intention, but rendered a work of this kind exceedingly necessary, lest in the general wreck of superstition, of false systems of government, and false theology, we lose sight of morality, of humanity, and of the theology that is true. . . . I do not believe in the creed professed by the Jewish church, by the Roman church, by the Greek church, by the Turkish church, by the Protestant church, nor by any church that I know of. My own mind is my own church.[28]

The Deists tried to demonstrate that faith was wholly compatible with what they saw as immutable science and universal modern standards of rationality. They upheld social and individual morality, rejecting any doctrine that included supernatural revelation or the miraculous, including the Christian doctrine of the Trinity.

Friedrich Schleiermacher (1768–1834) saw the same need for Protestant Christianity to relate to the rationality of the modern world, but looked for a middle road between traditional orthodoxy and natural religion. Schleiermacher was the founder of what is now known as liberal Protestant theology. This German pastor and professor saw religion as embracing a sense of the infinite, without which humanity was incomplete. He situated religious belief within the realm of human intuition and feeling, not in rational proofs for the existence of God, or even in God's self-revelation. Schleiermacher described this awareness or feeling of utter dependence on an infinite God as "God-consciousness" (*Gefühl*)[29] and saw this in Christian terms as complete reliance or trust in Jesus Christ as the reconciler of humanity to God. "God-consciousness," Schleiermacher argued, was a universal human trait with particular forms evident in particular religions.

Schleiermacher's Christology saw Jesus Christ as the one human being who had fully experienced God-consciousness as a "veritable existence of God in Him."[30] This was the way Jesus was able to be the saviour of humanity because of the potency of his God-consciousness and his ability

---

28. Paine, *Age of Reason*.

29. Olsen and English, *Pocket History of Theology*, 90.

30. Schleiermacher, *Christian Faith*, 385.

to communicate this through his followers, the church. Corporate piety and ethical behavior became the key to this theology. Schleiermacher thus rejected theories of atonement, the doctrines of Christ's divinity and the Trinity. These were not seen as verifiable by reason and were therefore unacceptable to the modern mind.

This kind of Protestant liberal theology was hugely influential in the early years of the twentieth century, especially in mainstream denominations in Europe and the United States. Two movements developed in opposition to this trend. The first was Fundamentalism.

In 1910, a series of tracts called "The Fundamentals" were published, outlining conservative tenets of Christianity, often in pointed negation of specific liberal propositions. The impetus for this movement began in the late nineteenth century in reaction to the development of biblical criticism and Darwin's theories of evolution. Interpretation of scripture was the lynchpin of this movement. Inerrancy of the Bible was stressed and led to very particular theological, social and political behavior. There was rapid adoption of Fundamentalism in many quarters in the early 1920s. This caused intense rivalries and passionate controversies between and within Protestant churches.

In *The Future of Christianity*, prolific Christian author, Alister E. McGrath, discusses research into the origins of Fundamentalism in the process of cultural or religious revitalisation under three general stages:

> 1. Social change takes place within a people or social grouping, which results in cultural tension.

> 2. Initially, this tension leads to an attempt to accommodate the changes. This inevitably leads to a change or perceived degeneration in social patterns, which in turn leads to social disruption.

> 3. In reaction to this, a reaffirmation of traditional cultural patterns takes place, usually through the emergence of charismatic figures who champion this return to such patterns.[31]

We will see how this development has replicated itself in the events of the early twenty-first century, and how this also facilitated the growth of the Emerging Church. Clearly, there were major historical occurrences that went hand in hand with the reaction against Protestant liberalism in the early 1900s. World War One had been the "war to end all wars." Never before had the world experienced such mass devastation and loss of life.

Also at this time, another movement was making itself known on the theological landscape. Sustained by twentieth-century theologians, Karl

---

31. McGrath, *Future of Christianity*, 74.

Barth, brothers Reinhold and Richard Niebuhr and others, the "Neo-Or-thodox" movement grew up and gained momentum. The theologians who were associated with Neo-Orthodoxy could not be portrayed as following a single particular theological theme. In fact they were incredibly diverse in their thinking. However, they "were as critical of reactionary orthodoxy as they were of the reigning liberalism, they resented the dismissal of their witness which put (neo-orthodoxy) down to a mere return to past theological conventions and biases."[32]

Karl Barth gives a theological account of modernity in his *Protestant Theology in the Nineteenth Century*.[33] Barth discusses the absolutism of Enlightenment rationalism displayed metaphysically as natural theology and the apotheosis of humanistic reasoning.[34] These are themes to which Barth critically returns on many occasions. Barth views Modernity's affirmation of these themes as part of Enlightenment's constant secularisation of theologically grounded truths.[35] He sees this process of secularisation as idolatrous in humanity, "placing [it]self in an absolute position."[36] Karl Barth critiqued this understanding of modernity *as* the gospel itself, writing in his *church Dogmatics*, "modernity with its obtrusion of seemingly indispensible viewpoints and criteria is not the measure of all things."[37]

In the early 1950s, H. Richard Niebuhr wrote the seminal *Christ and Culture*.[38] In many ways Douglas John Hall's portrayal of H. Richard Niebuhr sums up the complexity of the crisis for the Neo-Orthodox movement. Hall describes Niebuhr as:

> A Christian apologist fully conscious of the pluralist character of our society, and . . . a churchman living between the extremes of a conservative absolutism that substitutes the divinization of Jesus for incarnation of the Word, and an inchoate liberal theism that begs the question, Why Jesus?[39]

When viewed from the perspective of Niebuhr's *Christ and Culture*, the Emerging Church is, in many ways, a symptom and product of that very debate. The Emerging Church movement generally tends towards trying

---

32. Hall, *Remembered Voices*, 94.

33. Barth. *Protestant Theology*, 35ff.

34. Ward, "Barth, Modernity, and Postmodernity," 277.

35. Ibid., 278.

36. Barth, *Protestant Theology*, 90.

37. Barth, *Church Dogmatics Volume III/3*, 334.

38. Niebuhr, *Christ and Culture*.

39. Hall, *Remembered Voices*, 94.

to understand contemporary culture in order to work within it, pointing to an end to the secular/sacred divide of modernity or transforming the secular realm.[40] In *Christ and Culture*, Niebuhr discussed five ways which the church of Jesus Christ related to the surrounding (Modern) culture. The five models of relationship were characterised as (1) Christ of culture, (2) Christ and culture in paradox, (3) Christ above culture, (4) Christ against culture, and (5) Christ the transformer of culture. This thinking represented a radical breaking from Christendom-entrenched North America. Niebuhr observes that all models exist in various forms, sometimes overlapping. It is difficult to determine which of the options Niebuhr proposes as preferable, although as John Howard Yoder has noted, in view of Niebuhr's logical structure in presenting the five models, the *Christ the transformer of culture* option seems to claim favourable status:

> Transformation takes into itself all the values of its predecessor types and corrects most of their shortcomings . . . a presentation following the pattern of thesis, antithesis and synthesis constitutes an implicit argument in favour of the last option reported.[41]

Inherent in an emphasis on transforming culture is the danger that it becomes the whole reason for the church's existence. Some of the problems Niebuhr associates with the *Christ against culture* model seem to be based on his definition of culture. Niebuhr describes culture as "monolithic,"[42] an ultimate category covering every way that humanity acts in and on nature. Logically, this makes a complete rejection of culture impossible, since the rejection itself is enacted by human activity and hence within culture. The church too, exists and relates within the extant culture. There are elements of Western culture that may present as inconsistent with Christianity, such as materialism and consumerism. Such elements warrant careful and critical theological reflection by Christians. In much of the literature on emerging or postmodern ministry, Christian separatism is encouraged. Separatists reject certain aspects of mainstream culture, but not the totality of culture. Separatists aim to be countercultural, not dominated by cultural forces.[43]

American Emerging Church author Leonard Sweet notes that "too much of the church sees the culture through the gun-slits of its ecclesiastical bunkers."[44] Sweet views the culture as having a role "that leaves it in vibrant

40. Gibbs and Bolger, *Emerging Churches*, 65–88.

41. Yoder, "How H. Richard Niebuhr Reasoned," 41–42.

42. Ibid., 54.

43. Staub, *Culturally Savvy Christian*, 137–57.

44. Sweet et al., *A Is for Abductive*, 11.

creative relationship with the church."[45] The problem is that the church has often mistaken culture for the biblical notion of *the world*. John Howard Yoder has also identified the fallacy here, "[W]hen the New Testament speaks of 'world' it precisely does not mean all of culture. It means rather culture as self-glorifying or culture as autonomous."[46]

Yoder contends that the separatist is not opposed to culture in Niebuhr's sense, but to cultural idolatry, those aspects of culture that attempt to supplant primary allegiance to the Lordship of Christ. Yoder claims that, from this perspective, Niebuhr is clearly mistaken in identifying culture, monolithically conceived, with "the world."

The Emerging Church movement claims that those who follow Christ generally believe they are called and empowered to think and behave differently spiritually, relationally, and creatively to the prevailing self-glorifying and consumerist Western culture. This begets counterculturalism in the sense that Christians are called to be both citizens of God's reign and citizens of the earth.[47] This counterculturalism brings inevitable conflicts. In postmodern emerging ministry, this can be viewed as cause for informed discernment in dissonance with some elements, but also hope and opportunity in resonance with other elements of the surrounding culture.[48] Christian education has a role in giving Christians tools to assess, evaluate and discern those things in the culture that align with what they profess and live as faith. As we have already noted, Christian faith resides within the prevailing culture. It is not physically set apart from the world around it. The Emerging Church movement generally does not shy away from the fact that Christianity is shaped by the cultural context. Emerging Church writers indicate the importance of building capacity in Christians to distinguish those elements of culture that have overtaken the incarnation of the gospel.[49] Western society's rampant consumerism, for example, can create situations where worship is viewed as a commodity for purchase if the style is what we like. Christians need to be helped to understand that the gospel is subject to various cultural interpretations. In his seminal, *The Gospel in a Pluralist Society*, Bishop Lesslie Newbigin states, "we must start with the basic fact that there is no such thing as a pure gospel if by that is meant

45. Ibid.

46. Stassen, *Authentic Transformation*, 70.

47. Staub, *Culturally Savvy*, 137.

48. Ibid.

49. Examples include Borg, *Heart of Christianity*, 190; Kimball, *Emerging Church*, 215, 230–32.

something which is not embodied in a culture. . . . Every interpretation of the gospel is embodied in some form."[50]

Emerging ecclesiology displays this sense of critiquing the past, yet often wanting to retain or merge that which seems appropriately positive or useful.[51] However, it remains questionable whether the theological rigor of the Neo-Orthodoxy movement is always evident in emerging understandings. Emerging Church writers often characteristically criticise the mainstream church as turning a blind eye to the prevailing culture. Examples of such critique are often stated in terms that represent strongly modernist-styled truth claims. These statements are also usually tendered without seeing any need to substantiate such observations. In one such instance, Pastor Jimmy Long states:

> The unchanging church ignores culture. It views the church as having nothing to do with present culture. The church is above and beyond culture. People in this camp see tradition as paramount, and many of the people in this camp believe there is never a need to change. The unchanging tradition can primarily, but not exclusively, be found in independent, rural, fundamentalist churches.[52]

The Emerging Church movement generally sees itself as operating in and appreciating postmodern culture, or at least engaging with it. As a self-designated postmodern minister, Tim Wright's précis on God's economy of salvation boldly declares that "God, in the person of Jesus, decided to become like culture. He became like the people he wants to find—so that he can put his arms around them, affirm them, welcome them, and ultimately lead them."[53] This statement would indicate a decided movement away from the polemic *Christ against culture* conception of parts of the modernist church.

The Australian church culture is distinct, because of its historical and geopolitical peculiarities, but does not present as greatly dissimilar to the rest of Western Christianity. Wider Australian culture has been described as the epitome of secular.[54] Australian Anglican Peter Corney quotes social

50. Newbigin, *Gospel in a Pluralist Society*, 144. Newbigin is often referenced by Emerging Church authors.

51. Gibbs and Bolger, *Emerging Churches*, 217–34.

52. Long, *Emerging Hope*, 23.

53. Wright, *Prodigal Hugging Church*, 17.

54. Among others, James Denney, a Scottish Presbyterian of the nineteenth century described Australia as "the most godless place on earth." See Burns and Monro, *Christian Worship in Australia*, 19.

researcher Hugh Mackay, stating that Australian society in the late twentieth and early twenty-first century is "re-inventing Australia."[55] Corney goes on to suggest that in every part of Australian existence, major change is evident. He cites information technology and the new communications environment as impacting "on a new generation's experience and expectation of church."[56] He discusses social and structural change under the headings of family life, transience, multiculturalism, changing leisure patterns, politics, work and money.[57] This, he asserts, all goes to make up the culture in which the church, too, is changing. He says that the "DNA of the Australian Protestant church is being re-configured." Some of the developments that Corney discusses, under the heading "New Paradigm and New Edge Churches," include the Regional church, the Small Group Movement and "the emergence of 'new edge churches' often aimed at Busters or Gen Xers." He describes these new styles of church as encompassing radical ideas of community, participation, creativity, story, team leadership, outreach focus and their experiential, non-dogmatic nature.

The Emerging Church movement has been depicted as originating from research conducted around these kinds of generational approaches applied to worship and church life. The so-called Gen-X style churches were established in California as early as 1986 by Dieter Zander.[58] Generational approaches take historic eras usually in recent history (particularly pertaining to that of the United States) and designate characteristics to those born within each era, generally relating to the events of that time period. These approaches are commonly based on a cyclic sociological theory more fully developed by William Strauss and Neil Howe.[59] The generations Strauss and Howe define include the Lost Generation (1883–1900), the G.I. Generation (1901–1924), the Silent Generation or Builders (1925–1942), Baby Boomers (1943–1960), 13th Generation or Generation X (1961–1981), the Millennial Generation or Generation Y (1982–2001), and the New Silent Generation (2001–). Concomitant with growing postmodernism, from the latter part of the Baby Boomer generation on, there are significant sociological differences in the characteristics of each generation. These differences were considered so immense and the generations so diverse, that churches were specifically generated with worshipping styles closely reflecting the characteristics of particular generations, hence Gen-X churches. It was in 2000,

55. Mackay, quoted in Corney, *Change and the Church*, 1.

56. Ibid., 2.

57. Ibid., 3–6.

58. Gibbs and Bolger, *Emerging Churches*, 30.

59. Strauss and Howe, *Generations*.

while designing a website to inform mainline churches about the distinctive characteristics of Generation X that Lutheran Pastor, Karen Ward, coined the term "Emerging Church" as the title of her website.[60]

Tom Sine identifies the British house church movement of the 1970s and early 1980s, along with charismatic movements and elements within the Anglican Church, as the facilitators of the earliest signs of the Emerging Church.[61] Sine recalls these young leaders as being distinctive in their sharp postmodern critique of what they saw as outdated cultural and ecclesial practices. Passionate about the gospel, they embraced a more narrative approach to theology than their older, systematically influenced counterparts.[62] Professor of New Testament at Northern Baptist Theological Seminary, Scot McKnight, makes a similar observation: the emerging movement tends to be suspicious of the diversity of systematic theologies, claiming that "God didn't reveal a systematic theology but a storied narrative, and no language is capable of capturing the Absolute Truth who alone is God."[63] McKnight captures the ongoing and conversational quality of the Emerging Church movement, describing emerging theology as "radically Reformed. It turns its chastened epistemology against itself, saying this is what I believe, but I could be wrong. What do you think? Let's talk."[64]

Australians Michael Frost and Alan Hirsch in *The Shaping of Things to Come*[65] cite research done by the "Gospel and Our Culture Network"[66] into cultural trends and the re-visioning of a new approach to church. This research was the catalyst that incited the interest of a number of the current Emerging Church leaders in Australia.[67] The study outlines twelve hallmarks of this kind of church philosophy, including proclamation of the gospel, being a community where all are involved in learning to become disciples of Jesus, the Bible as normative, distinct from the world because of its participation in the life, death and resurrection of Jesus, discernment of God's missional vocation for all members, reconciliation, accountability, hospitality, worship as central, continuous revelation, as well as having a

---

60. Gibbs and Bolger, *Emerging Churches*, 30.

61. Sine, *New Conspirators*, 33.

62. Ibid., 34.

63. McKnight, "Five Streams."

64. Ibid.

65. Frost and Hirsch, *Shaping of Things To Come*.

66. Ibid., 7–12.

67. Examples include "Forge" founded ecumenically in New South Wales, as a network of emerging expressions of church, "Caféchurch" in Melbourne, and "Backyard Missionaries" in Perth.

vital, public witness. Frost and Hirsch describe these as new ways of "being church" for a postmodern world.

Is postmodernity the major determining factor in the development of the Emerging Church? Its leaders are not always entirely positive towards encroaching postmodernism. Some have expressed direct and serious reactions to many aspects of a move from modern thinking into a postmodern mindset. Paul Goodliff characterizes this, summarizing the change:

> Postmodernism says goodbye to big stories or metanarratives that are grand explanations of the truth (Enlightenment), history (Marxism) or faith (Christianity). In their place are a multitude of local stories, often conflicting, but celebrating their illogicality and diversity. This fragmentation applies to our cultural, social and religious realms where the consumer reigns. Everything becomes an item for consumption: education, health care, knowledge and religion make consumers of parents and children, patients, students and worshippers. . . . The confident culture of modernism, optimistic, utopian and progressive, has been replaced with a diffident, often hope-less and anxious spirit about our age.[68]

Undoubtedly, twenty-first-century cultural expectations have impacted on the life and practices of the church. A loss of confidence often leads to a regression to long-held certainties. As we have already observed, theological trends swing back and forth throughout history, reacting and counter-reacting to various societal crises. Once again, it has become increasingly apparent across the global Christian church, and even across the spectrum of religious faiths, that there has been a notable rise in all forms of Fundamentalism. This time the reaction is against the perceived creep of postmodern liberalism. In turn, Emerging Church leaders have often implicitly defined their project as a reaction against Fundamentalism.

Australian Anglican Muriel Porter insists, in *The New Puritans: The Rise of Fundamentalism in the Anglican church,* that there is more to a fundamentalist mentality than merely interpreting the Scriptures literally. She says that there are some key markers of a fundamentalist mentality, which has arisen as a direct correlation with the uncertainty of postmodern thinking and its rejection of the authoritative claims of meta-narratives. Porter lists these markers as: a rationalist, objective, conservative mindset, zeal to preserve doctrinal purity, charismatic and authoritarian leadership,

68. Goodliff, "Our Story," 21.

behavioral requirements, a tendency to separation, and a commitment to male "headship."[69]

Porter compares the culture of the Puritans with a response in today's church to contemporary cultural changes. She cites the Sydney diocese of the Australian Anglican Church as an example. She sees this growing fundamentalist mentality as paralleling the way the Puritans responded to the early Church of England in the mid-1500s. The Puritans wanted power centered in the local congregation, rather than an overarching hierarchy. They opposed ritual, ceremony and written liturgy as ungodly. They also had wider social reformation in mind, wanting to reform popular culture by abolishing such longstanding "pagan" rituals as the maypole, as well as plays, pubs, public games and even the celebration of Christmas.[70]

There was a well-documented rise in Fundamentalism in the cultural changes of the early twentieth century. The Great Depression and World War Two had followed the horrors of World War One. The once hailed progressive humanism of modernism had led to the stalemates of the Cold War and the distinct possibility that humankind could put an end to itself. Many in society questioned, "Where was God in all this?" Since the destruction and loss of September 11, 2001, terrorism has given war a new face, and Western society, particularly in the USA, has responded again with a rise in conservative Christianity and a postmodern-styled interest in spiritualities of all kinds.

The Emerging Church movement has been in existence for long enough for the novelty to have worn thin, and to have begun to sieve and filter those who are fully committed to the "emerging cause." Mark Driscoll, one-time Emerging Church leader, is a case in point. The chapter on the Emerging Church in his book, *Religion Saves: And Nine Other Misconceptions*, discusses his reversion back to theological conservatism, after an initial dalliance with the Emergents.[71] Now Driscoll describes himself as a *missional church* leader,[72] rejecting much of the Emerging Church movement as overly liberal. What does this kind of widely publicized action indicate for the future of the Emerging Church movement? I would see it as a healthy part of its development. Part of the ongoing dynamics of the Emerging Church thrust is that it is in a state of emergence. Naturally there will be those who will experiment with, adapt and even reject elements. This is consistent with growth and healthy formation. We will discuss further

---

69. Porter, *New Puritanism*, 23, 24.

70. Ibid., 20.

71. Driscoll, *Religion Saves*, 209–42.

72. Ibid., 210.

critiques of the emerging movement and how they have been dealt with later in this chapter.

EMERGING THEMES

The evolution of the Emerging Church has seen a number of similar themes becoming apparent. These themes often arise in practical response to particular contexts. Some of the most common of these central ideas will be discussed here. They include the following: the experiential nature of emerging churches, their missional nature, emphases on orthopraxy, community, hospitality, generosity and participatory worship. Naturally, Emerging Church leaders and authors have particular accents in their ministries as well.

Experiential

There are a number of leading Emerging Church writers who contend that the new church needs to be experiential in approach. The survey will be limited to the observations of two key authors, Scorer and Sweet. Tim Scorer's[73] main focus is on the experiential nature of the Emerging Church. Scorer heavily cites the teaching of Marcus Borg in a chapter in *The Emerging Christian Way: Thoughts, Stories and Wisdom for a Faith of Transformation*.[74] Scorer links experience with reflection, drawing on Borg's practical theological methodology which, Scorer says, frees people to move "beyond attachment to the belief-centered emphasis on sin and salvation, on requirement and reward" to a transforming journey with Christ as companion and center. According to Scorer, this is the mindset that is needed to enter "the emerging paradigm."

Leonard Sweet claims the experiential aspect of postmodern faith is the "Holy Grail of emerging culture."[75] Sweet observes a postmodern regard for this emphasis on the experiential which generates a cult of sensation.[76] Each sensational experience must outdo the last. With the unending array of entertainment options available, the issue of boredom seems more evident now than ever. "Apprised of the danger of seeing experience as a narcotic, postmodern Christian leaders nevertheless realize that human be-

---

73. Scorer, "Experience," 33–47.

74. Ibid.

75. Sweet, et al., *A Is for Abductive*, 119.

76. Ibid., 121.

ings abhor boredom as nature abhors a vacuum, so they seek to transform boring experiences into learning experiences."[77] It is worth noting in passing that this indicates enormous potential for Christian education in sourcing, creating, encouraging and interpreting learning and teaching experiences. It also infers that a much larger teaching base needs to be sourced than just a few Sunday School teachers on a Sunday morning. The resource pool for teaching needs to be continually widening to include increasingly far-ranging educational opportunities. It is possible to access other Christian communities across the globe immediately and without great cost.

It has been said that Generation Y is information rich but experience poor. Information does not equate to knowledge or experience. Leonard Sweet believes that people today are "experience gatherers. They don't know it when they see it; they know it when they experience it and enact it."[78] Contemporary Western society has moved from the empirically based, "I have to see it to believe it," to a mindset that has to experience something to believe it. In his *A Church for the 21st Century*, Leith Anderson notes, in agreement with Sweet, that "the old paradigm taught that if you have the right teaching, you will experience God. The new paradigm says that if you experience God, you will have the right teaching."[79]

Missional

Emerging leaders Brian McLaren[80] and Doug Pagitt,[81] among others, call for postmodern ministry to embrace new missional and relational understandings. "Doing mission" or "Being missional"[82] is a shift of focus for the age-old theme of mission as it relates to the praxis of the Emerging Church.[83] This is not about just sending missionaries or money overseas. Mission is viewed in the broadest sense as the *missio Dei* or God's mission in every context. The Emerging Church encourages leaders who are seen more as postcolonial missionaries[84] than pastors, in the sense of living out Christianity's call to service and justice for all of creation. In discussing postmodern Christian involvement in non-party political action, and the false dichotomy of sacred

77. Ibid., 122–23.

78. Ibid., 121.

79. Anderson, *Church for the 21st Century*, 21.

80. McLaren, *Church on the Other Side*; also *A New Kind of Christianity*.

81. Pagitt, *Church Re-imagined*.

82. Russinger and Fields, *Practitioners*, 24.

83. McKnight, "Five Streams."

84. Sweet, et al., *A Is for Abductive*, 197.

and secular, Steve Chalke notes that "Jesus' mission touched every part of life. It offered God's shalom, or well-being, for every part of life—spiritual, physical, emotional, social and, by extension, political. The church's mission is just as rounded and political. A gospel that offers anything less is no gospel at all."[85]

Scot McKnight's comments reflect those of a number of Emerging Church authors:

> The modernist church is critiqued for being more concerned with achieving eternal life than enacting a living compassion for the plight of widows and orphans. Protestant Evangelicalism has concentrated on the saving of souls for heaven at the expense of saving those who struggle here on earth. Jesus cared "not just about lost souls, but also about whole persons and whole societies."[86]

Orthopraxy

Emerging Church writers representing a wide range of theological commitments, including Sherry and Geoff Maddock, Brian McLaren, Eddie Gibbs and Ryan Bolger[87] question the church of Modernity about its inability to match praxis with its stated beliefs. In other words, they see that orthodoxy has often not generated orthopraxy. They make the point that the true worship which God requires is not in the offering of sacrifices for the salving of guilt or for the sake of duty, but worship as a just and compassionate way of living. They emphasise that God, speaking through the prophets, insists instead that true worship means to "learn to do good; seek justice, rescue the oppressed, defend the orphan, plead for the widow."[88]

Emerging Church leaders are largely unified on this point about orthopraxy as true worship. In Dan Kimball's *They Like Jesus but Not the Church*, this emerging pastor stresses, "Our goal should not be to get people to 'go to church.' We should be inviting people to participate in the life of the church community and to participate in the activity of God, not merely inviting them to attend worship services."[89] These emerging leaders view worship

85. Chalke and Watkis, *Intelligent Church*, 129.

86. McKnight, "Five Streams," 4.

87. Maddock, "Ever-Renewed Adventure," 80–88; McLaren, *New Kind of Christianity*, 215–29; Gibbs and Bolger, *Emerging Churches*, 47–64.

88. Isa 1:17. See also Micah 6:6–8; Isa 1:17; and many other biblical examples.

89. Kimball, *They Like Jesus*, 215.

as far wider than an hour on Sunday. They see that life as a Christian is not merely concerned with going to church. For them, worshipping God is not just singing songs and praying prayers and listening to someone make propositions about God. Worship is also *praxis* in the sense of informed action. True worship is the Christian follower's response to God's grace. This response occurs both inside and outside the formal worship hour.

Grace allows the opportunity of imagining living better by aligning life with the ways of God. Emergent, Rob Bell, in discussing Jesus as the way, the truth, and the life as recorded in John 14:6, claims that "this kind of life Jesus was living, perfectly and completely in connection and cooperation with God, is the best possible way for a person to live."[90] For Emerging Church writers, living better does not mean living more easily; it means living in friendship with the source of all being, the transcendent yet immanent lover of the whole cosmos. This means being aware of the needs of the wider society, the wider world. The Emerging Church literature overwhelmingly stresses that lives lived in this way are the most effective evangelism. The medium (the individual and the community) is seen as the most effective message, the example, the subject under observation by the wider world. For Christians, it is the triune God who challenges new imaginings in people's lives. It is ultimately Jesus whom Christians are called to follow. It is God's Holy Spirit who convicts, and converts. The Christian's response, according to these Emerging Church writers, is to worship and thank this triune God-in-communion. It is God who assists the community in worship, perfects that worship and indicates through Scripture and Tradition the ways that have worked before as constituting right worship, so that the wheel does not have to be continually re-invented.

Community Orthopraxy

The living-out of the gospel to ensure its integrity is of utmost importance to Emerging Church practitioners. Scot McKnight describes the church as "the community through which God works and in which God manifests the credibility of the gospel."[91] This is nothing new for the church. The emphasis, according to these Emerging Church leaders, must move away from individualized, privatized beliefs to credible, communal action. For the Emerging Church, the concept of the *community* in mission moves away from a modernist individualism. Brian McLaren discusses the idea that modern Protestant Christianity has also focussed too heavily on individual

90. Bell, *Velvet Elvis*, 21.
91. McKnight, "Five Streams."

or personal faith, to the detriment of the development of the faith of the group, community or Body of Christ.[92] McLaren sees this imbalance as associated with modern capitalism, which viewed the group as an illusion or as threatening the rights of the individual. The proclamation of the biblical story became biased by this lean towards individualism, in that it emphasized the salvation of individual souls and left everything else out of the equation. "The ultimate redemption of all of creation, including our larger group identities (tribes, nations, languages/cultures), a theme so important in the Bible, generally evaporated from our thinking about mission." Postmodern mission needs to utilize the church as community to connect with the wider, surrounding community—the world. The church is by nature a missional community, existing for the mission of God reconciling the whole world and all of creation to Godself and each other. McLaren adds that this "mission itself leads to the creation of an authentic community (aka the kingdom of God), in the Spirit of Jesus Christ."[93]

Emerging Church author and practitioner, Doug Pagitt, sees the community as essential to a holistic approach to spiritual formation, but also as a by-product of spiritual formation.[94]

> Community as a means of spiritual formation serves to immerse people in the Christian way of living so that they learn how to be Christian in a life-long process of discovery and change. Christian community can and should be context for evangelism and discipleship, a place where faith is professed and lived.[95]

To live and to be formed as a Christian means ongoing determining, in the power of God's Holy Spirit, to live in a way that follows the way of Jesus. This determination, Pagitt suggests, is not dependent upon one's individual strength of character or ability to persevere, or even a whole community's will to follow in this way. This constant choice is a gift from God who strengthens, heals and guides in formation. Pagitt, along with other Emerging Church writers, calls for communal spiritual formation, challenging a re-imagining of the gospel itself.[96] Ken Wilson critiques what he sees as the hypocrisy evident in much of the modern Western church, claiming that many postmodern spiritual seekers would be "repelled by the witch's brew of politics, cultural conflict, moralism and religious meanness that seems

92. McLaren, *Church on the Other Side*, 34–36.

93. Ibid., 36.

94. Pagitt, *Church Re-Imagined*, 23.

95. Ibid., 25.

96. Ibid., 31. See also McLaren, *New Kind of Christianity*, 183–95; Wilson, *Jesus Brand Spirituality*, 1–15, 56–58, 131–45.

so closely connected with those who count themselves as special friends of Jesus."[97] Wilson offers an alternative view for the formation of Christians, challenging seekers to consider "a way of living that Jesus modelled as a fellow pilgrim." This may not seem particularly revolutionary to many contemporary Christians, but the shift in focus Wilson describes moves from belief-based *orthodoxy* to the Emerging Church's focus on lived-out *orthopraxy*. Scot McKnight observes:

> Here is an emerging, provocative way of saying it: "By their fruits (not their theology) you will know them." As Jesus' brother James said, "Faith without works is dead." Rhetorical exaggerations aside, I know of no one in the emerging movement who believes that one's relationship with God is established by how one lives. Nor do I know anyone who thinks that it doesn't matter what one believes about Jesus Christ. But the focus is shifted.[98]

Over twenty years ago, George Barna pre-empted the emerging shift away from theologically informed faith to action-for-relevance based faith:

> Christianity can be neatly boxed and laid aside, as long as it is nothing more than a series of proverbs and teachings about man, God, life, eternity and the like. If, however, we expand people's concept of Christianity so they view it as a life-style and a purpose, rather than as a theology, perhaps we would challenge them to take our faith more seriously.[99]

This statement raises issues of great concern, and its sentiments are often repeated uncritically by a number of Emerging Church proponents. There is the issue of reliance on the action quality of orthopraxy without reliance on theologically secure underpinnings of orthodoxy. There is a frightening tendency towards *uninformed* action. Theology is reduced here to "a series of proverbs and teachings." The field of theology is sometimes viewed with suspicion from Evangelical quarters if it transverses literal biblical interpretations or moves too close to what is seen as humanly-generated tradition.[100] Other writers point to a post-systematic theology character about many in the emerging conversation.[101] Many born in postmodern

---

97. Wilson, *Jesus Brand Spirituality*, 1.

98. McKnight, "Five Streams," 4.

99. Barna, *Frog in the Kettle*, 125.

100. Examples include Mark DeVine's critique in "Emerging Church," 4–47. Also a number of the other contributors to that book.

101. McKnight, "Five Streams," 4.

generations do not know or understand the biblical story and "don't have one God as the predominant God to worship."[102] It goes without saying that any concept of Christendom is long gone. The laity's growing deficiency in the area of Christian knowledge which began in the demise of modernism[103] is still observed almost as commonly within the church as in the wider community (this will be discussed further in the next chapter). Biblical illiteracy has led to a general theological illiteracy. Pragmatism has often emerged to fill the vacuum of critical theological reflection. Christian education has an obvious role in restoring a balance between orthopraxy and orthodoxy, between the church's theology and mission. The reinstatement of critical theological reflection based in a sound knowledge of the Christian story in both Scripture and tradition, is paramount.

Hospitality

A key concept flowing out of this principle of community orthopraxy, and repeatedly occurring in various overviews of the changing church culture within the new paradigm, is that of hospitality. Closely related to a postmodern ministry concept of missional living and cultural engagement, hospitality "primarily is the creation of a free space where the stranger can enter and become a friend. It is not about changing people, but rather about offering them the space of belonging and acceptance."[104] In Mike Yaconelli's edited collection entitled *Stories of Emergence: Moving from Absolute to Authentic*,[105] almost all the contributors tell stories of anger and frustration over the lack of hospitality at every level of their "old church" life. Gibbs and Bolger identify "welcoming the stranger"[106] as one of their key characteristics of Emerging Churches. Drawing heavily on the theological insights of N. T. Wright, Gibbs and Bolger discuss the concept of inclusive practices, starting with the exile of ancient Israel, through to the practices of Jesus and then compare these practices with those of modernity, where they claim the sacred/secular divide had its heyday. They challenge the exclusivity of modernity and note that the Emerging Church embraces plurality and difference, "knowing that the 'other' both clarifies and defines the boundaries of their faith."[107] They observe some particular practices of the Emerging

102. Kimball, *They Like Jesus*, 15.

103. Driscoll, *Religion Saves*, 211.

104. Russinger and Fields, *Practitioners*, 38.

105. Yaconelli, *Stories of Emergence*.

106. Gibbs and Bolger, *Emerging Churches*, 117–34.

107. Ibid., 119.

Church with regard to hospitality, including moving Eucharist from an occasional observance to the central act of worship, and moving from private, personal faith to a faith that is active in the public arena.

The attention to the importance of hospitality, combined with growing interest in ritual and mystery, has led to this re-engagement with the centrality of the Eucharist in the worshipping life of the Christian community. The Eucharist is, of course, much more than an expression of hospitality, but it does indicate the welcome each person is to receive at the table of the Lord and into the Body of Christ. The idea of "welcoming the stranger" is not limited to the stewards who stand at the front door of the church on a Sunday morning. Worship is seen as being expressed in all aspects of life, whether it be acts of kindness, service or social justice. The Eucharist is the gathered worshipping community entering into communion with God in God's very self as Triune. The sacraments are the central formative acts in the life of the church. Many Emerging Church leaders encourage this trend toward more regular celebration of the Eucharist as the core element in the sharing of a meal within worship. Mark Palmer, an Emerging Church leader, observes that "through shared meals, open to everyone, [God's] kingdom is extended and the gospel is proclaimed."[108] Another well-known Emerging Church leader, Karen Ward, likens the ministry of hospitality to the concept of the "monastic guesthouse,"[109] where all who came to the door were to be welcomed as if they were Jesus himself.

Generosity

Closely linked with the development of a more broadly based hospitality, the encouragement of generosity constitutes another critical reaction against the modern church. This critique, which may stem generationally from Old Church leaders having been formed in the contexts of economic depression or war, is the attitude that Old Church often embraced and lived by a perception of scarcity, paucity, and protection rather than a sense of providence or abundance in giving. British Emerging Church leader, Steve Chalke, devotes an entire chapter to the subject of the church's generosity in his book, *Intelligent Church*.[110] Chalke notes:

> The moment has come for the church to abandon, once and for
> all, a theology of judgement, a theology of in or out, sinner or

---

108. Palmer, quoted in Gibbs and Bolger, *Emerging Churches*, 120.

109. Karen Ward, quoted ibid.

110. Chalke and Watkis, *Intelligent Church*, 91–102.

> saint, forgiven or not. . . . Generous churches see the good in oth-
> ers and respond with a spirit of kindness and open-handedness
> rather than judgement. . . . A generous church recognises that its
> tone and emphasis are as important as the core of its message.[111]

God's free gift of unmerited love and forgiveness in Jesus Christ, the gift of grace, shows that God's very nature is generosity. Theologically rediscovering generosity as an important practice of the Emerging Church is also tied to the critique of the modern church as consumerist and driven by the market forces of capitalist Western culture. Consumerism is roundly criticized as a major threat to genuine, life-giving Christ-centered community. The notion of Christian formation, which embraces discipleship as the following of Christ above all else, is challenged by the enticement of "getting and spending."[112] Alan Hirsch and Darryn Altclass, Emerging Church authors and church planters, call consumerism "the major challenge" to Christian allegiance today and "a very significant religious phenomenon."[113] They continue, "If the role of religion is to offer a sense of identity, purpose, meaning, and community, then it can be said that consumerism is a type of religion."[114] For many postmoderns, this is how church is viewed: as another in a long stream of spiritual options—a prospective "purchase." This also affects the church's missional and worshipping ideology in that worship and service can be reduced to marketable items, shaped by market considerations. The customer is always right, so the customer must be given what they desire. This has led to the down-playing of biblical theology which presents countercultural views such as living simply, sharing generously and depending on God's providence.

Participatory Worship and Spirituality

The notion that the church's worship and service are entertaining commodities to be used for personal benefit is rejected in the literature of the Emerging Church's postmodern ministry.[115] A dramatically different view of worship is promulgated. Worship is seen as returning to a New Testament expression of worship as a participatory act of love and the Christian's gift to

111. Ibid., 99–100.

112. A phrase attributed to William Wordsworth's poem "The World Is Too Much with Us" (1807).

113. Hirsch and Altclass, *Forgotten Ways Handbook*, 64.

114. Ibid., 65.

115. Gibbs and Bolger, *Emerging Churches*, 138–39. Also Labberton, *Dangerous Act of Worship*, 22.

God.[116] Debra Dean Murphy describes this paradigm shift as "startling"[117] to many Protestant worshippers who think of worship "in starkly utilitarian terms, . . . as an instrument for personal growth or evangelistic outreach or moral exhortation or the stirring of our souls." Worship is viewed by the Emerging Church movement as a part of everything that the follower of Christ does in their daily life; it is not restricted to an hour on Sunday morning. Worshippers are discouraged from seeing themselves as passive recipients or mere spectators.[118] Each worshipper has his or her gifts to build up the Body of Christ in worship and service of God. To see worship as giving to God and others has become practically alien to some with a modern mindset. Emerging Church leaders generally note that this is one of the most difficult of all the new paradigm shifts to enact. Consumerism remains a constant feature in contemporary culture, and is no less real a feature in the contemporary church. Some Western Christians would feel that worship should be designed predominantly to build them up, personally. Thus, they are as content to sit back and relax when it comes to worship as they are to watch their favorite TV show. British Emerging Church proponent, Jonny Baker, observes that "participation and involvement are key. In a consumer culture, it's all too easy for worship to be something else we consume."[119] Here, Baker echoes what many mainline Christian leaders have been saying for a number of years.

Church shopping, where people pick and choose the worship styles that appeal to them at the time, has pragmatically led to a number of diverse approaches being attempted, and continuing to develop. The emphasis on participation and creativity is critical, however. New Zealand born Emerging Church leader, Steve Taylor, discusses a variety of forms of church as a major means of bridging the gap between what he calls "spiritual tourism" and "redemptive community."[120] Taylor notes:

> On the ground, the emerging church is exploring these tensions in a number of ways. The emerging church is in reality the emerging *churches*, which represent an assortment of redemptive forms: house churches, art collectives, weekly participative

116. Gibbs and Bolger, *Emerging Churches*, 155–56ff. Also, Labberton, *Dangerous Act*, 13ff. See also, Murphy, *Teaching that Transforms*, 14–17.

117. Murphy, *Teaching that Transforms*, 14.

118. Gibbs and Bolger, *Emerging Churches*, 157.

119. Quoted in Gibbs and Bolger, *Emerging Churches*, 159.

120. Taylor, *Out of Bounds Church*, 81–97, 102–11.

communities, incarnational church plants, and postmodern monasteries.[121]

In *The Out of Bounds Church*, Taylor then proceeds to discuss each of these forms in the chapter titled *Missional Interface*. The section called "Postmodern Monasteries" is a consideration of a postmodern monastery as one way of preserving knowledge "within the rhythms of prayer."[122] Taylor claims that if this were the case, it could effectively encourage and sustain biblical literacy. He compares the copying of the text of *The Book of Kells* by medieval monks, with their use of the esthetic illumination, to contemporary expressions of emerging styled worship: "a dedicated group of people combining text with creativity, within the rhythms of prayer, to pass on knowledge." This style of intentional worshipping community will be discussed further in the next chapter. Taylor, like many other Emerging Church leaders generally, is enthusiastic about using ancient rituals and practices in new and creative ways. He states:

> The mission of the emerging church starts in cooperation with the God of play. It calls for a willingness to live out the creative imago Dei in ways that touch the culture in which we live. I'm not suggesting play as a wanton, unconstrained act of irresponsibility or irreverence. In one sense we as Christians play with a set number of paintbrushes: Scripture, tradition, orthodoxy. . . . To these we add the unique experiences of life in our world. Like the Renaissance painters or the early Greek fresco artists, we create out of the belief that God is present in the act of rebirth, of new life.[123]

Another characteristic that distinguishes emerging churches is this strong emphasis on the arts and creativity, especially as a means of greater participation in worship. Australian Emerging Church leader and author, Michael Frost, recognizes that Western culture today is powerfully stimulated by visual images, mainly due to the dominance of television and film as communicators and entertainers. He notes that "this takes the emerging church back to its roots, where the imagery of stained-glass windows, icons, illustrated books, and sculpture were used to convey truth and arouse the believers to worship."[124]

---

121. Ibid., 115.
122. Ibid., 126.
123. Ibid., 68.
124. Frost, *Exiles*, 295.

The merging of ancient and creative contemporary practices and spiritualities holds increasing significance in postmodern sensibilities. This reflects the growth of interest in spirituality generally, especially in the United States of America since the September 11, 2001 attacks. Ken Wilson discusses this contemporary curiosity as an "explosion . . . —whether the fad over angels, or the varied New Age practices, or Kabbalah (a form of Jewish mysticism), or the Pentecostal and charismatic movements within Christianity—it is a kind of early gasping for air, as if we've been holding our breath for too long."[125] It is as though Western society has been yearning for the satiation of spiritual hunger in a more diverse, captivating way. In *Emerging Hope*, Jimmy Long observes that "worship and prayer are making a comeback in the postmodern world, since postmodernity has brought openness to the supernatural."[126]

A return to a more credal, intentionally liturgical approach has been suggested by some postmodern ministry leaders including Karen Ward,[127] Tom Harpur,[128] and Mark Labberton.[129] This appears to be symptomatic of the interest in blending of ancient rituals and practices with renewed contemporary spiritual inquisitiveness.

LINKS TO ESTABLISHED MAINSTREAM DENOMINATIONS

Some Emerging Church author-practitioners such as Jonny Baker,[130] George Lings,[131] and Steve Taylor[132] have remained linked to mainstream Christian denominations, preferring to relate "around the edges of it."[133] There is growing interest in the Emerging Church from mainstream church leaders.[134] In chapter 2, we noted some of these, including *Fresh Expressions* in the United Kingdom. In another example of explanations about the Emerging Church devised specifically for interpretation by the mainstream,

125. Wilson, *Jesus Brand Spirituality*, 90.

126. Long, *Emerging Hope*, 154.

127. Ward, "Welcoming the Stranger," 208.

128. Harpur, "New Creeds," 51–64.

129. Labberton, *Dangerous Act of Worship*, 47, 58.

130. Baker, "Emerging, Missional"; also Baker, et al., *Alternative Worship*.

131. Lings, "What Is 'Emerging Church'?"

132. Taylor, *Out of Bounds Church*, 115.

133. Baker, "Religion Report."

134. See the *Fresh Expressions* Movement in UK Anglicanism, for example, and Mobsby, *Emerging and Fresh Expressions*.

Robert Bos contributes to a definition on the Uniting Church in Australia National Assembly's Theology and Discipleship website. Bos compares the noted emphasis in the Emerging Church on Christian community to similar statements by the World Council of Churches and the Uniting Church in Australia itself.[135]

BLOGS AND OTHER NET-BASED APPROACHES, VIRTUAL COMMUNITIES

Descriptive blogs on emerging cultural and ecclesial issues abound, and the discussion generally reacts against definitions of emerging theology and emerging ecclesiology *per se,* as this is seen as a modernist way of thinking, or too restrictive.[136] In fact, blogs, websites, social networking sites, and chat-rooms are major participants in the ongoing Emerging Church conversation. A number of books published recently are, in actuality, compilations of weblog material, for example Michael Moynagh's *Emergingchurch. intro,*[137] Spencer Burke and Colleen Pepper's *Making Sense of Church,*[138] and Dan Kimball's *They Like Jesus but Not the Church.*[139] While this blog literature is current and "at the coal face," it can also tend to be fairly insular, repetitive, and often uninformed and unedited.[140] The role of the internet and other emerging technologies as major purveyors of the emerging conversation, however, is not in question. The use of net-based technologies has enhanced and hastened the spread of the Emerging Church conversation. It has also meant that critique is immediate and often devastatingly damning in its personal candor and unconsidered spontaneity. A number of Emerging Church leaders have been savagely personally attacked by opponents via the blogosphere. Brian McLaren has attracted much of the salvo. In 2005 McLaren, supported by some key Emerging Church leaders, especially those associated with Emergent Village, responded to these often vitriolic criticisms. The response was offered online on the Emergent Village

---

135. Bos, "Emerging Church."

136. See Rowse, "What Is the Emerging Church?"; Jones, *New Christians;* Rogers "Coming out of the Cocoon"; and Bessey "Walk Like an Emergent."

137. Moynagh, *Emergingchurch.intro.*

138. Burke and Pepper, *Making Sense of Church.*

139. Kimball, *They Like Jesus.*

140. Tim Bednar's blog discusses this issue in detail: http://www.e-church.com/Blog-detail.asp?EntryID=301&BloggerID=1).

website[141] in June 2005 and was published as an appendix in Tony Jones' *The New Christians: Dispatches from the Emergent Frontier.*[142]

MODELS OF CONGREGATIONAL/COMMUNITY LIFE

As the Emerging Church movement grows and develops, the literature describing models of congregations and innovations in worship increases exponentially. The models are many and diverse in style and substance. Jonny Baker and Doug Gay's *Alternative Worship: Resources from and for the Emerging Church*,[143] Dan Kimball's *The Emerging Church: Vintage Christianity for New Generations*,[144] Mike Yaconelli's edited collection, *Stories of Emergence: Moving From Absolute to Authentic*,[145] Doug Pagitt's *Church Re-Imagined: The Spiritual Formation of People in Communities of Faith*,[146] and Michael Frost's *Exiles: Living Missionally in a Post-Christian Culture*[147] describe the "look" of church in a postmodern culture. Each of these writers, and many others tackle aspects of the church's life such as worship, spirituality, social justice, mission, hospitality, and generosity, the arts, community building and leadership from an increasingly postmodern perspective. Emerging Christian worshipping communities meet in pubs, parks, beaches, cafés, and on the net. Worship may be held on any day of the week and at any time of the day or night. Groups sometimes intentionally cater for shift workers, so that their worship times may be in the middle of the night. Small groups and house churches are common strategies used to deal with an emphasis on all members' creative participation in worship and formation.

In literary compilations discussing the Emerging Church such as Doug Pagitt's and Tony Jones' *An Emergent Manifesto of Hope*,[148] key leaders within local Emerging Churches describe their on-the-ground experiences, including a Christian community in prison, existing and beginning church mergers in the Catholic, Methodist and Presbyterian churches in the United States of America, and house churches in many contexts. A number of these

---

141. Emergent Village, http://www.emergentvillage.com/weblog/our-response-to-critics .

142. Jones, *New Christians*, 227–32.

143. Baker, et al., *Alternative Worship*.

144. Kimball, *Emerging Church*.

145. Yaconelli, *Stories of Emergence*.

146. Pagitt, *Church Re-Imagined*.

147. Frost, *Exiles*.

148. Pagitt and Jones, *Emergent Manifesto of Hope*.

authors challengingly detail critical consideration of the ongoing theological implications of what is happening in the church, now and into the future.

DEVELOPING EMERGING THEOLOGY

Theology is a key component in the emerging discussion and has been an integral part of the discussion herewith. It would be foolish to say that theological reflection does not exist in the Emerging Church conversation. In fact it would be more accurate to say that theology and philosophy have almost everything to do with this discourse. The problem arises when people imitate practices and styles of ministry without prior rigorous engagement theologically. Another concern is the sometimes *laissez-faire* attitude with which the place and understanding of worship and the nature of the church can be held in postmodern ministry. Consumerism is a difficult trait to convert. The Emerging Church can easily be portrayed as the "next big thing" or "Silver Bullet" that will bring in the crowds and heal the church's every ill. This kind of poorly-conceived pragmatism undermines ongoing potential for God's creative Spirit to be heard.

We have already seen how the theology of Emerging Church leaders has been formative in the development of the Emerging Church. In a 2007 publication, *Listening to the Beliefs of Emerging Churches: Five Perspectives*,[149] five key Emerging Church leaders write on various strands of theology, including Biblicist, incarnational, missional, embodied and communal theologies. Editor Robert Webber then responds, and an assessment of emerging theology forms the conclusion of this insightful project. Adrian B. Smith, in *Tomorrow's Faith: A New Framework of Christian Belief*, compares "familiar traditional understanding" theologically with "a contemporary understanding" on topics such as the Bible and Revelation, God, Jesus, Human Beings, and the Church.[150] As the movement grows and matures, more work has been done in developing theology that relates specifically to the emerging conversation. More recent works like Brian McLaren's *A New Kind of Christianity*,[151] Tony Jones' *The New Christians*[152] and Ken Wilson's *Jesus Brand Spirituality*[153] indicate important expansion and strengthening in the theological thought of emerging leaders. These works generally display more rigorous theological attention to the issues around being the

149. Webber, *Listening to the Beliefs*.

150. Smith, *Tomorrow's Faith*, chapter subheadings.

151. McLaren, *New Kind of Christianity*.

152. Jones, *New Christians*.

153. Wilson, *Jesus Brand*.

church in the third millennium, along with a movement away from purely pragmatic responses to these issues.

Former systematic theologian, Ray S. Anderson, who now prefers a practical theology approach, compares theological understandings of the "Old" and "New/Emerging" church to those of the earliest Jerusalem and Antiochian churches. In his book, *An Emergent Theology for Emerging Churches,*[154] Anderson draws sharp distinctions between the established church of first-century Jerusalem and that of the Apostle Paul's Antioch. Anderson uses biblical quotes to show how Antioch was the equivalent of today's Emerging Church, in its missional and "spirit of the law" theological understandings of Christ, God's kingdom, and the community of the Holy Spirit.[155] This is possibly the most comprehensive and systematic of monographic discourses on the particular theology of the Emerging Church. Much of the other literature in this area develops theology around particular practices such as worship and mission, and concepts like culture and creativity.[156]

CRITIQUES

When the theological pendulum swings far enough in one direction, there will always be those who will want to pull back in the other. One of the most serious critiques, for the purposes of this study, is found in Kevin DeYoung and Ted Kluck's, *Why We're Not Emergent; By Two Guys Who Should Be.*[157] In their chapter titled, "Doctrine: the Drama is in the Dogma," DeYoung gives voice to many of my concerns about the Emerging Church movement with regard to neglect and even rejection of doctrine and doctrinal formulations. DeYoung concedes that not every emerging leader "has thrown doctrine out the window." He does observe that a number of Emerging Church authors are ambiguous and uncritical on issues of contemporary missiology, amongst other theological and ecclesial questions. He quotes emergent leader, Barry Taylor's comments on Paul's sermon in the Athenian Areopagus recorded in Acts 17:22–31:

> His [Paul's] declaration that God is not far from any one of us
> (see Acts 17:27) is a profound missional lesson for us all; we

---

154. Anderson, *Emergent Theology.*

155. Ibid., 19–42.

156. Gibbs and Bolger, *Emerging Churches*; Sine, *New Conspirators.*

157. DeYoung and Kluck, *Why We're Not Emergent,* 105–28.

don't have to take God anywhere; we just have to discover where he is already at work.

God is nowhere. God is now here. God is present; God is absent. The future of faith rests in the tension between these words, and it is from this place of discomfort and complexity that new life emerges.[158]

DeYoung observes that this type of hyperbolic "double-talk"[159] does little to enhance Christian understanding of God or God's mission in the world. Emerging Church leaders, he notes, are "suspicious of orthodoxy, putting it several notches below orthopraxy."[160] He argues that Paul's sermon clearly goes on (recorded in verses 30 and 31) to proclaim the doctrine of Christ's resurrection for the sake of the world. Paul, in fact, uses doctrine for his defence of Christianity in his mission to the Greeks.

DeYoung suggests that the power and challenge of the gospel is weakened when it becomes just like the thought of the contemporary age. "Nobody objects to a nondoctrinal Christianity because there is nothing to object to."[161] Incidentally, this also points out the dependence that some emerging and other church leaders have in the lingering sense of Christendom that still survives in parts of the North American Protestant church. The issue of handing on of orthodox faith is not seen as imperative because Christianity is basically in accordance with the commonly held contemporary mindset.

Despite criticisms that can rightly be leveled at the Emerging Church movement, especially in the areas of theological pragmatism and undue subservience to contemporary cultural mores, trends, preferences and approval, Western Christianity needs to be open to fresh movements of God's Holy Spirit in the church and in the world. Some of the critique is descends to caricature and merely reinforces the twentieth century literalist versus liberal biblical interpretation argument. Certainly the modern church is in dire need of evaluation. Postmodern generations are discovering spirituality, many for the first time. This is an opportune time for the Christian church to be involved in a re-imagining process. In exploring some characteristics and insights of the Emerging Church, we may uncover ways of enhancing the appeal of Christianity generally and Christian education specifically, that will help both to relate to an ever-changing society.

158. Ibid., 109.
159. Ibid.
160. Ibid., 111.
161. Ibid., 108.

CHRISTIAN EDUCATION IN THE EMERGING CHURCH

How is the Christian faith being passed on in the Emerging Church? How are people being formed as disciples of Jesus Christ? Explicit references to the term *Christian education* are rarely found in the Emerging Church literature. The notion of *paradosis* (passing on the faith) has rated meagre mention and has been implicit at best. This is changing. More attention has recently been paid to this area by Emerging Church leaders. Formation and discipleship are more commonly referred to, often closely related to this process for the whole community.

The Emerging Church vanguard proclaim postmodernism as their contextual framework. They rightly emphasize the gifts that the whole community brings to the table: God, speaking God's word through all. The tenets of postmodernism recognise the pluralistic nature of the world, and are more open to valuing world views equivalently. In this light, a pedagogical schoolroom idea of education may seem quite modernist in nature. This modern concept of education reflects the importance of experts and authorities. How does learning occur in the postmodern era, where there are no longer overarching common narratives or universal truths?

Australian educator, Susan Burt, is one of the few writers to use the terminology, *Christian education*, or even to discuss it with reference to the Emerging Church. Writing in *The Emerging Christian Way: Stories and Wisdom for a Faith of Transformation*,[162] Burt observes:

> Exciting things are happening in congregations seeking an authentic Christian life in our culturally diverse and religiously pluralistic world. New settings, enthusiasm, and ways of being are emerging, as those at the grassroots respond to the changing dynamics of family, church, and community life. We are being motivated by a new story, an emerging vision that embraces search and meaning, not certainty. We no longer hold to the "jug to mug" model of teaching—an approach that is always telling and seldom listening, always trying to fill the other person up with our own understanding. Instead, we are listening for the word in others.[163]

Burt underscores the importance of imagination in emerging Christian formation. Quoting the *Seasons of the Spirit* Christian Learning Curriculum Theological and Educational Foundations document, she notes:

162. Burt, "Christian Education," 201–18.
163. Ibid., 204.

> The Bible contains meaning and mystery beyond the printed word . . . [the curriculum seeks to] encourage children, youth, and adults to enter imaginatively into scripture, and to experience the message that transcends the printed words, inviting congregations and individuals to discern God's message for this time.[164]

Burt asserts that intentionally bringing the imagination, as well as the emotions and experiences, to every biblical story will help the learner to discover the voices that are not included, to enliven the story, and to make meaning for the contemporary context. This is not a particularly new suggestion. Religious imagination has long been a component of Christian education. A strong example comes in the work of well-known Christian educator, Maria Harris. Harris discusses the importance to Christian formation of religious imagination in her *Teaching and Religious Imagination*:

> Teaching, when seen as an activity of religious imagination, is the incarnation of subject matter in ways that lead to the revelation of subject matter. At the heart of this revelation is the discovery that human beings are the primary subjects of all teaching, subjects who discover themselves as possessing the grace of power, especially the power of re-creation, not only of themselves, but of the world in which they live.[165]

Harris draws on the work of theologians Tillich and Rahner, as well as that of psychologist Philip Wheelwright, to develop an approach to teaching the Christian faith as a work of religious imagination.[166] Harris' paradigm sources four forms of imagination from a psychological perspective which she re-envisages in religious terms: contemplative, ascetic, creative and sacramental imagination. Thus, religious imagination is not an innovation of the Emerging Church, but it is a renewal of this kind of teaching and learning, drawing in the non-scientific, non-rational aspects of Christian knowledge.

Christian educator, Debra Dean Murphy, discusses "faithful imagination"[167] as far from being frivolous or individualistic, but "a community's capacity for envisioning an alternative way of being, doing, seeing and living in the world."[168] This she relates to the forming of active partici-

---

164. Ibid.

165. Harris, *Teaching and Religious Imagination*, xii.

166. Ibid., 22.

167. Murphy, *Teaching That Transforms*, 147.

168. Ibid.

pation of the Christian community in the reign of God. This understanding of education moves from a mere transference of knowledge towards thoughtful, informed contextualisation of that knowledge for creative use today. Murphy cites the practice of the Eucharist as transforming human imagining as it conforms those imaginings to alignment with God's ways and to communion with the triune God.[169]

Even though solid attempts are more recently observable, there still remains a gap in the specific area of Christian education within the Emerging Church movement. Longterm thought concerning the development of Christian identity and ethos, beyond discipleship, is lacking. I had expected the Emerging Church to be innovative in its Christian education practices, and there is growing evidence of this. There is, however, still much to be challenged in Modernity's handling of Christian education. The Emerging Church movement has challenged other aspects of the modern church. How can it challenge Christian education? Intentionally formative Christian teaching and learning must develop beyond evangelism or proselytization. The Emerging Church's ministry in this area needs far more consideration if it is to live the Christian story faithfully. We will deal with this in further detail in the next chapters.

The field of Christian education can, however, derive learnings from these and other insights gathered from the general practices and attitudes of the Emerging Church. The themes apparent in the Emerging Church can offer fresh inspiration to Christian education. These include renewed focus on the experiential aspects of faith and orthopraxy, as well as a movement away from an individualistic piety and towards an emphasis upon community orthopraxy. Postmodern thought has begun to drive some shifts in missional paradigms and some attempts in restoring worship to its central countercultural place in the ongoing life of Christians. Worship is re-envisaged as more participatory, hospitable and generous. This leads to the contention that the worshipping community must again become the key context for formation of Christian identity and ethos. This too will be discussed more fully in the next chapters.

169. Ibid., 189.

Chapter 4

Key Influences on the Development of Christian Education

WE HAVE SEEN SOMETHING of how the Emerging Church movement has arisen and developed. We have also observed that, especially in its earlier iterations, Emerging Church leaders could be accused of overlooking the place of Christian education. This accusation, of course, in an ongoing sense, can also be leveled at the mainstream church. It is crucial, then, to consider the parallel emergence and evolution of Christian education for a transmodern and postmodern world.

A number of the proponents of the Emerging Church argue that Christianity should look to its ancient roots, in order to get "back to basics," to the core values and beliefs which truly shape Christian faith. We have discussed the new interest that has been generated by the renewal of some ancient rituals and practices in worship and life. So that we might get "back to basics" with Christian education, in this chapter we will engage in a brief historical overview of some key developments in its early emergence. From the very beginning of our exploration here, reflection on Christian education must be placed firmly within the domain of theology and practical theological method. As an entity, Christian education has often been studied from a purely pragmatic perspective—"This is *how* you do it"—instead of starting at the roots of understanding *what* we are doing in Christian education and questioning *why?*

In keeping with this latter perspective, we will briefly examine some of the ways people learned faith in the early church. In a necessarily curtailed sense, considering the wide-ranging realm of doctrine, we will then look at examples of *what* early Christians learned and *why*. Some key questions will be contemplated. What knowledge was needed to embrace a new lifestyle, a new understanding of God? How was the content of Christian history, knowledge, rituals and practices (*traditium*) formulated, and how did the passing on or transmission (*traditio*) of that knowledge and those rituals and practices impact on Christianity's emerging theology? How were early Christian communities engaged in the passing on of the faith? And, perhaps most importantly for our purposes, how is *traditio* and *traditium* still impacting on Christianity's ongoing practical theology in a postmodern world?

Our first task, however, needs to be: what do we mean by Christian education—*traditio* and *traditium*?

WHAT IS CHRISTIAN EDUCATION?

One of the difficulties associated with the study of Christian education has been the term *Christian education*. There have been myriad definitions, along with just as many understandings of both *education* and *Christian education*. A popular definition of *education* is that of American educator, Laurence Cremin: "The deliberate, systematic, and sustained effort to transmit, evoke, or acquire knowledge, attitudes, values, skills, or sensibilities, as well as any outcomes of that effort."[1]

Educational philosopher P. H. Phenix gives a definition of education that is perhaps more appropriate to this discussion of *Christian* education, particularly in terms of formation in faith: "Education is the process whereby persons intentionally guide the development of persons."[2]

Contemporary philosopher Mortimer J. Adler notes that the word *education* "is used so loosely that to talk about 'education' without qualifying adjectives attached to it is not informative; or worse, it is misleading."[3] The word "education" is derived from the Latin *educare* which means to bring up, to raise, or to rear.[4] With the addition of the qualifying adjective *Christian*, Christian education is thus raising a person in the Christian faith, or as a Christian. The aspect of *intentionality* helps to distinguish education from a more generic *learning*. Thus, adapting Phenix's definition, Christian education implies *an intentional process where persons are guided in their Christian development*. A further framework of Christian education will be

1. Cremin, *Traditions of American Education*, 34.
2. Phenix, *Philosophy of Education*, 13.
3. Adler, *Adler's Philosophical Dictionary*, 83.
4. Simpson, *Cassell's Latin and English Dictionary*, 77.

discussed in detail in chapter 6, but for our purposes here, the adaptation of Phenix's definition will suffice.

The context for Christian education has been and remains, generally, the Christian community. Here we will be focussing primarily on community of faith/congregationally based Christian education as distinct from the more generic religious education whose context is commonly associated with formal (church or public) school subjects. With regard to the educational task of a community, Christian educator Charles Foster quotes biblical scholar Walter Brueggemann's observation "that it requires a functional balance between those efforts designed to sustain the continuity of a people's identity and those designated to introduce enough novelty and freedom to help a community adapt to new situations and circumstances."[5] The notions of continuity and a distinctive group identity are thus important factors for Christian education. The Latin terms *traditium* and *traditio,* and the Greek term *paradosis,* referring to the conceptualisations of the handing on of faith, thus become essential tasks of Christian education. Foster concludes: "It is [from] the urgency with which a community seeks to incorporate succeeding generations into its life that we discover its concern for and commitment to education." This has been the case in the Emerging Church movement. As it has grown, there has manifested in the movement a greater urgency to incorporate succeeding generations into its life. The enthusiastic, international take up of Fresh Expressions' "Messy Church" is one example of this.[6]

THE EARLIEST EMERGENCE OF CHRISTIAN EDUCATION

Throughout history, educational theory and practice has been defined and redefined. *Traditium* and *traditio*—crudely stated as theory and practice, or, to use the equivalent educational terms, *content* and *process*, have often become entwined within the field of Christian education. It is difficult to establish the content of distinctly *Christian* knowledge apart from its culture, time, or environment. In the teaching and learning of any content area, the process of knowing is governed, at least in part, by what is understood as knowledge at that time and in that place. Here, we are interested in examining emerging patterns in contemporary Christian teaching and learning. One of the features of the Emerging Church is a great interest in re-discovering the rudiments of Christian faith and "getting back to basics."

5. Brueggemann, quoted by Charles Foster in *Educating Congregations,* 71.

6. Moore, *Messy Church,* among a growing number of resources published by BRF.

In order to see how Christian knowledge and practice has emerged, and has been shaped by the full gamut of contextual forces, it will be valuable to look back briefly at some of the earliest foundations of Christian education.

The first of these foundational elements is the influence of ancient Greek educational philosophy on the earliest development of Christian knowledge, teaching, and learning—its *traditium*. The Greek impact sits alongside the more commonly acknowledged Hebrew heritage of Christian education. This factor will also be important in preparing the ground for a new proposal in the following chapters.

Secondly, we will focus on the catechumenate of the early church, which exhibits a particular style of *traditio*. This style has left some interesting legacies, which will be analyzed in terms of parallels in contemporary Christian education and Emerging Church settings. In selecting these particular features, I make no claim to be able to cover their breadth and complexity comprehensively. What is under scrutiny is their correspondence and relevance to a postmodern context.

THE INFLUENCE OF ANCIENT GREEK EDUCATIONAL PHILOSOPHY

The three major schools of ancient Greek philosophy that most heavily influenced the earliest Christian writers and teachers were Platonism, Aristotelianism and Stoicism. These schools developed in the second and third centuries BCE. Plato, who founded the Academy as a centre of learning, used his most comprehensive writing, *The Republic*, to set out his views on society and its highest virtue: education.[7] Identifying the necessary functions to be performed in the ideal society, his educational plans elaborated the processes by which people were to be selected and trained to perform those functions.[8]

Commenting on the myth of Er in Book X of Plato's *Republic*,[9] Greek physician Galen (AD 129–199)[10] discusses Plato's teaching methodology as compared to that of the Christians of Galen's time:

> Most people are unable to follow any demonstrative argument consecutively; hence they need parables, and benefit from them
> . . . just as now we see the people called Christians drawing their

7. Wyckoff, "Education: Theories of," 208.

8. Weate, *Young Person's Guide to Philosophy*, 15.

9. Stevenson, *A New Eusebius*, 137.

10. Kirby, *Early Christian Writings*, 1.

faith from parables (and miracles), and yet sometimes acting in the same way (as those who philosophize). For they include not only men but also women who refrain from cohabiting all their lives; and they also number individuals who, in self-discipline and self-control in matters of food and drink, and in their keen pursuit of justice, have attained a pitch not inferior to that of genuine philosophers.[11]

The use of stories and parables has always been an integral part of Christian learning. The philosophers used this method as well. In *The Republic*, Plato outlines his Theory of Forms[12] by way of the allegory of the cave. In this parable, the human condition is depicted as people chained to the wall of a dark cave. From the inside of the cave the only vision those people have is the shadows of the things of the world outside. Those trapped in the cave mistakenly believe that the shadowy drama they experience is all there is to life. Plato, as a philosopher and a teacher of philosophy, held the key for escape to the real, perfect world. He claimed that training in philosophy would guide an individual to realise that the perfect world of Forms exists. Students of philosophy would come to know true goodness and become the highest echelon of rulers or guardians in society. Once one had escaped the cave, they were not to remain in the higher world, but were to return to the cave to free others. The duty of the philosophically trained guardians was to teach and share the knowledge. This, Plato stressed, would not be easy, as the returning ex-prisoner would be mocked and ridiculed by those still incarcerated in the cave. The returning guardians would talk of a seemingly impossible perfect world, and they would not be able to see the old shadows on the wall of the cave as they once had. They would thus be persecuted and would find their message often hopelessly rejected.

The message of the allegory of the cave and the Scriptural advice from, for example, Rom 12:2, often used by contemporary Christian educators, are surprisingly similar: "Do not be conformed to this world, but be transformed by the renewing of your minds, so that you may discern what is the will of God—what is good and acceptable and perfect."

This emphasis on Christian learning as a means of being ontologically transformed and thus being more closely aligned with God's intentions for one's life is an integral feature of Christian education. In a particularly emerging Christian sense this transformation comes from God's revelation to us that some aspects of ourselves keep us trapped in darkness. Brian McLaren compares old and new ways of discussing Jesus' mission in his

---

11. Walzer, *Galen on Jews and Christians*, 15.

12. Stokes, *Philosophy*, 23.

book, *Everything Must Change*. McLaren compares emerging understandings of the salvific work of Jesus, to the emphases of "old church" on sin and the Devil. He claims that in an emerging view, God in Jesus is the light, enabling us to see the way out of our own darkness. Jesus came to earth in human form to free humanity from its limited vision of life, and to offer a new vision, God's vision or Kingdom.[13]

Plato's Theory of Forms was influential in later Christian thought, especially in relation to the concept of humanity being made in the likeness of God (*imago Dei*). In Plato's metaphysical system, the Earth that is here and now is a world of mere shadows of what is real. Beyond this, there is a transcendent, invisible yet real world that exists eternally after death. This world of intelligible "Forms" or "Ideas" consists of perfect models of all things on the Earth. Earth represents shadowy reflections of an ideal world. Humanity is trapped in an environment of shadows, mistaking the shadows for what is real.[14] According to Plato, the eternal nature of this perfect world is obscured from most people, who may only be able to grasp it clearly by sound education and training in that which is eternal. Reality is the realm of eternal, unchanging *being;* the present changing world of *becoming* is but a pale reflection of reality.

Plato saw the soul (psyche) and body of a person as existing separately before birth and after death. Writing in *The Republic*, Plato describes the soul as the invisible essence of a human being, made up of the intellect, spirit (emotions and will), and appetites (drives and basic impulses). He aligns the balance of a healthy individual with the good order of the well operating State.[15] In *The Meno,* Plato examines the nature of knowledge. He argues that the soul, or mind, has passed through many existences. Knowledge for Plato was about remembering these previous experiences.[16]

Aristotle (384–322 BC) was educated in Plato's Academy and later founded his own learning institution, the "Lyceum." His philosophical style and content differed from that of his former teacher, Plato. Aristotle categorised learning into various strands or fields of inquiry. He is sometimes known as "the father of science." He also classified arguments into valid and invalid types, thus formulating the science of logic. In his work, *De Caelo* (*On Heaven)*, Aristotle delineated his cosmology.[17] He wrote that the world

13. Emerging Church leader Brian McLaren distills Jesus' purpose as transformative in "Reframing Jesus," part three of his book, *Everything Must Change*, 79.

14. Weate, *Young Person's Guide,* 14.

15. Plato, *Republic*, 436(C), 440(B), 433(E).

16. Weate, *Young Person's Guide,* 51, 52.

17. Kennedy, *Modern Introduction to Theology*, 221.

was eternal, without a beginning or an end. He said the earth was spherical, surrounded by another sphere of heaven, and that outside that, there was nothing. He stated that all matter could be divided into four basic elements: earth, water, air, and fire. In Book VIII of Aristotle's *Physics*, he claims that everything in the cosmos is always changing except the power that initiated the motion. This transcendent power he called the Unmoved Mover. He identified the Unmoved Mover as God, thus drawing his physics and cosmology into his theological conception. Aristotle's methods for scientific understandings of nature and humankind implied a formal education that enabled citizens, along with the State, to achieve their ends in harmony.[18]

Aristotle was convinced that everything in the universe was striving towards the realisation of its potential, its own form of perfection and *telos* or purpose. He claimed that the behaviour of all things, animate or inanimate, could be explained by their teleology, their reason for being or function. Aristotle used the idea of function to relate his theories about ethics to his thoughts on physics. He believed that the natural purpose of humanity was to reason. Aristotle saw reasoning as the most critical of human functions, and in order to reason well, one must apply the specific virtues of one's character. It was not until the Middle Ages that much of Aristotle's thinking was accepted by the church, through the mediation of Aquinas. Virtue ethics, based on Aristotelian thought, came back into vogue especially in the field of education, in the late twentieth century.

Stoicism had its roots in the key question for Socrates: how was one able to lead a good life? Stoic philosophy was thus essentially concerned with ethical matters. According to the Stoics, human beings are all citizens of the cosmic State (*polis*) and that each citizen's duty is to each other.[19] Stoics believed that humankind was part of a divine plan and that whatever happened was meant to be. Because of this, children were seen as important to the Stoics because the future was contained in this divinely ordained design.[20] To the Stoics, a good life meant a virtuous one. They refused to be led by their emotions, because feelings stood in the path of good judgment and wisdom.

Formal education in Plato's Athens started at around the age of seven, depending on the family's financial position. Classes were held for boys only, led by a *paedagogos* or nanny cum tutor, who taught his students to read, write and to undertake some elementary mathematics. The boys then engaged in physical training where they learned instrumental music,

18. Wyckoff, "Education: Theories of," 209.

19. Turnbull, *Get a Grip on Philosophy*, 74.

20. Weate, *Young Person's Guide*, 18.

gymnastics, dancing and singing, as well as exposure to Greek literature passed on in the oral tradition,[21] often through the medium of songs.[22] Education was designed to create good citizens who could serve the State. Its aim was also the development of students' individual talents.[23]

By the third century CE, a revised form of Platonism, the Neo-Platonic school, had developed, stressing the ultimate transcendence of God. Neo-Platonism (especially in the form of Gnosticism) became an alternative to the steadily growing Christian faith. Gnosticism was influential in the thought of many Christian scholars into the fourth century and beyond. The idea of one supreme and unknowable God had become central in much of Greek philosophy by this stage.[24] This philosophical monotheism was a connecting point for early Christian writers.

Platonism and Christianity could, it seemed, be harmonised. Both were other-worldly. Jesus had said, "My kingdom is not of this world." (John 18:36). Plato had said the same thing about his world of Forms.[25] Both Greek philosophy and Christianity had a common belief in the immortality of the soul. For the early Jewish Christians, the question was philosophy's place in God's economy.

Early church Apologist, Clement of Alexandria, wrote in his *Stromateis:*

> Philosophy then before the coming of the Lord was necessary to the Greeks to bring them to righteousness, but now it is profitable to bring them to piety, seeing that it is a sort of training for those who gaining the fruit of faith for themselves by means of demonstration for "you will not stumble" [Prov 3:23] if you attribute all good things to providence, whether they be Greek or to Christian. For God is the cause of all good things, but of some primarily, as with the old and new covenants, and of others consequently, as with philosophy. Peradventure also it was given to the Greeks primarily, before the Lord called also the Greeks. For philosophy educated [*epaidagogei*—was the *paedagogos*] the Greek world, just as the law did the Hebrews to bring them to Christ. Philosophy therefore is a preparation, making ready the way for him who is being perfected in Christ.[26]

---

21. Power, *Evolution of Educational Doctrine*, 55.

22. Sundquist, *Harper's Encyclopedia*, 278.

23. Ibid.

24. Rauche, *Student's Key*, 74–76.

25. Stokes, *Philosophy*, 23.

26. Clement of Alexandria, "Stromateis," 183, 184. Scripture citing and Greek transcription my addition.

For the Greeks there was the question of Jesus himself. Where did the notion of the Christ fit? How could Christ be both human and divine? This presented a problem when the early Christian teachers wanted to think about the Hebrew and Christian God. How could a god have any direct contact with this temporal world? The early church Apologists had to grapple with the inherent contradictions between the Greek and Christian concepts of God. If God could have no direct contact with this world, he must have a mediator to go between the divine world and the human world. A common title used in Greek thought for this mediating power or principle was *Logos*, meaning both *Reason* and *Word*.[27]

This concept has clear parallels with ideas inherent in the Gospel of John 1:1–4, 10–14, and 18. The author writes:

> In the beginning was the Word, and the Word was with God, and the Word was God. He was in the beginning with God. All things came into being through him, and without him not one thing came into being. What has come into being in him was life, and the life was the light of all people . . .
>
> He was in the world, and the world came into being through him; yet the world did not know him. He came to what was his own, and his own people did not accept him. But to all who received him, who believed in his name, he gave power to become children of God, who were born, not of blood or of the will of the flesh or the will of man, but of God.
>
> And the Word became flesh and lived among us, and we have seen his glory, the glory as of a father's only son, full of grace and truth. . . . No-one has ever seen God. It is God the only Son, who is close to the Father's heart, who has made him known.

There were, of course, other problems for early Christian thinkers and teachers. For the Greeks, the need for a mediator (*Word*) was not necessary because of human sin, but simply because an unchanging god cannot directly involve himself in a changing, temporal world. In addition, the Greek *Word* was clearly separate from, and inferior to, God.[28] The natural extension of these ideas created immense theological difficulties for Christian thinkers into the fourth century and later, as the divinity of Christ the Word was questioned, along with his status as part of the Trinity.

The teachings of the Greek philosophers clearly influenced those in the early church who were interested in keeping this new Christian faith alive and passing it on to the next generations. The dominant conception of

---

27. Lane, *Lion Concise Book*, 12, 13.

28. Ibid., 13.

Greek education was the need to serve and function well as part of the State. In order for the State to operate expeditiously people had to be taught to fulfill various roles beneficial to the good ordering of the State. The teachers of philosophy were seen as the ones who could free people from the prison of ignorance of living in the shadows.

Postmodern minds still seek this kind of transcendence. Modernity saw transcendence in the development of the scientific age (ironically brought about in many ways by the influence of Greek philosophy). As Western society shifts from Modernist scientific universalism to greater acceptance of the plurality of spiritual views and values, there is an opportunity for Christian formation to shift too. Some of the styles and techniques used by the ancient Greeks might not sit well with today's educators, but teaching and learning concepts like individual and peer mentoring, and small group interaction instead of mass produced learning, have found contemporary favor. The early Greek philosophers serve to remind us of the importance of education in the creation of well-functioning society. Christian community is likewise enhanced when there is openness to learning about the ways of God in the Christian story. Ancient Greek philosophy emphasizes the importance of reflective thinking and critical problem solving, along with practical wisdom, as ways of knowing that influence behavior. These must become vital components of postmodern Christian education. Christian education must move away from the idea held by some that knowing facts and figures pertaining to Scripture will make better Christians; but Christian ethos should be active and practiced, reflective and learning. Of course Greco-Roman society was the backdrop for the earliest Christian communities, so Greek philosophy also served as something of a counter to emerging Christian thought, as we have seen. In many instances the early Christians were forced to distinguish their doctrine from that of the extant culture. In contemporary, post–Christendom times Christians have begun to recognize that they are in a similar position. This will entail moving back to a more thorough understanding of normative Christian practices and doctrines as foundational to developing Christian ethos. We will discuss this further in later chapters.

THE HEBREW HERITAGE

The second major influence on early Christian education is the Hebrew way of thought. It is to a discussion of this important topic that we now turn.

The ancient Hebrews did not embrace Platonic dualism.[29] The Hebrew worldview held that God, self-revealed throughout history, had created and sustained the world. This God was emphatically unitary, yet remaining actively involved in a covenant relationship with the Hebrew people. The word of God represented God ontologically, spoken from the center of God's being, which was understood to be God's heart. This word, as a dynamic entity, entered the listener's being, leading to obedience to the word first spoken. God creates by God's word. "This word of God is the extension of his person and therefore his power. It does things. What his word says, God does."

It is into this understanding that Jesus of Nazareth was born. Jesus was brought up learning in the Hebrew educational tradition. This tradition emphasized the purity and distinctiveness of the Hebrew people. Educators Elmer H. Wilds and Kenneth V. Lottich note that "the greatest lesson to be drawn from the history of [Judaism] is that a strict adherence to an educational system based on a peculiarly high religious and moral ideal has preserved their unity in a way that no political system could approximate."[30] Education was viewed as a way of maintaining the culture. The Hebrew Scriptures stressed the responsibility of the family in passing on the Jewish faith. In Deut 6:4–9 the writer exhorts Israel thus:

> Hear, O Israel: The Lord is our God, the Lord alone. You shall love the Lord your God with all your heart, and with all your soul, and with all your might. Keep these words that I am commanding you today in your heart. Teach them diligently to your children and talk about them when you are at home and when you are away, when you lie down and when you rise. Bind them as a sign on your hand, fix them as an emblem on your forehead, and write them on the doorposts of your house and on your gates.

The Hebrew word *shanan* is used in this passage, translated as "teach them diligently," when the author discusses the methodology of the educational task within the family and the wider community. This word can also mean *to bring into focus, to whet* or *to sharpen*.[31] This indicates that Hebrew parents were to encourage the sharpening of their children's minds, whetting their intellectual appetites for the questions of their faith. This was to be achieved through ritual, family life and oral instruction in faith. The father of the family had the responsibility for the education in the Law at home.[32]

---

29. Knight, *Christ the Center*, 2, 7, 8.

30. Wilds and Lottich, *History of Educational Thought*, 80.

31. Gangel, "Towards a Biblical Theology," 60.

32. Watson, "Education: Jewish and Greco-Roman," 311.

Girls did not attend public school, but were often taught to read, and were made familiar with the written, but not the oral Law. Girls at this time were also encouraged to learn Greek.[33]

According to the Jerusalem Talmud, Jewish Scribe Simon ben Shetach had instituted formal educational reforms in the century before Jesus' birth. Schools had previously existed but attendance was made compulsory around this time.[34] Early Jewish historian Flavius Josephus[35] (AD 37–c100) contrasts the Israelite education system with that of the Spartans' emphasis on practice, and that of the Greeks, who centred more on theoretical instruction. Josephus declares in his *Against Apian*: "But our law-giver very carefully combined the two. For he neither left the practice of morals silent, nor the teaching of law unperformed."[36]

The content of Hebrew learning in Jesus' time was the Law or Torah. The Torah was the basis of all sectors of Jewish life. Its teaching pertained to social, religious, as well as legal requirements. Jewish boys were taught the Scriptures, as Greco-Roman boys learned the classics like Homer and Virgil. Extracts from the Torah were produced on small scrolls. Later, students would graduate to memorisation of entire books, starting with the Torah, then the Prophets, and finally the Writings.[37] Writing itself was taught separately to reading, as a professional proficiency, whereas in the Greco-Roman system these skills were integrated. For Jewish students this was because it was forbidden to transcribe Scripture from dictation.[38]

The Gospels of the New Testament were Greek documents written between the end of the first century and the middle of the second century. In T. W. Manson's *The Teaching of Jesus: Studies in Its Form and Content,* the author notes that "the substance of the Gospel is neither a dogmatic system nor an ethical code, but a Person and a Life."[39] The Christian faith sees Jesus as the son of the God of the Jews and, at the same time, of the same being as God.[40] This unique understanding took some centuries to resolve and was formalised at the Council of Chalcedon in the fifth century.[41] Richard Osmer, a renowned Christian educator, notes the significance of what he

33. Cheyne and Black, *Encyclopaedia Biblica*, 111–13.

34. Ibid.

35. Feldman, in *Dictionary of New Testament Background*, 590.

36. Josephus, quoted in Schurer, *A History of the Jewish People*, 489.

37. Marthaler, *Harper's Encyclopedia*, 294.

38. Watson, "Education: Jewish and Greco-Roman," 312.

39. Manson, *Teaching of Jesus*, ix.

40. Although not named as such until the fourth century.

41. Pazmiño, *God Our Teacher*, 60.

calls the Chalcedonian *form and grammar* for the *traditium* of Christian education. Osmer states, "the grammar consists of three rules that characterize the relationship between the human and divine in Jesus: indissoluble differentiation, inseparable unity, and indestructible order."[42] The writer of the letter to the Colossians affirms that in Jesus, "are hidden all the treasures of wisdom and knowledge" (Col 2:3). Christians see Jesus as more than a great teacher or scholar, or even prophet. Jesus is God in human form. Thus, Jesus' wisdom is the wisdom of God. One of Christ's most critical teachings centered on the coming of God's Kingdom, where God's wisdom would prevail. "This divine Wisdom overthrows the dominant logic of the world (hierarchical, authoritarian, juridical, dualistic) in favor of a new logic, that of grace, love, freedom, of uncoerced and fully reciprocal communicative practices."[43]

THE CATECHUMENATE

The educational landscape, even in far flung Palestine, included Hellenistic institutes of higher learning, the Stoic philosophers' schools. Their alumni moved around as traveling teachers, giving instruction in ethical principles.[44] This, of course, was also the way Jesus had lived and taught. It seemed appropriate, then, after Jesus' ascension and final instructions ("Go . . . and teach")—known as the Great Commandment—that his followers would also become itinerant teachers. These were the earliest of the new faith's prophets visiting the fledgling Christian communities to celebrate the presence of Christ with them, in the sharing of the Eucharist.[45] As they grew and matured, these communities were also interested in teaching about the practical living of the new faith and how it related to their previous beliefs. This led to the separation of the ministries of prophecy and teaching. The prophets continued to travel from place to place, whereas the teaching ministry became more settled within the communities.

As the new Christian beliefs spread, the teaching ministry grew, as evidenced in writings such as *The Didache: The Lord's Teaching through the Twelve Apostles to the Nations*.[46] The *Didache* was part of the earliest curricula material. It was written some time before 150, as a kind of teaching guide for learning the practices and order of the Christian faith, purportedly

42. Osmer, "New Clue," 188.

43. Hodgson, *God's Wisdom*, 140.

44. Marthaler, *Harper's Encyclopedia*, 294.

45. Ibid.

46. Zdziarski, *Didache*.

from eye-witnesses of Jesus. It was written in the style common to that of similarly dated collections of Jewish moral teachings. *The Didache* gives the impression that the resident teaching ministry of the church had been accorded at least equal, if not greater, authority to that of the transient prophet. In fact, true and false prophets were discerned by the way their words and actions aligned with *The Didache*'s accepted teachings: "And not everyone who speaks in the spirit is a prophet, but only if he has the ways of the Lord. From his ways the false prophet and the prophet shall be known."[47]

As Christianity continued to expand and more extensive organisational structures were established, the ministry of teaching moved into the hands of the leaders of the faith communities, the bishops and presbyters. The four main functions for these early Christian teachers were similar to those of the rabbis. These interrelated roles included the instruction of children and new members of the community; the conservation, interpretation, and application of the tradition in new contexts; the maintenance of a distinctive religious identity over against that of the dominant culture; and the answering of criticisms of non-believers.[48]

As the episcopal structure of the church consolidated, formal Christian teaching developed by way of the catechumenate. The catechumenate was a designated period, often up to three years, of formal instruction climaxing at Easter, for those wishing to be baptized and thus attain membership in the church. Training was to be undertaken by candidates or *catechumens*, instructed by the bishop or a delegated presbyter. The catechumens were usually the children of believers and adult Jews or Gentile converts to Christianity.[49] Baptism constituted full participation in the worship of the church and figured prominently in the church's life. "Year after year, crowds of new believers flocked to be enrolled for the sacrament."[50] The church's celebration of the resurrection of Jesus at Easter was enhanced by the solemn baptism of the candidates who believed that they too could participate in this resurrection to new life. Baptism was the culmination and pinnacle of years of earnest preparation.

Before their baptism, catechumens at different levels of probation were allowed to participate at the worship gathering according to their level. Martin describes the three levels as "hearers," who could listen to the reading of the Scriptures and sermons, "kneelers," who could also stay for

---

47. Zdziarski, *Didache*, 11:7, 8.

48. Marthaler, *Harper's Encyclopedia*, 295.

49. Gangel and Benson, *Christian Education*, 89.

50. Field, *From Darkness to Light*, 19.

the prayers, and "the chosen," who were given further doctrinal training.[51] Each group also had to show that their conduct matched their academic learnings regarding following Christ. The curriculum covered the Scriptures, the Apostles' Creed and Christian writings including *The Didache* and *The Shepherd of Hermas*.[52] The teaching was given in a question and recited answer format or catechism.[53] Instruction in the sacramental liturgy or *mystagogy* was not given until after baptism had occurred.[54]

Catechists also initiated their students into Christian practices like fasting, kneeling to pray, and keeping night vigils. Daily exorcisms were performed, which were designed to lessen the influence of evil on the catechumens and to rid them of their old way of life.[55] At each level, the catechumens were stringently monitored on their moral behaviour and living, and then promoted accordingly. Some occupations were precluded as they were seen as not being compatible with Christian living at that time. Obvious prohibitions were roles involving pagan worship (including officials of the State) and the gladiatorial games (which also included spectators). Soldiers, who had to swear allegiance to the Emperor, actors in the theatre, and artists who depicted pagan gods were not admitted to the catechumenate either.[56]

In *De Catechizandis Rudibus* (On Catechizing Beginners in Faith), Augustine, Bishop of Hippo, elaborates on his understanding of teaching practice around the end of the fourth century.[57] Deogratias, a Deacon in Carthage, had asked Augustine to provide instruction in doctrine and method. Augustine describes Deogratias as "enjoying the reputation of possessing a rich gift in catechising, due at once to an intimate acquaintance with the faith, and to an attractive method of discourse."[58] In contemporary educational parlance we might call this a "Train-the-Trainer" model of instructing and encouraging catechists. Augustine even includes a type of lesson plan,[59] along with a comprehensive coverage of Christian knowledge, predominantly from the Hebrew Scriptures, as well as from the apostolic tradition. Augustine also stresses the need for a cheerful disposition on the

---

51. Martin, "Catechumenate," 113–14.

52. Gangel and Benson, *Christian Education*, 89.

53. Martin, "Catechumenate," 113.

54. Sawicki, in *Harper's Encyclopedia*, 295.

55. Field, *Darkness to Light*, 20.

56. Ibid., 19.

57. Turner, "Role of the Catechist," 17.

58. Augustine, "On the Catechising of the Uninstructed," 1:1.

59. Ibid., 16:24–25.

part of the catechist so as to ensure that the catechumens (or in fact, the teacher himself) will not become weary.[60]

Children of believers were often influenced in the ways of the Christian faith by their families. John Chrysostom (ca.347–407) addressed parental responsibility with regard to Christian instruction in *On Vainglory and the Raising of Children*.[61] Chrysostom discusses the importance of teaching children about the faith and its practices as moral protection against the worldly forces of evil. He declares: "The downfall of society stems from this disregard for children. Many seek the preservation of their estates, but not the preservation of the souls of those in their care."[62]

The catechumenate existed primarily for adult new believers, and did not develop on the Greek model of philosophers' schools of higher learning until the second century establishment of the first Catechetical School at Alexandria, under the leadership of Pantaenus, Clement and Origen. The work and influence of these teachers will be discussed further, below.

Formal Christian education gradually became the domain of these catechumenal schools, which were often held in the home of the teacher. It remained so into the fifth century, when the growth of the practice of infant baptism meant basic teaching of faith was seen as the duty of the family, after a child had been baptized. This understanding of baptism led to people putting off the commitment to the sacrament until later in life, or even until their death was imminent. By doing this, one could avoid the rigorous obligations of the catechumens, and die in the new-birth innocence conferred by baptism. Bishops and other church leaders strongly opposed this notion, "stressing the danger of sudden death."[63]

Catechumenal education was at its peak between 325 and 450, continuing into the fifth century. The catechumenate and catechesis, as a style of teaching, still exist in a much revised form in some Christian churches today. In its emergence and evolution, the catechumenate sowed the seeds for later developments in episcopal, cathedral and monastic schools.[64]

THE EARLIEST TEACHERS OF THE CATECHUMENATE

We will now look at a few of the key teachers of the catechumenate and briefly discuss their contribution to the development of Christian doctrine

60. Ibid., 10:14–15.

61. Marthaler, *Harper's Encyclopedia*, 295.

62. Chrystosom, "On Vainglory," 39–41.

63. Gangel and Benson, *Christian Education*, 89.

64. Ibid., 91.

and ultimately to the *traditium* of Christian education. The early Christian bishops were the main overseers and teachers of the fledgling Christian communities from the second century. It is no surprise that many used Greek philosophical understandings as their educational foundations, having been raised in this way themselves.

In his youth, Justin Martyr searched Greek philosophy for the truth, attaching himself to Stoic, Aristotelian and Platonic teachers, as well as becoming a student of Pythagoras. But in his *Apologies* he vigorously defends the Christian faith to the Roman emperor and the Roman senate.

In his *Apology*, II.13, Justin writes:

> I confess that I both boast and with all my strength strive to be found a Christian; not because the teachings of Plato are different from those of Christ, but because they are not in all respects similar, as neither are those of the others, Stoics, and poets and historians. . . . Whatever things were rightly said among all teachers, are the property of us Christians.[65]

Another apologist of the second century important to the development of Christian education was Irenaeus (c. 130–200). Irenaeus was influenced by the Greeks but was mainly concerned with refuting the heresy of Gnosticism. He felt that the coherence of emerging Christian doctrine was dependent upon a tradition of faithful instruction. The heresies of the Gnostics must be opposed at all costs, and this could be best achieved by the scattered statements of Scripture being drawn together within a system.[66]

Irenaeus appealed to the apostolic teaching handed down through the churches that had been founded by the Apostles themselves. He himself had been tutored under the martyr Polycarp, a follower of the apostle John.[67] For Irenaeus, apostolic tradition was the essence of the Christian faith and he railed against the Gnostics, who did not accept apostolic teachings.

African church Father, Tertullian (c. 160–225) was also highly critical of Greek philosophy, even though he had been brought up a Stoic.[68] He was another strong opponent of the heresy of Gnosticism. Before Tertullian, Christian thinkers wrote mainly in Greek, but this early church teacher was a Roman in his thinking. He placed many of his ideas within a typically Roman legal framework. Tertullian emphasised the paradoxical nature of faith and the contrast between Christianity and philosophy, which was a considerably different understanding from that of Justin and earlier apologists.

---

65. Martyr, in *A New Eusebius*, 61–62.

66. Chadwick, *Early Church*, 82.

67. Dowley, *Christians*, 25.

68. Knight, *Christ the Center*, 35.

Another of the apologists who was a key figure in the development of Christian knowledge was Clement, Bishop of Alexandria. Second century Egypt saw a burgeoning in the popularity of Gnosticism, with a number of its greatest proponents originating from or being taught there. Pantaenus, Clement's teacher, was the earliest known supporter of orthodox Christian doctrine in North Africa. Because of the size of the Gnostic following in Egypt, there was a problem of *obscurantist obscurity,*[69] viz., simply believing without trying to overcome or think out the difficult questions. By contrast, Pantaenus, Clement, and Origen after him, attempted to present an orthodoxy that was intellectually viable. They sought to show that philosophical and intellectual quandaries could be challenged and investigated without being heretical, but at the same time "respectable to people familiar with the highest forms of Greek culture."[70]

In Clement's *Miscellanies* 1:5 he notes:

> Before the coming of the Lord, the Greeks needed philosophy for righteousness. And now it leads to piety. It is a kind of preparatory training for those who reach faith through demonstration. . . . For God is the cause of all good things: of some directly, as with the Old and New Testaments; of others indirectly, as with philosophy. Maybe philosophy was even given to the Greeks directly, until the Lord should call them. For it was a schoolmaster to bring the Greek mind to Christ, as the Law did for the Jews. Thus philosophy was a preparation, paving the way for those who are brought to perfection in Christ.[71]

Incidentally, the parallels between this thought and the writings of Paul to the church in Galatia are significant. As we have already seen, Paul often represents the Jewish Law as a *paedagogos*—the Greek moral school teacher or punitive nanny whose role it was to drill, protect and even aggressively discipline the children of God until faith was revealed in Jesus Christ. In Gal 3:23–26, for example, Paul states:

> Now before faith came, we were imprisoned and guarded under the law until faith would be revealed. Therefore the law was our disciplinarian until Christ came, so that we might be justified by faith. But now that faith has come, we are no longer subject to a disciplinarian, for in Jesus Christ you are all children of God through faith.

---

69. Lane, *Christian Thought,* 20.

70. Gangel and Benson, *Christian Education,* 90.

71. Lane, *Christian Thought,* 21.

The Church Fathers, it is clear, often were attempting to understand and explain Christian doctrines in the light of their own education in ancient Greek philosophy and the context of Hellenistic culture in which they did their work. Christianity needed to present an intellectually respectable face to the ancient world. By using and adapting the philosophical understandings, language and approaches of the time, greater credibility was assumed. There were questions, philosophical, ontological and axiological, that seemed to have little apparent "coverage" in the recorded teachings of Jesus. How could Jesus have been of two substances—divine and human? What is the nature of the triune God? How did God create the world from nothing (ex nihilo)? Early Christian thinkers, trained in the grammar and conceptions of Greek philosophy, naturally turned in that direction to assist them in their explorations and speculations on these difficult questions.

As a part of a lived and practiced belief system, Christian education needs to be viewed as more than a passing on of knowledge. Ontological and axiological questions are also an essential component of the Christian faith. The Christian ethos is not encompassed in a set of inscribed, finite units of knowledge. What does it mean to be a Christian? How is one to behave? What can be known about God, and what is unknowable?

Augustine, Bishop of Hippo (354–430), disturbed by the problem of evil, asked some of these questions. Born in North Africa, Augustine had studied in Italy and had been strongly influenced in his ideas by Plato. Augustine sought to combine an understanding of the Christian faith with reason. He believed that understanding is a reward of faith.

As a theologian, Augustine's thought shaped the subsequent development of Christianity and has been arguably the greatest influence on the Western, Latin-speaking church. His influence was widespread and lasting. Not only did his thought dominate the Middle Ages, but both Reformation and Counter Reformation thinkers lodged their arguments in Augustinian thought. Thinkers like Anselm, Aquinas, Luther, Pascal and Kierkegaard were indebted to Augustine.[72] In Augustine, the church's traditium was being set for future generations, and is still influential in the contemporary church.

Augustine sums up his philosophy of learning and faith: ". . . let us seek to understand this, praying for help from him whom we seek to understand. . . . Faith seeks, understanding finds. This is why the prophet says, 'Unless you believe, you will not understand.' "(Isa 7:9).[73] Augustine's ideas about epistemology and its relationship to developing some understanding of God

---

72. Raeper and Smith, Beginner's Guide to Ideas, 18.
73. Augustine, Trinity, 9:1, 15:2 in Lane, Christian Thought, 43.

are important to Christian education. For Augustine, philosophy became "the study of God and the human soul."[74] What is the domain and purpose of Christian knowledge, and ultimately then, of Christian education, but to explore God and humanity?

The content of Christian education is, as has already been discussed, only partly cognitive knowledge. As Augustine and the Christian thinkers before him saw, an empirical pedagogy is not sufficient for formation as a follower of Jesus. Christian educator Thomas Groome describes Augustine's theological purpose as "a quest for practical spiritual wisdom, and his method is based on an experiential/relational way of knowing."[75] The nature of Christian education means it must include components of epistemology, ontology and axiology—context and experience interpreted by Scripture and Tradition, with practical wisdom, and Christians believe, guidance by God's Holy Spirit. Both the *traditium* and the *traditio* must reflect these components, and be based in the Scriptures along with the recognized confessional statements of the church—its dogma.

The results of such understandings of Christian education have often seen the formalizing of Christian education. In the early centuries of Christianity, as we have seen, schooling, following the Greco-Roman model of the Roman Empire, had ostensibly supplanted the academic teaching role of the family.[76] With the rise of the catechumenate, and then catechetical schools for advanced theological study and the training of clergy being established in Alexandria, Antioch, Edessa, Caesarea, Nisibis, Jerusalem and Carthage, Christian faith education also moved from the hands of the laity.

Around the time of Emperor Constantine's conversion to Christianity and the subsequent Edict of Milan in AD 313, and certainly in its wake, the catechumenate flourished. The Edict of Milan ruled that Christian worship, which had suffered considerable persecution until then, would be tolerated along with the other religious practices of the Empire, most notably monotheistic Sun worship.[77] Christians could now openly *evangelize* or teach the message of their faith. The implications of Constantine's conversion were to define the history of the church and of Europe for at least the next millennium. This was much more than an end to the persecution of the Christians. The union of church and State was entwined socially, politically and even justified theologically. "The sovereign autocrat was inevitably and

---

74. Raeper and Smith, *Beginner's Guide to Ideas,* 20.

75. Groome, *Christian Religious Education,* 159.

76. Gangel and Benson, *Christian Education,* 55.

77. Ibid., 91.

immediately involved in the development of the church, and conversely the church became more and more implicated in high political decisions."[78]

The concept of Christendom was born. The official acceptance of "Christendom" or the Christian State across the Roman Empire meant that the church now had to carefully define orthodoxy, so as to preserve the purity of its teaching and attack heresy. This led to the ecumenical Councils of Nicaea (325), Constantinople (381), Ephesus (431) and Chalcedon (451), where major doctrinal statements, particularly on the Trinitarian being and nature of God, were formulated and accepted. The institutionalization of the church's *traditium*, and thus of the church itself, was being cemented.

The Roman Empire gradually declined in the West until its fall late in the fifth century. This demise was accompanied by, and in some ways facilitated by, a decline in the vitality of secular thought. Christianity had thus far been dependent on formal secular schooling for the teaching of reading, writing, logical thinking and debating. This was vital for Christian clergy and others in order to pass on the faith. The catechumenate had fallen into disuse by the mid-fifth century and was non-existent by the seventh century.[79] These factors, coupled with the invasion of imperial cities by barbarian tribes, weakened the educational enterprises of both church and State.

ONE LEGACY OF THE EARLY CATECHUMENATE: MONASTICISM

Monasticism had come to be part of the post-Constantine Christian understanding in the middle of the third century. People opposed to the new style of State-sanctioned Christianity withdrew from society, seeking "white martyrdom" (as opposed to "red martyrdom," which meant physically dying for one's faith). This lifestyle reflected some of Paul's teachings about the struggles within oneself between so-called desires of the flesh and those of the spirit. The ascetic movement followed in the footsteps of hermits such as Antony. This gradually led to the formation of settled regulated communities, and later, monasteries. In Asia Minor, Basil of Caesarea (330–379) established one of the earliest such communities, emphasizing love and service to others over the indifference to the needs of secular society and individualism of the hermits.[80] An emphasis on the denial of the flesh fueled a movement eventually dominated by a monastic rule, developed by

---

78. Chadwick, *Early Church*, 125.

79. Sawicki, in *Encyclopedia of Religious Education*, 296.

80. Chadwick, *Early Church*, 179.

Benedict of Nursia (c. 480–547) that upheld initially poverty and chastity, then obedience.

Educationally, monasteries contributed much to the development of Christian learning in the medieval period and in later times. Along with cathedral schools which continued to be overseen by the local Bishops, monastic schools were set up for training in the ways of a particular order or rule, but later accepted students for general as well as religious education. Learning was conducted in Latin and included rigid discipline, fasting and prayer, along with the liberal arts (grammar, logic, rhetoric, arithmetic, geometry, astronomy, and music). Monasteries were able to preserve and pass on formal Christian knowledge (albeit in a fairly limited way) by protecting and copying ancient manuscripts. This, along with other social and historical antecedents such as the Crusades and the subsequent rise of Islam, paved the way for the development of renaissance universities encouraging the thought of theologians such as Anselm, Duns Scotus and Aquinas.[81] These and other Christian teachers or "Schoolmen" gave impetus to a period of the history of Christian education known as Scholasticism. Influenced by Aristotle, Aquinas saw a sharp divide between issues of revelation and those of reason. Faith, however, could also be reasoned, and Aquinas developed a rational defence of belief, and "proofs" for the existence of God based on cosmological and teleological arguments.

There are a number of parallels that are evident between these historical antecedents and the contemporary situation of the church today. One strand of the Emerging Church that is attempting to recall and re-imagine some of the roots of Christian education is New Monasticism.

A POSTMODERN PARALLEL: THE NEW MONASTICISM OF THE EMERGING CHURCH

New Monasticism is a movement which first started in the 1920s and 1930s in post World War I Germany[82] and has received attention again with the rise of the Emerging Church. The concept originally developed in reaction to the horrors of the War, and the economic depression left in its wake. Eberhard Arnold and his family founded the Bruderhof (place of brotherhood) Community to live simply and authentically as Christian disciples. Arnold stated:

---

81. Gangel and Benson, *Christian Education,* 110.

82. Wilson-Hartgrove, *New Monasticism,* 33.

> We want a genuine school of life, where the simplest work be-
> comes a physical and artistic experience, where there is free-
> dom from intellectualism and its pitfalls, where a new man can
> emerge, a creative man whose culture expresses what is real. We
> do not need theories or idealistic goals or prophets or leaders.
> We need brotherhood and sisterhood. We need to *live* Jesus'
> Sermon on the Mount. We need to show that a life of justice and
> forgiveness and unity is possible today.[83]

Around the same time, theologian Dietrich Bonhoeffer wrote to his
brother, Karl-Friedrich Bonhoeffer:

> The restoration of the church will surely come from a sort of
> New Monasticism which has in common with the old only the
> uncompromising attitude of a life lived according to the Sermon
> on the Mount in the following of Christ. I believe it is now the
> time to call people together to do this.[84]

Thus the name and notion of intentional Christian communities
re-emerged and, paradoxically, developed through such disparate entities
as the urban US Catholic spirituality of Dorothy Day, co-founder of the
Catholic Worker movement (which promoted Catholic social teaching in
the 1930s in the slums of New York, and later established Catholic Worker
communal farms), and the conservative pietism of the Anabaptists into the
1950s.[85] Later, in the 1960s and 1970s, groups like the Jesus People evolved,
and more recently, under the umbrella of the Emerging Church, New Monasticism has again been re-invented.

Generally, the literature concerning New Monasticism concurs that its
most recent reincarnation was developed by Jonathan Wilson in his 1998
book, "Living Faithfully in a Fragmented World: Lessons for the church
from MacIntyre's 'After Virtue.'"[86] In this book, Wilson responds to moral
philosopher Alasdair MacIntyre's plea, which concludes his influential *After
Virtue*, written in 1981. In *After Virtue*, MacIntyre critiques Modernity's
ethical decay and calls for "the construction of local forms of community
within which civility and the intellectual and moral life can be sustained
through the new dark ages which are already upon us. . . . We are waiting for
another—doubtless very different—St Benedict."[87]

---

83. Arnold, quoted in Mommsen, *Homage to a Broken Man*, 21 (Mommsen is Arnold's great grandson).

84. Bonhoeffer, quoted in Freeman and Greig, *Punk Monk*, 7.

85. Wilson-Hartgrove, *New Monasticism*, 33.

86. Wilson, *Living Faithfully*.

87. MacIntyre, *After Virtue*, 263.

The form of New Monasticism developed by Wilson attempts to bring about a renewal of morality and graciousness through community. Wilson proposes four features distinguishing his vision: (1) it will be "marked by a recovery of the telos of this world" revealed in Jesus, and aimed at the healing of fragmentation, bringing the whole of life under the lordship of Christ; (2) it will be aimed at the "whole people of God" who live and work in all kinds of contexts, and not create a distinction between those with sacred and secular vocations; (3) it will be disciplined, not by a recovery of old monastic rules, but by the joyful discipline achieved by a small group of disciples practicing mutual exhortation, correction, and reconciliation; and (4) it will be "undergirded by deep theological reflection and commitment," which may lead to the recovery of the church's life and witness in the world.[88]

The Twelve Marks of New Monasticism give a sense of continuity to the movement, which seeks to found communities that value hospitality, generosity especially to the poor, contemplation, prayer and communal life. The Twelve Marks are:

1. Relocation to the "abandoned places of Empire" at the margins of society

2. Sharing economic resources with fellow community members and the needy among us

3. Hospitality to the stranger

4. Lament for racial divisions within the church and our communities combined with the active pursuit of a just reconciliation

5. Humble submission to Christ's body, the church

6. Intentional formation in the way of Christ and rule of the community along the lines of the old novitiate

7. Nurturing common life among members of intentional community

8. Support for celibate singles alongside monogamous married couples and their children

9. Geographical proximity to community members who share a common rule of life

10. Care for the plot of God's earth given to us along with support of our local economies

---

88. Wilson, *Living Faithfully*, 72–75.

11. Peacemaking in the midst of violence and conflict resolution within communities along the lines of Matthew 18

12. Commitment to a disciplined contemplative life[89]

This movement has now spread across the US, back to Europe and the United Kingdom, where a related strand, 24–7 Prayer, 24–7 Boiler Rooms and Communities, is quietly growing.[90] The distinguishing factor of this sub-section of the Emerging Church is its emphasis on learning as a Christian practice, and the importance of intentional Christian formation and discipleship. With the Benedictine monks as their models, 24–7 Prayer, a New Monastic group in Britain, sees a vital difference between the scholarly approach of academia and the monastic heritage of learning. "While scholars look to debate and critique, monks rely on meditation on the Bible, the writings of the Desert Fathers and classic literature. Their aim is devotion."[91] The worshipping, praying community is the learning community. The Boiler Rooms are set up to pray ecumenically for issues globally and locally, on a 24 hours a day, 7 days a week basis, hence "24–7." The 24–7 Movement has now grown to include small, contemporary monastic communities world-wide. One of the founders, Andy Freeman notes:

> As we began to consider the place of learning in 24–7 Boiler Rooms, we felt led not to the classroom, but to the prayer room—to the disciple gazing in wonder at the Lord, reverencing and worshipping Him. Isn't it fascinating how often God speaks to us when we worship? When we change the subject of our attentions from ourselves to Christ, we put ourselves in the true place of learning.[92]

When learning is central to and expected by the whole community of faith, there is the possibility for lifelong participation in Christian formation, and worshipping that genuinely begins to grasp the Christian ethos.

ANOTHER PARALLEL: THE SUNDAY SCHOOL MOVEMENT

Mention needs to be made of a major component of the *traditio* on the modern Protestant Christian education landscape: the Sunday School. In

89. Rutba House, *Schools for Conversion*, xii–xiii.

90. Freeman and Greig, *Punk Monk*, 100–123.

91. Ibid., 67.

92. Ibid.

some ways the Sunday School has had parallels with the learning *traditio* of the early church. However, the Sunday School movement stems from different presuppositions to those foundational to the catechumenate. Whilst the catechumenate was designed to make the most of and incorporate the worshipping community as the learning community for beginners in faith, the Sunday School movement did not value the worshipping community in the same way. The Sunday School was seen as the complete learning community in itself. Once a student had graduated from the Sunday School, they were generally understood to have completed their Christian education. In many ways, the notion of Sunday School's existence has contributed to the fact that Christian education has not evolved in the same way as the Emerging Church movement.

In many Protestant congregations today, it would be true to say that Sunday School is still commonly perceived as *the* Christian education component of congregational life. Much that has been written with regard to Christian education has limited it to children and young people, working in terms of stages of physical, cognitive and faith development, predominantly within the context of the congregational Sunday School. This restriction has also limited Christian education's ability to survive as a central part of the church's ongoing mission.

The Sunday School has been understood at various times in the church's more recent life as instruction for the under-privileged, an evangelistic outreach tool of the church, and a church growth organization.[93] Since its inception in the late 1700s, Sunday School has been organised to emulate secular schooling, with age group divisions ranging from pre-school through children, youth, and even to adults. Robert Raikes (1736–1811) is usually associated with the founding of the Sunday School concept in Britain.[94] In 1780 this Gloucester newspaper publisher, already committed to efforts in prison reform and the education of offenders, established a school for poor children in "Sooty Alley," Gloucester. The purpose of the school was to teach working children the basics of reading and writing so that they could better themselves socially. Classes took place on Sunday, their only free day.

Sunday Schools were replicated around the world, especially in countries colonised by the British. With the notion enshrined in the American Constitution of the separation of church and State, the Sunday School movement thrived in America. Similar structure was employed, usually organised around territorial boundaries, with denominational differences

93. Borchert, *Harper's Encyclopedia*, 623.
94. Knoff, *World Sunday School Movement*, 24, 25.

being ostensibly ignored. The Sunday School catch-cry was, "Doctrine divides, service unites." The laity of the churches volunteered as teachers, seeing it as their duty to those less fortunate.

In this way, for over two centuries, Christian education became formalized, regimented, segregated from the rest of life and from the worshipping community. Sunday School conformed Christian education to the model of the secular school of the time. Participants were known as "students" and were divided into "classes" according to age groups. There were examinations, graduations, and prizes for achievement.

At the heart of the Sunday School movement, two key concepts were accepted: sectarian doctrine was seen as divisive; and instruction was chiefly a ministry of the laity. Today, many would agree that sectarianism has had its time. Postmodern minds see no place for this kind of separatism. The contemporary Protestant Church, and especially the Emerging Church would generally applaud the strong involvement of the laity in this kind of ministry.

So, why has the Sunday School movement ostensibly been rejected as a model of Christian education by the Emerging Church? Clearly, Christian education needs to recapture its place as an intersection of *doxology* and doctrine. The worshipping community must regain its place as the learning community. Sunday School's function in many instances has become that of child minding during the congregation's service of worship. By itself, making paper pinwheels does not ensure any understanding of the happenings of the Pentecost narrative! Whereas the catechumenate saw the necessity for beginners in faith to achieve a standard of behavior and knowledge that allowed them to participate more fully in the worshipping life of the church, Sunday School often has the beginners in faith separated from the gathered worship of the community so that worship may proceed quietly, without interruption from noisy youngsters. Insights from this study of the worship of the Emerging Church indicate that intentional learning needs to be a part of the design of worship events. The whole community (for good or ill) is, in fact, engaged in the education of the beginners in faith of all ages, as I will show in later chapters.

When the Sunday School movement began, and throughout its heyday, education was thought to be a force for freedom from poverty and servility. Sunday School continued in similar modes for over one hundred years, gradually becoming more closely aligned with particular churches. By the late 1800s there was a strong evangelical focus.

After World War II, a growth in industrialization and specialization saw secular education and training as increasingly vocationally related. The whole of society, including the religious landscape, was starting to become more pluralistic. The clergy was becoming increasingly "professionalized," which tended to lead to a greater marginalisation of lay teachers in congregations. All this contributed to a decline in religious education generally.

By the 1960s and 1970s secular education was looking to expand its horizons beyond the standard classroom, through the influence of the deschooling movement. The best known advocate of deschooling was Ivan Illich. He believed that schools:

> stifle curiosity, penalise initiative, destroy the will to learn; that they discriminate against the working class child, that they inculcate middle class values, that they foster competitiveness and discourage cooperativeness; that they perpetuate useless knowledge, that they erode critical awareness and reward mindless conformity.[95]

The Deschoolers rejected formal education out of hand, placing education into the hands of the broader community. Their efforts led to a reformation of schooling that continues to the present day. In the later decades of the twentieth century, the church on the whole, however, continued with an outdated and separatist classroom-based approach to learning, usually restricted to the young, and with a general lack of interest in its relationship with theology, doxology or doctrine. Life-long Christian learning was not a high priority. Sunday School became a place to send the children, while church was for the adults. To the detriment of the whole church, Christian education and formation in faith became understood almost solely in terms of Sunday School. Its role had changed from social reformer to an evangelical tool, and then to a vehicle for providing adult worshippers an hour of peace and quiet, and thus maintaining the institution as appropriate only for adults. The development of doctrinal and doxological understandings of the church had been largely neglected by Sunday School proponents. At the same time, Sunday School and its teachers tended, on the whole, to be caricatured by both Christian and secular commentators.

At the end of the twentieth century, evangelical American author Tim Stafford, among numerous others, painted a grim picture of the decline of Sunday schools. Stafford suggested a reason for this is that churches do not see education as a critical part of their mission, channelling resources elsewhere.[96] In 2005, *The Christian Century* reported a growing trend in mainstream American churches to cut Sunday School classes and youth education programs because of a lack of teachers.[97]

95. Illich, *Deschooling Society*, 71–72.
96. Stafford, "This Little Light of Mine," 29–32.
97. "Slight Decrease," 15.

For some time Christian education has not enjoyed the central place it once held in the life of the church. Meanwhile, interest in the mainline church as a whole has not fared well in many arenas of postmodernist society, whereas there seems to be a spike in the interest in the more amorphous notion of spirituality. The practices of the Emerging Church reveal an attempt to face the fresh demands of a post-structural, postmodern world. We have seen how, as a field, Christian education has seemingly become caught in a mid-twentieth century, Modern schooling paradigm. Can insights learned from our study of the Emerging Church help resuscitate teaching and learning in Western Christianity? In the next chapter we will examine some causes for the withering of growth in Christian education, and offer a new paradigm that it is hoped will complement and challenge both the Emerging and mainstream church.

Chapter 5

The Current Crisis of Christian Education

IN THIS CHAPTER WE will explore the current situation of Christian education in the Western Protestant church. I will argue that Christian education
has suffered a loss of theological place in the life of the church. There will
be a clarification of the approaches and outcomes that will form the understanding of Christian education for this study. These will then be considered
in greater depth, in correlation with the insights gained from our examination of the Emerging Church literature. The nature of Christian knowledge
and epistemology will be discussed in order to introduce a new interpretive
framework for Christian education, especially designed for use in emerging
postmodern ministry.

In previous chapters we have seen how Modernist thinking infiltrated
every aspect of Western life, including the life and faith of Christians as the
church. We have looked at postmodernism as a reaction against many Modernist understandings. In so many ways, the Emerging Church movement
has reflected this postmodern reaction, and its response provides a relevant
and timely means for considering paths ahead for Christian education as
well. As a stimulus to some fresh thinking in this area, we will first briefly
consider two pieces of research that examine the state of Christian education in Western Protestantism over the last twenty years.

In his book, *The Teaching Church*, Eugene C. Roehlkepartain quotes
the Minneapolis Search Institute's study of US Christian education entitled,
Effective Christian Education: A National Study of Protestant Congregations.[1]

1. Roehlkepartain, *Teaching Church*, 18–22.

95

This study was undertaken from 1990 to 1993 and surveyed 11,122 adults, teenagers, pastors and Christian educators across five mainline denominations in the United States of America. Roehlkepartain observes that this research revealed four central points with regard to Christian formation. Firstly, in general, US Christians do not have what is described as "mature" faith. In this study, faith maturity was measured under eight marks or expressions. These were: "Trusting and Believing," which included the actions that stemmed from the practice of faith; "Experiencing the Fruits of Faith," which examined the subjects' sense of well-being, peace and security; "Integrating Faith and Life," which studied faith as a hermeneutic for life; "Seeking Spiritual Growth," which noted the movement from childhood concepts and changes in the nature of belief; "Nurturing Faith in Community," which focussed on participation in the life of the Christian community; "Holding Life-affirming Values," which looked at lifestyle; "Advocating Social Change," which examined concern for the public sphere of life; and "Acting and Serving," which looked at subjects' involvement in acts of love and justice.2 According to the criteria used in the study, only 32 percent of adults were considered to have a mature faith, and most young people (64 percent) were considered to have an undeveloped faith. Roehlkepartain notes that "for most people in our churches, faith is dormant and inactive."

Secondly, Christian education was identified by the study's participants to be the most important vehicle within congregational life for helping people grow in their faith. Roehlkepartain gives no further explanation or analysis here, except to comment on the obvious potential for Christian education in promoting faith, and to quote Christian educator, Richard Robert Osmer:

> The restoration of a church that can teach with authority . . .
> may be the pressing issue before mainline churches today. . . .
> The American mainline Protestant churches are at a crossroads.
> Which path they take may very well rest on whether they can
> restore the teaching ministry of the Church to its rightful place
> of importance.[3]

Thirdly, it was found that most congregations were not involved in what was seen as effective Christian education at all. Roehlkepartain laments that "most Christian education in congregations revolves around outdated processes, methods, and content."[4] The original report concluded:

2. Ibid., 36, 37.

3. Osmer, quoted in Roehlkepartain, *Teaching Church*, 19.

4. Ibid.

Christian education in a majority of congregations is a tired enterprise in need of reform. Often out-of-touch with adult and adolescent needs, it experiences difficulty in finding and motivating volunteers, faces general disinterest among its "clients," and employs models and procedures that have changed little over time.[5]

Fourthly, *Effective Christian Education* showed that concrete changes within churches can improve educational effectiveness and help people to grow in faith.

A survey of Christian education in the Uniting Church in Australia studied over 300 congregations in 2000. The study, *Making Disciples,* was conducted by the then national body for that church's Christian education, Uniting Education. Although conducted over a significantly smaller target audience than the Minneapolis study, the outcomes reflect similar findings. The *Making Disciples* survey questions intentionally attempted to help respondents view Christian education in wider terms than merely Sunday School. The results of the survey, *Making Disciples,* revealed a number of critical issues, including:

Community development and private faith

- Members and ministers in congregations agree that the primary outcome of Christian education is to relate faith to life, but disagree about what that means
- Members connect Christian faith to life mainly in terms of personal and private piety and values
- Ministers want members of congregations to connect faith to life with more communal, social and public expressions of Christian religious practice and ethical behaviour
- While members think that congregations' education programs should give more attention to relating faith to everyday life, they are reluctant to participate in such programs unless 'everyday life' means personal piety and private morality
- Members expect the congregation to provide high quality religious and social services but are reluctant to invest in the training that will develop quality leadership for those services

---

5. Benson and Elkin, *Effective Christian Education,* quoted in Roehlkepartain, *Teaching Church,* 58.

- Most people, both ministers and members, consider Christian education as something that happens "within the Church"— their needs and the religious needs of the Church constitute the majority targets of educational activities

- For most Uniting Church attenders, relationships with family and friends are more important for a sense of peace, wellbeing and meaning than are the Church's teachings, traditions or life.

Growth in the life of faith

- Members report that the most growth in Christian faith has occurred in their personal experiences of and understandings about God

- Members see close personal relationships and participation in the church community as contributing more to their growth in faith than structured programs or activities

- Members reflect imbalance in the degree of integration between the two dimensions of Christian faith—the vertical (or God/person relationship) and the horizontal (or person to person relationship)—in favour of the vertical dimension.

Congregations' practice

- Ministers and members reveal significantly different understandings of the educational ministry of the Church at many points

- Several significant barriers to participation in intentional Christian education are noted—ministers mention time, motivation and leadership as the most significant; members suggest relevance to daily life as the most significant

- The fundamental connection in congregations between education and discipleship has been lost

- There is evidence that the teaching ministry of the Church is being resisted; and there is some loss of confidence among those with a responsibility to teach in the Church

- Few ministers have a coherent plan for intentional educational ministry

- Few congregations have a structure for sustained Christian education

- Few congregations have a systematic, structured or sustained process for helping people discover and develop their gifts for ministry and mission

- Little attention has been given to the education of those beyond the congregation.[6]

The results of these two studies are disturbing for many in the church. Both studies reflect the sluggish state of faith formation in Western mainline Protestant Christianity. Both studies reveal not only biblical and liturgical illiteracy, but the loss of the ability to allow faith to inform reflection on and behavior in life. Many Christians view faith as personal and private, reflecting a Modernist view that it is unscientific, perhaps even irrational and therefore risky to admit or discuss. The Christian community is thus commensurately impoverished. Church leaders are not unaware of the problem, but often feel inadequate to the task of finding ways forward. There is a strong sense of pessimism evident. The Emerging Church, in many ways, can be seen as a reaction against this state of affairs. The call to "walk-the-walk" of faith as well as "talk-the-talk" of faith comes from many Emerging quarters, as we have seen. It becomes apparent that a new paradigm for Christian education is long overdue. What has been done in the past clearly cannot move Christian communities creatively into the future. A fresh appreciation for the ways of knowing that relate to active Christian faith and faith formation is needed for new generations of people who seem to be eager to explore faith and the whole area of spirituality generally.[7]

First, however, let us briefly describe some of the main understandings that have developed regarding Christian education, to see how these understandings have, in many ways, been catalytic to the problems we have discussed.

CURRENT APPROACHES, METHODOLOGIES AND DESIRED OUTCOMES OF CHRISTIAN EDUCATION

Traditionally, Christian education has been approached and carried out in a number of ways, for many different purposes, and with various "metaphors,"

6. Hughes, *Making Disciples*, 1–2. Bulleted points have been used in the *Making Disciples* study, so I have chosen to retain them here.

7. Cox, *Future of Faith*, 14–20.

to use Seymour and Miller's descriptor.[8] In their book, *Contemporary Approaches to Christian Education*, they discuss five contemporary methodologies: religious instruction, faith community, spiritual development, liberation, and interpretation, each with a corresponding metaphor—education, community of faith, person, justice and meaning.

For Seymour and Miller, religious instruction as an approach emphasises the structures of formal education and ordered learning within the church. The faith community focuses upon the power of the life of the congregation to teach. Spiritual development builds on psychological research about human growth. Liberation is a reflection of the liberation theologians, whose aim is to empower people to live the reign of God in the midst of oppression. Interpretation, finally, emphasises the connection between faith and daily life.

In *Mapping Christian Education*, published fifteen years after *Contemporary Approaches*, Jack Seymour provides a revised and updated overview of his and Miller's approaches to Christian education. Seymour makes an important statement about the state of play in Christian education at the turn of the twenty-first century:

> Christian education that relies on the practices of public education is under considerable scrutiny. Contemporary studies look to congregational life and public mission for Christian education theory. Therefore, in the last decade, even more attention has been given to the relationship of biblical methodologies, the study of religions, and theology to Christian education.[9]

Distinct approaches to Christian education within the contemporary Australian context have generally fallen into three main strands that reflect vastly differing hermeneutics and particular desired outcomes:

1. Education in religions/faiths, and specifically education about Christianity;

2. Pre-evangelism and evangelism or information about Christianity with a view to Christian conversion; and

3. Christian formation and transformation.

These strands roughly follow Seymour and Miller's model of approaches, but social, historical, and geopolitical differences in the make-up of Australian Christianity have given rise to some different emphases. The Australian landscape, ethos and diverse cultural make-up are among the

8. Seymour and Miller, *Contemporary Approaches*, 16–34.

9. Seymour, *Mapping Christian Education*, 15.

many factors shaping the style and understanding of Christian knowledge and its application within this context.[10]

I will use the term *desired outcomes* here, instead of Seymour and Miller's *approaches*. These desired outcomes are not always explicitly or even consciously defined, and tend to encompass wide-ranging approaches in practice. Often the methodologies employed to achieve particular desired outcomes are limited by a specific environment or context—Religious Education in a State school, for example. Desired outcomes and methodologies can be entwined, as part of the tacit or often unarticulated awareness inherent in a particular community's life. The experience of Catholic School children attending a weekly School Mass is one example of this. Let us now briefly describe each of these desired outcomes.

1. Education about Religions, Including Christianity

Education about religions, including Christianity, pertains to identifying a purportedly objective, scientific study of religion, religious beliefs or faiths. This is distinct from a theological and confessional study for the purpose of increasing the faith, understanding and institutional commitment of an individual student in a particular religion.

Examples of this type of education include secondary school "Study of Religion" courses and religious studies at secular universities. In parts of Australia, Religious Education and "Scripture Classes" in State Schools can also contain elements incumbent in this strand, although they tend to be predominantly focussed on teaching about Christianity to the exclusion of other religions.

This is where we see in practice the fact that conceptions of the nature of Religious Education are "divided into those which emphasise religious education as a religious activity and those which emphasise it as an educational activity."[11] So we come to the distinction between Religious Education and Christian religious education.

Where Religious Education is viewed as a religious activity, it has been understood as "that process of teaching and learning by means of which religions have sought for their transmission and self-perpetuation."[12] Clearly, this is specific to a particular religion or faith, and thus we may speak of Jewish or Buddhist or Christian religious education to give just some of the possibilities.

10. Bouma, *Many Religions*, 101.

11. Hull, "RE, Nature of," 284.

12. Ibid.

> In this accepted traditional sense, religious education would proceed through a convergent teaching procedure, in which the personal commitment of the teacher, the content . . . and intentions . . . would converge. Traditionally it was the nature of religious education to speak from faith to faith.[13]

If Religious Education is understood as a predominantly educational activity, rather than as a religious activity, its nature and context will be different. As an educational activity, it must be justified on general educational grounds rather than being undergirded theologically, having its roots in the philosophy and sociology of education and in the theories of curriculum development. During the 1970s and early 1980s, under the influence of writers such as Edwin Cox, J. W. D. Smith, and Ninian Smart, the theory and practice of Religious Education as a branch of secular education became more established. Therefore it has become necessary to express and understand the "religious activity" differently. The theological standpoint will always affect the nature, characteristics and purpose of the education being undertaken. Christian education is education about Christianity, but it also encompasses education about being Christian, which will be described later as *Christian formation and transformation*.

2. Pre-Evangelism and Evangelism

Christian education can take other guises and exist in other contexts as well. This leads us to the second strand of Christian education that we will consider here, viz., *evangelism*. Mary C. Boys, in her book, *Educating in Faith: Maps and Visions*, notes four of what she calls *classic expressions of religious education*, namely *evangelism, religious education, Christian education,* and *Catholic education*.[14] She views evangelism as a classic approach that remains the most difficult to define. "Moreover, the task of tracing its paths with any degree of accuracy requires a point of departure earlier than that for the other expressions—a consideration suggesting . . . its formative power." Boys maintains that the umbrella term *evangelism* deserves close attention because its dynamics established much of the agenda of religious education in the twentieth century.

With Boys' observations in mind, I have termed this outcome of Christian education "Pre-evangelism and evangelism," or information about Christianity with a view to conversion. If evangelism is sharing the

---

13. Ibid.
14. Boys, *Educating in Faith*, 9.

good news—the *euaggelion*—or "communicating the gospel to those outside the faith with the intent of evoking commitment to Christ,"[15] then *pre-evangelism* is what comes prior to this. The term has sometimes been used as an excuse for covert evangelising without being seen to be doing evangelism (making new Christians). In other words, pre-evangelism is presenting information designed to lead the hearer (at some time in the future) to conversion to Christianity. The difference is that pre-evangelism infers that the hearer may not become converted on the spot!

Evangelicalism has continued to stress education as a central means of making the gospel known. But education in this context has often had a strictly didactic, instructional and transmissive flavour, with biblical literacy through memorization and song its chief goal.[16] Christian education has often been hijacked by evangelicalism that is disguised as the more overarching "mission." Mission, in this understanding, can be concentred on the numbers game that is the quantitative measure of growth of the Church Growth movement. Christian education needs to avoid establishing this kind of numerical competition as its objective. The primary goal of Christian education needs to be the Christian formation and transformation of each person as a follower of Jesus, learning, teaching and living the Christian story. This in turn builds, strengthens and nurtures the whole community in its grasp of Christian ethos, character and way of life. A key question for evangelicalism as an entity is, *What happens to all these numbers of people once we get them through the church door? How is the worshipping community actually fulfilling this lifelong teaching and learning role?*

The journey of faith clearly begins with a first step, but in Christian education we are concerned with guiding each other in moving on in faith, in the many more steps involved in following Christ. The writer to the Hebrews describes this as moving from milk to meat, not being blown about by every new spiritual whim:

> For though by this time you ought to be teachers, you need someone to teach you again the basic elements of the oracles of God. You need milk, not solid food; for everyone who lives on milk, being still an infant, is unskilled in the word of righteousness. But solid food is for the mature, for those whose faculties have been trained by practice to distinguish good from evil. Therefore let us go on toward maturity, leaving behind the basic teaching about Christ, and not laying again the foundation.[17]

---

15. Fackre, *Harper's Encyclopedia*, 236.

16. Boys, *Educating in Faith*, 31.

17. Heb 5:12–14; 6:1.

Christian education must include an ongoing quality, the ability to reflect theologically on the experiences of journeying with the Christian story. A Christian life is not completed at conversion; rather, that is a beginning point. The disciples of Jesus followed him and learned from his teaching for at least three years, and at the end of his time on earth, the writer of the Gospel of Matthew notes of the disciples that: "[W]hen they saw him, they worshipped him; but some doubted."[18] This is a profound statement for Christian education. As followers, Christians are inevitably traveling along the way. Grasping Christian ethos is a life-long task. The Christian faith is not a destination, the body of knowledge associated with it can never be fully known. It concerns, after all, a growing knowledge of the infinite, transcendent God, along with a growing knowledge of oneself in relation to this God and God's people. Christianity also has other complexities which it must face, including the task of discovering, understanding and dealing with its social, cultural and political context for Christian engagement. Christian formation and transformation comes by being immersed in whole-of-life worship of God.

3. Christian Formation

As the third outcome for Christian education, Christian formation is concerned with the way in which individuals and communities perceive themselves and their life, their attitude towards others, and how their vision and values are shaped by their understanding of God, of themselves and of God's people. Christian formation involves the development of character as individuals and as the Christian church—the Body of Christ. As Paul implores in his letter to the Romans: "Do not be conformed to this world, but be transformed by the renewing of your minds, so that you may discern what is the will of God—what is good and acceptable and perfect."[19]

Christian formation is a lifelong process that permeates every aspect of one's life. It is an ongoing work of God. Empowered by God's Holy Spirit, it is determining and growing progressively into alignment with God's will as one participates in the Christian story. The shaping of "beliefs, intentions and actions"[20] is the domain of Christian formation, whether it is the moulding of an individual or a whole community.

In the majority of the discourse informed predominantly by the thinking of the Emerging Church, Christian formation or discipleship is

18. Matt 28:17.

19. Rom 12:2.

20. Hauerwas, *Character and the Christian Life*, 16.

the most important desired outcome of Christian education. There are, of course, those within Emerging Church ranks who would rather nominate evangelism as the desired outcome of choice in their communities. Sharing the good news of Jesus Christ through proclamation is vital, and this is profoundly achieved by living out the good news in the worship of God and worshipping God by responding to God's grace in loving the neighbour. This is the transformed action that the Emerging Church proclaims. This action is community oriented, and embraces diverse ways of knowing; it is centered in worship of God in Jesus Christ by the power of the Holy Spirit as distinctive to the identity of Christians, and profoundly countercultural in attitude and purpose. Christian formation should not be separated from worship, and the worshipping life of the people of God cannot be limited to attending church services.[21]

By its very nature, Christian formation is essential for the continuation of the church into the future. As we have seen, it is also a major area in need of renovation for the sake of the whole church, so it will remain the focus of our discussion. It has been necessary to be clear as to our primary concern in the discussion here. With the help of insights gained from our observations of the Emerging Church, we will now reconsider what it means to be formed in Christian faith as individuals and communities in a postmodern world.

THE WORSHIPPING COMMUNITY AS THE CONTEXT FOR CHRISTIAN EDUCATION

The eschatological goal of the human vocation is enunciated in strongly doxological terms in the opening of the Westminster Shorter Catechism:

> What is the chief end of man (*sic*)?
>
> Man's chief end is to glorify God, and to enjoy God forever.[22]

Human beings essentially were created to worship God and enjoy God. Human beings were also granted free will and intellect by God in order to choose and explore, to discover, learn about, and actively participate in this worship and enjoyment of God. Thus, as Christians worship God, there is the potential to grow in understanding of who God is, what God is like, and how God is to be worshipped. This is a key to greater enjoyment of God and knowledge of ourselves. In any loving relationship, as one grows to

21. Murphy, *Teaching That Transforms*, 13.
22. Westminster Shorter Catechism.

understand and appreciate the personality of the other, the initial awkwardness of unknowing and being unknown gradually tends to dissipate and enjoyment may follow. Worship as the glorification of God is a core means of knowing and enjoying God. Individuals may worship God privately, but in essence, worship is always relational.

Jesus said, "Where two or three are gathered in my name, I am there among them."[23] When people gather to worship God in Jesus' name, Christian community is constituted. This Christian community is formed doxologically by sharing in the sacraments of Baptism and Eucharist. The sacraments anticipate the parousia, the second coming of Christ. Orthodox theologian John Zizioulas notes that in Holy Communion, "the Church becomes a reflection of the eschatological community of Christ . . . an image of the Trinitarian life of God."[24] In its sacramental life, Christian community is given the gift of reflecting the communion or perichoresis within the triune God. This eschatological community looks forward to the time when Christ's Reign will be made complete.

When Christ's Reign (or Kingdom) comes in all its fullness, all divisions—natural, cultural and social—will be transcended. It is these divisions which fragment and disintegrate the world, leaving it in need of transcendence, reconciliation and redemption.[25] In the celebration of the Eucharist there should be no discrimination in terms of age, gender, ability, culture or economic status because this Communion, as representative of God's new covenant, is an anamnesis of both past and future.[26] It is not only a recollection or re-enactment of the past, but an anticipation of the coming Reign of Christ. The Christian community exists in the time between the life, death and resurrection of Jesus Christ and his second coming, to be Christ's Body on earth. In order to share this good news of God's reconciling love, the Christian community must learn, teach and live this Christian story.

The Christian community is physically wide ranging and diverse, yet spiritually unified in its worship of God in Christ by the power of the Holy Spirit. All manner of diversity is unified in Christ. In the Letter to the Galatians, the Apostle Paul teaches that "there is neither Jew nor Greek, there is neither slave nor free, there is neither male nor female; for you are all one in Christ Jesus."[27] "One in Christ" does not mean one in total compatibility

---

23. Matt 18:20.

24. Zizioulas, *Being As Communion*, 254.

25. Ibid., 255.

26. Ibid., 254.

27. Gal 3:28.

with one another.[28] Christian unity is found in Christ alone. History reveals that Christian community is not designated by homogeneity. Neither is homogeneity to be its goal. The purpose of the Christian community is to glorify God in all of its life. Adoration of God in Christ as the ultimate source and ground of Christian formation is the Christian community's destination and means of transportation.[29] As Christ's Body on earth, "the Christian community is the repository for and continual proclaimer of those stories which make the Christian message come alive for the average person."[30] So the Christian community cannot exist for itself alone. It exists to share and learn and teach and live the Christian message of love and reconciliation with God, each other and the world through Jesus Christ.

This sharing comes not only at the superficial level of acquaintance with Scripture or dogmatic information or even in moral living. This teaching and learning comes as a gift of God's Spirit, through worship of God in all parts of everyday life. Worship needs to be understood as more than the Sunday morning service. Emerging Church culture demonstrates an awareness that postmodern minds tend to shun legalistic bondage to unbending tenets and unthinking duties. There is not a rejection of ritual but of rigidity. Worship is approached as experiential and communal.[31] The essential context in which Christian formation and transformation occurs, clearly, is the worshipping community. The Christian community's role to incarnate God's love by participating in God's redemptive transformation in the world means that its members will need to live this transformation in themselves.[32]

The Christian community is, in this sense, vital and necessary to the formation of Christian character.[33] Part of this formation is the development of a Christian ethos—a call to an understanding of who God is and so to the worship of God, along with witnessing God's presence and participating in service in the world. This is where the truth of Christian ethos is learned, taught and lived. Christian ethos is developed and nurtured by ongoing reflection and praxeology to help Christian people form their community consistent with their conviction that the story of Christ is a truthful

---

28. Dawn, *Royal Waste of Time*, 179.

29. Murphy, *Teaching That Transforms*, 13.

30. Crossan, *What Are They Saying About Virtue*, 44.

31. Anderson, *Worship and Christian Identity*, 6, 18–24.

32. Foster, *Educating Congregations*, 55, 56.

33. On this see Hauerwas, *Community of Character*; see also Anderson, *Worship and Identity*; Murphy, *Teaching That Transforms*; Crossan, *What Are They Saying*.

account of human existence.[34] This community is made up, however, of fragile, broken, ordinary sinful human beings. The Christian worshipping community in all its frailness and humanity is still the most appropriate and pressing context for Christian education because of its unique relationship with Christ. Theologian Dietrich Bonhoeffer, in his *Life Together*, sums up the essence of Christian community generally:

> Christianity means community through Jesus Christ and in Jesus Christ. No Christian community is more or less than this. We belong to one another only through and in Jesus Christ. What does this mean? It means, first, that a Christian needs others because of Christ.[35]

Bonhoeffer's words point to the centrality of Christ for any ministry of the church. Christ is the central element of a Christian ethos. Christ is to affect all of Christian action and orientation. As the core of the Christian's ethos, Christ calls people to be his disciples, to follow his ways. At this point it is necessary to briefly clarify the difference between discipleship and Christian education, as understood here. The studies discussed at the start of this chapter indicated that something of a division has developed between Christian education and discipleship. The Emerging Church, as we have also seen, has tended to focus on Christian formation as discipleship. Discipleship, of course, is vital, but Christian education is able to bring learnings from the wider field of education, in domains such as human development, psychology of learning and teaching, human behaviour and theological anthropology, knowledge management and tools, which can enhance discipleship in a postmodern era. Christian education presents a larger overview, including the formation of disciples who are able to discover daily what it means to be called to be the Body of Christ. The concepts of Christian community and the Christian worshipping community must also be taught and learned. This is most appropriately achieved by being an active part of the Christian community and actively worshipping with the worshipping community. Discipleship is part of this teaching and learning. Before any of the thrust of the Emerging Church movement had been fully encountered, Stanley Hauerwas wrote an article entitled "Discipleship as a Craft, Church as a Disciplined Community." Here he argued that

> Christianity is not beliefs about God plus behaviour. We are Christians not because of what we believe, but because we have been called to be disciples of Jesus. To become a disciple is not

34. Hauerwas, *Community of Character*, 10.
35. Bonhoeffer, quoted in Childs, *Faith, Formation, and Decision*, 3.

a matter of a new or changed self-understanding, but rather to become part of a different community with a different set of practices.[36]

The church is at somewhat of a transition point in its life, as we have seen. There is a great opportunity now to re-explore what it means to be a part of this different community with its essential practice—Christian worship. The different set of practices that Hauerwas observes flow out of and help constitute worship of God. It can be argued that this community and its worship of God is the central medium by which Christian knowledge, attitudes and practices are formed. The difference is that this community's identity is found in Christ and the Christian story. This difference can also be exhibited in different ways of knowing. We shall discuss this further shortly.

In many Western Protestant churches, worship has not been recognized as a key source for formation of Christian identity. Christian education has been separated from worship where Sunday School, as the only intentional educational ministry, has been viewed as merely inculcating a body of information or even as childminding during Sunday worship. Both Christian formation and worship now require greater understanding by Christians, with intentional teaching and learning of major importance. The Emerging Church movement has invited a re-imagination of worship as active, participatory and creative, simultaneously lighting and reflecting the rest of Christian life. Worship is a primary context for Christian education's *traditio*, the ongoing reflection on the ways of teaching and learning the living customs and attitudes of its community. Worship is also a starting place for the teaching and learning of the doctrines or *traditium* of the faith. The aim of worship is to glorify God, but it also has the effect of teaching doctrine and helping to form Christian identity. As Geoffrey Wainwright notes:

> Worship . . . is a source of doctrine in so far as it is the place in which God makes himself known to humanity in a saving encounter. The human words and acts used in worship are a doctrinal locus in so far as either God makes them the vehicle of his self-communication or they are fitting responses to God's presence and action.[37]

In any Christian worshipping community there will be situations where further discussion of particular doctrinal and other issues will need more time and space, but the liturgical connection remains crucial. The

36. Hauerwas, "Discipleship as a Craft," 881–84.

37. Wainwright, *Doxology*, 242–43.

re-introduction of Christian education into the context of active worship is of utmost importance. But how is this to be achieved?

To recall the Westminster Catechism again, the role of the Christian educator is to help learners glorify God and enjoy God forever. If the Christian worshipping community is the context for Christian formation, who, then, is the Christian educator? A story may help to illustrate.

In one of the congregations where I have ministered, there are a number of people with intellectual impairments. They interact well in the church community and participate in all of its activities, especially enjoying worship. One woman, Julie, sits in the front row and vies to be the first to "pass the peace" when the time comes. One Sunday, Julie came in more exuberantly than usual. She had a brand new Bible, which she told me she had bought just the day before. She said she needed it for church (Julie is not able to read). When the time came to read the scriptures, Julie held up her Bible and yelled, "Help!" One of the women sitting nearby came over, sat with her and pointed to the place as Julie listened and followed along. She joined in as we repeated, "Thanks be to God" in response to the Scripture readings. Then she sat through the rest of the service with the broadest of satisfied smiles on her face.

The Christian worshipping community is also the Christian learning and teaching community—the Christian educators. Christian education happens in many places other than the Sunday school room. People learn how to be Christians by being with Christians, by living with and living out the Christian story. Probably most often, Christian *learning* happens unintentionally. There is a difference between Christian learning and Christian education. Education is an *intentional* practice. Intentional learning (education) does not have to imply institutionalized learning. In the previous chapter, we looked at how the *traditio* of Christian education has happened historically. So far in this chapter we have entered into a discussion about the most appropriate context for Christian education being the worshipping community. This discussion will continue as we now consider the *traditium* or knowledge content of Christian education.

CHRISTIAN KNOWLEDGE

In chapter 4 we briefly discussed a rough definition for Christian education as incorporating the overarching understanding of Cremin[38]: "The deliberate, systematic, and sustained effort to transmit, evoke, or acquire knowledge, attitudes, values, skills, or sensibilities, as well as any outcomes

---

38. Cremin, *Traditions of American Education*, 34.

of that effort," with the wording of Phenix,[39] ". . . the process whereby persons intentionally guide the development of persons," as well as our own adaptation of Phenix's definition: "an intentional process where persons are guided in their Christian development" founded on the *a priori* presupposition of God's will and essential action in this process and effort. Christian education is more than Christian knowledge, but at this point, we should consider what we mean by Christian knowledge.

Augustine understood the knowledge of Christian faith as knowledge of God and knowledge of self. "O unchanging God, that I may know Thee and that I may know myself."[40] At the beginning of his *Institutes*, Calvin added:

> Our wisdom, in so far as it ought to be deemed true and solid wisdom, consists almost entirely of two parts: the knowledge of God and of ourselves. But, while joined by many bonds, which one precedes and gives birth to the other is not easy to discern.[41]

What is knowledge and how do we obtain it? This question has been asked over the centuries since the time of the early Greek philosophers. We have seen how the developments of the Enlightenment and modernity caused a change in the understanding of the nature of knowledge and its sources. Any theory of knowledge must explain how the knower processes experience to formulate conclusions about reality and truth.

Calvin's view of knowledge of God and knowledge of ourselves as "joined by many bonds" would seem to indicate that the Christian story is God's relationship with creation and, notably, humankind throughout history. To learn and grow in Christian ethos means to know at least part of the story, even though it is always "looking through a glass darkly," to quote from Paul's letter to the Corinthians. How do we know what God is like? What can we know? What do we have to know about God in order to worship God? What does this knowledge comprise and how did it come into being?

---

39. Phenix, *Philosophy of Education*, 13.

40. Augustine, *Soliloquies of St. Augustine*, 2:1.1. Also, Augustine said about faith and knowledge, "The knowledge by which we know that we live is the most inward of all knowledge, of which even the Academic cannot insinuate." (*Trinity*, 402). "But, without any delusive representation of images or phantasms, I am most certain that I am, and that I know and delight in this. In respect of these truths, I am not at all afraid of the arguments of the Academicians, who say: 'What if you are deceived?' For if I am deceived, I am." (*City of God*, 1:468).

41. Calvin, *Institutes of the Christian Religion*, Book IV, i, 10, 37.

Epistemology

The scope of epistemological study covers and addresses four main questions: *What can be known? What is the process of knowing? Who is the knower? What is the criterion for distinguishing truth from error?*[42] The question, *What can be known?* sets up the boundaries between ontology and epistemology. For what *is* known will affect what can be known.

Christian education must constantly strive to search for appropriate ways of knowing for this discipline. More than ever, ways of knowing in Christian education are tied to the nature and scope of knowledge.[43] In other words, how we know about God and ourselves is closely related to what can be known about God and ourselves. Christian educator Thomas Groome discusses an epistemology for Christian formation in his book, *Christian Religious Education.* Citing Paulo Freire, Groome notes that "educators usually pose the epistemological question as, How may knowing be promoted? But the answer to that question is shaped by our understanding of a prior one, What does it mean to know?"

As we have already seen, in order to begin to answer epistemological questions for Christian education, one must be aware of the nature and purpose of the task, and take into consideration the context within which it takes place. When discussing Christian education in the context of the Christian community, where it most appropriately belongs, the epistemological questions must necessarily use a particularly Christian hermeneutic. What is Christian knowledge and where does it come from?

In thinking about the process of knowing, the contrasting poles in the epistemological argument have already been briefly discussed. These poles can be described as *rationalism versus empiricism,* and as *idealism versus realism,* with both groupings being, in many ways, variations on the same theme. The Rationalist view—that truths about reality can be deduced by human reason alone—means that knowledge essentially comes from within the knower. The Empiricist belief that experience is the source of all knowledge, leads to the conviction that knowledge comes from the outside world. Idealism is the view that the essential nature of reality lies in the consciousness; the mind and spiritual values are posited as fundamental in the totality of what is, with knowledge being based on ideas. Realism is the notion that knowledge is gained by studying and examining what exists in actuality (i.e., what is real).[44]

---

42. Loder, *Encyclopedia of Religious Education,* 219.

43. Groome, *Christian Religious Education,* 139.

44. Ibid., 150.

Let us return, for a moment, to the ancient Greek philosophers. Plato, for example, can be identified as a rationalist as well as an idealist.[45] For Plato, the world that can be known by the senses is not reliable. The sensate world is changeable and a source of relative opinion rather than truth. Above the sensate world exists what Plato saw as the true source of knowledge. This was the transcendent, eternal and superior world of forms or ideas like justice, truth, and freedom. By what is within a person, their human soul or mind, the ideal and eternal objects of the world "above" can be accessed. The forms, known by reason, are for Plato the source of real immutable truth, distinct from the relative opinion provided by the senses and the present world "below."

In contrast to Plato, Aristotle could be described as an empiricist and a realist.[46] Aristotle concurred with Plato that knowledge is always of some "universal," in that humans know particular things as instances of universals. However, Aristotle rejected Plato's view regarding a separate transcendent world of forms. For Aristotle, what is known is an expression of what is real, and the senses inform the mind. The soul is a set of faculties within the body, with knowledge arising from the senses. These faculties provide the data for appropriation and judgment by reason. Aristotle divided knowledge into three kinds: theoretical (*theoria*), practical (*praxis*), and productive (*poiesis*). Aristotle believed that these types of knowledge were three human activities through which learning or understanding could take place. These are "three different ways for a reflective subject to relate to the objective world, and therefore three different ways of knowing."[47] One of the insights I have gained from this study of the Emerging Church is that Christian educators should be encouraged to undertake ongoing reflection on their Christian teaching, learning and relating to the world through each of these lenses or ways of knowing.

These divisions, or ways of knowing, can be very helpful in the present argument wherein Christian education is interpreted theologically as an intersection between doxology and dogma. As we have seen, Christian education is more than the imparting of Christian information or theory. It is learning and teaching life in the light of the Christian story. Dogma, as the Confessional Statements of the church, may be viewed in pedagogical terms as *theoria* knowledge, or perhaps, part of the Christian historical and theological "story." Dogma, as particular doctrines, was often formulated as correctives against teachings promulgated by heretics. Thus dogma can

45. Turnbull, *Get A Grip on Philosophy*, 66.
46. Stokes, *Philosophy*, 23, 25.
47. Groome, *Christian Religious Education*, 153.

be seen as setting boundaries or guidelines for orthodoxy within the whole story of the Church. Dogma, by its very nature, is theoretical, critical and, to a certain extent, cognitive, however, it is *lived* in *doxa*. That is not to say that dogma is passive or static, but it should be seen in this context as the guideline for a more reflective style of knowledge. Dogma protects and defines. It is the *recipe* or the *map*, by which the action or *praxis* or *doxa* takes place. The Gospel writers were aware of the need for these kinds of delineators for Christian knowledge. An example of their awareness may be seen in the prologue to the Gospel of John. The writer of this Gospel highlights a doctrine of the nature of God in the first lines of the book:

> In the beginning was the Word, and the Word was with God, and the Word was God. He was in the beginning with God. All things came into being through him, and without him not one thing came into being. What has come into being in him was life, and the life was the light of all people. The light shines in the darkness, and the darkness did not overcome it.[48]

The Word is not apart from God, or after God. The Word was God. In the Word, God acted to bring life and to be life and light to all people. These are the boundaries or delineators. These are some of the guidelines or "lessons" about God and humanity. Dogma must be re-captured not as rigid laws and precepts. Dogma gives guidance for normative Christian action. This will be further discussed later. The *praxis* or action, when viewed from this Aristotelian perspective, is Christianity lived as worship of God, or *doxology*. This is life in Christ, where daily living is to reflect one's worship of God. As the writer of the Letter to the Philippians encourages this early church, "Keep on doing the things that you have learned and received and heard and seen in me, and the God of peace will be with you."[49] Aristotle's use of the term *praxis* in its broadest sense refers to almost any kind of intentional and deliberate outward activity that an individual or community is likely to perform. "Intentional" and "deliberate" are the key concepts here. *Praxis* is behavior based on and generated in some form of informed or ethical reflection.

Accordingly, *praxis* is action from which knowledge arises through participation in a social situation. For Christian education, this view of *praxis* aligns with some of the thinking of faith development theorists such as James Fowler and John Westerhoff, along with community-focussed Christian education proponents including Charles Foster and C. Ellis Nelson. Many modernist Christian educators would claim that this was a

48. John 1:1–5.
49. Phil 4:9.

relatively observable, measurable, even predictable and quite linear process. By growing up within the community of faith, a child may experience ways of becoming an adult of faith. The child, however, may learn ways that she chooses not to follow.

But by actively participating, as an equal, in a worshipping, witnessing and serving life based on Christ, one has an opportunity to learn something about oneself, about God and about God's people. By experiencing some of the Christian story within one's own life, by engaging in it, one becomes more aware of what it is like to begin to live by that story, and one has the potential to choose to continue living that story. An approach to Christian formation that enlists more holistic metaphors like a journey or a dance, as does Maria Harris,[50] for example, seems to be more appropriate in a contemporary context than a structured, linear method. The metaphors of journey and dance are particularly attractive to postmodern minds because of their open-endedness and flexibility. In a free-form dance, or on a journey, just as in Christian living, sometimes one tries to follow, sometimes one tries to lead, sometimes one gets weary and sits out for a while, sometimes there is exuberance and vitality, sometimes it is slow and deliberate. The uniform "ages and stages" of some developmental theories do not allow for unique differences and situations.

In our current discussion, *praxis* relates to living the Christian life as worship. *Praxis* also involves some form of intentionality. In Rom 12:1, Paul asks the Roman Church to "present your bodies as a living sacrifice, holy and acceptable to God, which is your spiritual worship." Spirituality may be defined as lived faith, so *praxis* in this context has an explicitly spiritual component. Worship of God is to saturate all parts of everyday living, with *doxology* or praise of God being a crucial, life-giving element of knowledge of God and of oneself. Christian praxis means crafting life worshipfully.

Consideration of a life crafted worshipfully leads to the concept of *poiesis*. For Aristotle, *poiesis* is a way of knowing in which something concrete is created or crafted. The concrete product embodies a certain kind of knowing, and its production involves a knowing process. This is the knowing expressed in the work of the sculptor, the craftsperson, the tradesperson, and, in its highest expression, the poet.[51]

There is technique or skill involved in this way of knowing. Doxology can certainly involve a sense of craft or artistry. Liturgy could be described as poetry or a work of art used to give praise to God. For a sculptor, *poiesis* is knowing and discovering the "clay-ness" of clay or the unique properties of

50. Harris, *Teaching and Religious Imagination*, 23.

51. Groome, *Christian Religious Education*, 155.

stone or wood. For the Christian learner, *poiesis* is knowing and continuing to discover the "Godness" of God, the ethos or properties of Christianity—what it means to know and live faith. Doxology is creating worship that, perfected by Christ, and in the power of the Holy Spirit, praises God. At the same time, doxology helps the worshipper to know more of God. The Psalmists understood this dual task of doxology:

> O come, let us sing to the LORD;
> let us make a joyful noise to the rock of our salvation!
> Let us come into his presence with thanksgiving;
> let us make a joyful noise to him with songs of praise!
> For the LORD is a great God,
> and a great King above all gods.
> In his hand are the depths of the earth;
> the heights of the mountains are his also.
> The sea is his, for he made it,
> and the dry land, which his hands have formed.
> O come, let us worship and bow down,
> let us kneel before the LORD, our Maker!
> For he is our God,
> and we are the people of his pasture,
> and the sheep of his hand.[52]

This praise of God, as evident in many of the Psalms, is an example of doxological *poiesis*. Psalm 8 is another good example. In this sense, *poiesis* is the "sacrifice of praise to God, that is, the fruit of lips that confess his name" that the writer to the Hebrews is talking about.[53] Christian education has a certain "skilling" function in helping people know *how* to rightly praise God.

Aristotle regarded *theoria* as being grounded in *praxis*; and *poiesis* cooperating with *praxis* to make possible the life of *theoria* and the highest form of wisdom, *sophia*. Thus, he believed his three ways of knowing were interwoven. Through centuries of philosophical and theological interpretation, theory and practice have tended to drift apart, to the extent of having almost become opposites. This rift has been reflected in the realms of Christian epistemology as well, as we have seen. For Christian education, the divide has, in modern times, become cavernous. Theology has often become divorced from *praxis*. With a lack of appreciation for its foundational role in promoting the Christian faith, and usually for pragmatic reasons, Christian education has sometimes been reduced to a mere time filler or child minder.

52. Ps 95:1–7.
53. Heb 13:15.

Constitutively, the idealist-realist debate concerns the construal of the essential nature of reality and human perception of it—both sides use reason to build their arguments. *Dialectic* is the highest form of reason in Platonic thought,[54] in which a kind of conversation or "back and forth" occurs by rational inquiry, in order to reveal from sensory experiences the *esse* or truth about a given topic or concept like freedom or love. The goal of the dialectic is an intellectual grasp or synthesis of an idea in its purest form, not tainted by experiential contingencies.[55]

In the early 1800s, philosopher, Georg Hegel (1770–1831), expanded the concept of dialectic where ideas grow and gradually move towards a better grasp of reality. Hegel's dialectic is concerned with the struggle between different dynamic concepts which each claim to be an accurate description of reality. Any concept or *thesis* will automatically give rise to its opposite or *antithesis,* and the resulting discussion between them may eventually achieve a higher, more truthful *synthesis.*[56] The aim of Hegel's process of dialectic is to finally reach "absolute knowing."[57] Hegel believed that the study of history through this process would eventually reveal something like the mind of God. Hegel was an Idealist, believing that the world is never experienced directly through the senses, but is always filtered or mediated by one's consciousness.[58] He claimed that human consciousness itself is never fixed, but is continually changing and developing new categories and concepts. These new ideas and paradigms determine how we experience the world, so that knowledge is always contextually dependent and comes about as the result of facing off of antithetical positions.

When used rigorously within Christian education, the focal point of this process of dialectic reasoning or dialogue is the leading out (as in the Latin *e-duco*) of some innate knowledge of God. This may happen within the individual and with others, including other Christians. The dialectical sharing of this knowledge makes the narratives of *traditium* an essential component of Christian formation. *Traditium* itself must be open and willing to be critiqued and questioned dialectically. Rigor, in this sense, implies the necessity of a sound knowledge of doctrine, history and the human condition.

Epistemological inquiry is part of a theological agenda. The self-revelation of God in Jesus Christ is a good example. This is made known

---

54. Groome, *Christian Religious Education,* 151.

55. Pence, *Dictionary of Common Philosophical Terms,* 14.

56. Robinson and Groves, *Introducing Philosophy,* 78.

57. Hegel, *Phenomenology of Spirit,* 493.

58. Robinson and Groves, *Introducing Philosophy,* 79.

through God's grace working by faith. The "knower" (believer) is one who knows/believes they are redeemed from the brokenness and separation of sin by God's gracious faith. The knower, thus, is a member of the Body of Christ, the church. The criteria for such a claim include Scripture, variously interpreted and supplemented by different traditions, along with critiqued experience and reason.[59]

As discussed earlier, Positivism based in British Empiricism viewed all experience as perceived through the senses and thus arising from outside the body. This empirical experience is presupposed by the positivist as given, factual and irrefutable. Reality has an observable causal effect on the knower. In this Cartesian dualism, even "the mind" was an abstract conception, not able to be proved, and thus thought of as a kind of epiphenomenon,[60] and as having only a passive role in the acquisition of knowledge.

In this view, there is a sharp distinction drawn between fact as objective and belief as subjective. Belief and value are not able to be proven by the senses, therefore are not given. Belief and value are imposed on reality from within the knower. They are, as such, seen as subjective.

Epistemologically, the acceptance that reality consists only of matter leads to an ontology which can only be one-dimensional. Following that assertion, in an Empiricist/Positivist theory of knowledge, the notions of the mind and of understanding are reduced to minor physiological components of the knowing process. There is also no need for a metaphysics or theology if one's ontology is limited to nothing but matter. In Modernist thought, belief and value are subjective, personal and therefore not as worthy of respect as objective knowledge. A scientifically detached and impersonal reason alone is seen as the means for gaining knowledge.

One important postmodern thinker opposed to this Modernity-inspired view is Michael Polanyi. In his *Personal Knowledge: Towards a Post-Critical Philosophy*, Polanyi argues against the modern epistemological project, introducing a concept of personal knowledge. Writing in the mid-twentieth century, from a physical chemistry background, Polanyi primarily argues that there are solid reasons for considering "theoretical knowledge as more objective than immediate experience."[61] Polanyi rejects the either/or polemic of objectivity opposed to subjectivity. In discussing Einstein's theory of relativity, Polanyi notes:

> We cannot truly account for our acceptance of such theories without endorsing our acknowledgement of a beauty that

---

59. Ibid.

60. Hill, *Knowledge of God*, 58.

61. Polanyi, *Personal Knowledge*, 4.

exhilarates and a profundity which entrances us. Yet the prevailing conceptions of science, based on the disjunction of subjectivity and objectivity, seeks—and must seek at all costs—to eliminate from science such passionate, personal, human appraisals of theories, or at least minimize their function to that of a negligible by-play.[62]

He stresses that the personal element of knowing does not destroy a valid sense of objectivity. In Polanyi's view, humans are not unconnected from their environment, they participate personally in it, with human commitments, innate skills and passions informing discovery and validation in a profound way. With the starting point of Gestalt psychology, Polanyi discusses the nature of skill as comprising more than a set of rules which may not even be known to the person following them.[63]

> Rules of art can be useful, but they do not determine the practice of an art; they are maxims, which can serve as a guide to an art only if they can be integrated into the practical knowledge of the art. They cannot replace this knowledge.[64]

Polanyi advances the role played by inherited practices, the kind of knowledge that cannot be prescribed in detail and thus must be transmitted by example, traditionally from master to apprentice.[65] This is the kind of tradition I have named *traditio*, the sense of living customs of a community. Polanyi contends that people know more than they can articulate by words alone. Thus knowledge is often passed on by non-explicit processes, as is the case with the apprenticeship model: observing a master, and then practising under their tutelage, guidance and discipline. On many levels, this is an understanding of knowledge which is crucial for postmodern Christian education. Christian education is so much more than the ability to regurgitate trivial information from Scripture or to recite the names of the books of the Bible. Christian education is about forming people in all aspects of living. Rejecting the modern ideal of an authoritatively-rational knowledge,[66] Polanyi advances a different form of knowing authority:

> To learn by example is to submit to authority. You follow your master because you trust his manner of doing things even when

62. Ibid., 15–16.

63. Ibid., 49.

64. Ibid., 50.

65. Ibid., 53.

66. "Postmodernism," *Economic Expert*. http://www.economicsexpert.com/a/Postmodernism.htm.

> you cannot analyse and account in detail for its effectiveness. By watching the master and emulating his efforts in the presence of his example, the apprentice unconsciously picks up the rules of the art, including those which are not explicitly known to the master himself. These hidden rules can be assimilated only by a person who surrenders himself to that extent uncritically to the imitation of another.[67]

This is an extraordinary account of the habits of discipleship. Christian education, especially when viewed as Christian formation, has often been used interchangeably with the term, *discipleship*. The proponents of the Emerging Church are keen on this description of Christian formation because it encapsulates for them a more holistic notion of teaching and learning. Discipleship is the methodology or way of Jesus. Christian discipleship connotes Christian community. A community's identity and culture, in this way, may be described as performative. Postmodern French philosopher, Pierre Bourdieu, labels this kind of practical knowledge that constructs, defines, and enacts culture as *habitus*. As a synthesis of structure and agency a *habitus* is a "system of structured, structuring dispositions . . . constituted in practice and . . . always orientated towards practical functions."[68] Bourdieu uses the term in the general sense of a system of dispositions, of acquired patterns of thought, behaviour and taste that, taken together, constitute a social practice.

Duncan Forrester uses the term in a slightly different way, returning to the origin of the term in Aristotelian virtue ethics. Here, a *habitus* is viewed as a readiness to act in a virtuous way. One is trained in the virtuous life and is therefore ready to act virtuously when called upon to do so. Forrester is more specific, describing a *habitus* as:

> . . . a disposition of the mind and heart from which action flows naturally, in an unselfconscious way. . . . The habitus means that action springs not from rational calculation of interests or possibilities, but from the depths of the personality, where the habitus has been slowly formed from early childhood.[69]

Bourdieu claims the *habitus* as embodied action within a social structure "creates tangible institutions."[70] Polanyi notes that "a society which

67. Polanyi, *Personal Knowledge*, 53.

68. Bourdieu, *Logic of Practice*, 52.

69. Forrester, *Truthful Action*, 5.

70. Graham, *Blackwell Reader*, 109.

wants to preserve a fund of personal knowledge must submit to tradition."[71] Tradition in its dual facets of *traditium* and *traditio* is represented here. Certainly, this understanding of the notion of tradition incorporates the Aristotelian sense of the term *habitus* as the values and dispositions gained and regulated by being formed at a time in history and in a place in a culture, and as generally transposable into new contexts.[72] These embodied actions help generate and encourage tangible institutions like particular communities of practice. Although not entirely generated this way, Christian worshipping communities can and do behave similarly. It is the bringing of this *habitus* into conscious and explicit awareness, and exploring their sources, purposes and meanings as *practices* in the Christian community, that constitutes the greatest part of the task of the Christian educator. The practices of the Christian faith find their source, purpose and meaning in discipleship—following Christ. The embodied action then can fall back to tacit understanding, and thus contribute to new dimensions of faith experience.

For Polanyi, knowledge is dependent upon understanding and the engagement and participation of the knower in their understanding. Meaning is brought about through understanding. Meaning, for Polanyi, is generated by the integration of diverse parts into some kind of unified whole. The awareness of meaningful parts gives an understanding of the whole, or what could be described as "the bigger picture." The Indian story of the blind men and the elephant gives a good illustration of Polanyi's theory in action. The traditional story is summarized thus: Some blind men are given the task of explaining what an elephant is, by feeling particular features of the whole elephant. The man who feels only the trunk describes an elephant as being long, narrow and flexible, like a snake. The man who touches the leg describes an elephant as being thick and cylindrical like a tree trunk. The man who feels only the skin describes an elephant as flat, dry and vast like a huge piece of paper and the man who takes hold of the tail describes the elephant as hairy and stringy like a piece of rope. It was not until the men were able to feel all the other parts that they could recognise the whole elephant.

The men in the story had made meaning of their individual parts, but did not yet understand a whole elephant as made up of all these diverse parts. Once there is knowledge of the whole, the parts can be perceived as components of the whole, but the parts are not the whole in its entirety. The parts must function in an auxiliary or subsidiary way, pointing to a recognition of the whole, and not just pointing to themselves. Awareness of the whole elephant implied awareness of the parts, but this was tacit

71. Polanyi, *Personal Knowledge*, 53.
72. Bourdieu, *Outline of a Theory of Practice*, 78.

awareness, not explicit awareness. Once the elephant was recognized, it was possible for the men to concentrate on the parts, and not lose the concept of the elephant as a whole, but from then on, the trunk would always be an elephant's trunk, the leg would always be an elephant's leg and so on. The process of moving from tacit to explicit knowledge moves in one direction. On a practical level, many Christian individuals and communities fail to grasp the whole ethos of the good news of Jesus Christ, for example, because they focus too heavily on certain particulars.

Another way of explaining the movement from tacit to explicit awareness became clearer to me when I (a person who knows very little Latin) wanted to grasp the meaning of a Latin sentence which was used liturgically in the Roman Catholic Church. I looked up each of the individual words in a Latin dictionary. I even Googled the phrase. The words each made sense as words, but when they were put together I could not understand the meaning. So I took the sentence to a Catholic priest who knows the Latin language and the context of the sentence. He was able to artfully explain the meaning of the whole sentence as it was used in the context of the Mass. The words of a sentence each have meaning in and of themselves, but when those words are combined into a sentence, new meaning is created by the whole sentence. The particular words take on even greater meaning because they have now been understood in the whole sentence, within the context of a larger whole, the Mass.

Tacit knowledge functions in the background, as the basis from which new meaning is derived. Knowledge becomes explicit when a framework is introduced from which to see more of the whole—the bigger picture, so to speak. The framework for the Latin words was the whole sentence. When placed in a context, and explained by a "master" of that context, more complex meaning was experienced. Explicit knowledge can be articulated as knowledge and used to understand new situations, where it may become tacit knowledge for that new situation, adding to and defining the framework. Polanyi acknowledges that not all tacit knowledge is inarticulate knowledge. At its lowest level, however, inarticulate knowledge is that which is acquired through participating in and being nurtured by a community of belief or ethos that develops from birth and is different from one culture to another.[73] Inarticulate knowledge and its counterpart, inarticulate intelligence, where Polanyi says people know more than they can tell, acts as the subsidiary basis for explicit knowledge.[74]

73. Hill, *Knowledge of God*, 60, 61.

74. Polanyi, *Personal Knowledge*, 74–77.

The suppositions which underlie the method by which particular beliefs or assertions come about can be difficult to articulate. Polanyi suggests that we assimilate most of these pre-suppositions by learning to speak the languages surrounding these beliefs, naming and classifying them, and making distinctions between them and other assertions.[75] Bourdieu might describe the outcomes of this assimilation in behavioural terms as *embodiment*.[76]

The understanding of particular events requires some kind of framework of beliefs. This interpretative framework may be named as part of a community's hermeneutic. An interpretative framework is a way of creating specific and defining boundaries, or definition around the lens through which that community views itself and interprets new occurrences. These kinds of frameworks, when a person or community commits to them, operate at a subsidiary or tacit level. Persons and communities view particular events from the perspective of the beliefs that Polanyi says, in this way, "indwell"[77] them.

All areas of learning and interpretation are affected by this movement from particulars through a framework to understanding. The relationship between particulars and framework flows in both directions as well. The understanding of an event also feeds back onto the framework, enabling a person or community to reshape the framework and further their understanding.

Along with these, the relationship between framework and particulars that Polanyi sees as most important for learning is the case where the particular does not fit into the established framework. This creates a crisis point that necessitates dialogue between the particulars and the framework. This may require the framework to be adjusted in some way, or even to be completely rejected, and a new framework adopted. The adoption of a new framework entails a major conversion[78] in the life of a community or of an individual. Polanyi notes that science has undergone some of these paradigm shifts, such as the movement from Newtonian physics to the theory of relativity (to give a classic example).[79]

In the work of Polanyi, we see an example of a paradigm shift in the way knowledge is understood, and a movement from a Modern towards a postmodern epistemological perspective. A number of the principles

75. Ibid., 59.

76. Bourdieu, *Outline*, 79.

77. Polanyi, *Personal Knowledge*, 279.

78. Ibid., 319.

79. Ibid., 12–15.

described here, along with some of the insights gained by studying the Emerging Church, will be used to assist in the formation of some new thinking about Christian education designed to move towards a more postmodern approach.

I have been describing how we can apply a Practical Theological framework to create dialogue between practices of mainstream Christian education and practices of the Emerging church to develop a more effective framework for Christian formation. Using this methodology, we have already engaged in some reflection upon the current situation of Western society and ways the Christian church is emerging to relate to that society. We have looked at how Christian education has emerged, and some current parallels with ancient practices. From what we have seen, it seems that Christian education has, in some ways, stalled, and is not emerging in harmony with some of the fresh expressions of church evident from the Emerging Church movement. From this assumption, the pivotal question arises, *How can the practices of the Emerging Church help the whole church's Christian education emerge in fresh and effective ways?* Parallel with this question comes the inverse, *How can an informed understanding of Christian education practices help in the development of the Emerging Church?*

The next steps in the practical theology methodology will be to interpret Scripture and Tradition in the context of these questions and to respond, making our choices for transformed action. This will entail the outlining of a new interpretive framework.

Chapter 6

An Interpretive Framework

THIS EXAMINATION OF EPISTEMOLOGICAL considerations and *habitus* of Christian faith, along with insights from the Emerging Church leads to the development of a new interpretive framework. The framework I will utilize has been forming through the course of this argument. From the examination of the practices and attitudes of the Emerging Church, we have gleaned the significance of participatory worship. We have discussed the importance of the worshipping community as the learning and teaching community. Now we will bring some of those particulars into sharper focus by recognizing and outlining an interpretive framework for Christian learning and teaching.

The starting point in the interpretive framework to be developed here is the contention that a person learns what it means to be a Christian primarily by worshipping God through Jesus Christ in the power of the Holy Spirit with others who are trying to do the same. One is formed in learning with other community members, from them and despite them at times! The Christian worshipping community must grow to recognize itself as a Christian learning and teaching community, empowered by God's Holy Spirit. A major aspect of worship is engaging in reflection on our living in relation to God.

In the widest context of worship, Christians can begin to understand that worship is an ongoing way of living and reflecting on the whole of life. Week after week, people are able to find out what it means to be a Christian by hearing the story of God's action throughout history to reconcile creation to God. People can learn what God is like by hearing the stories of how others have discovered what God is like. These stories include the stories in

Scripture, in salvation history, in the traditions of the people of God. These are the stories of how people have responded to God and to each other in the whole of creation.

We learn how to live as a Christian by living *with* the story, and with the Holy Spirit's sanctifying action, we start to *live* the story. We live with the Christian story by hearing the gospel proclaimed, and we grasp the character of Christianity—Christian ethos—by asking questions like: What does this mean for the way I live my life? What framework will I use to help characterize what I believe?

We have seen the necessity in a Christian life for continuous, critical theological reflection and praxeology. We have briefly discussed the place of Christian dogma as grammar for Christian praxis, and we will further explore this point later. We have located the most important context for Christian formation as the Christian worshipping community, this being key in understanding and experiencing Christian ethos.

Following from this, the interpretive framework for Christian education offered in this discussion becomes: *an ongoing process of learning, teaching and living the Christian story in order to grasp Christian ethos.* In regard to the current discussion, the framework is to be set in the context of the worshipping community. This interpretive framework has been implicitly active in the discussion thus far, but will clearly require some further, more explicit clarification.

The theological premise of the framework is the Christian contention for the need of an active, chosen and deliberate living of the Christian (faith) story, as expressed in the life, death and resurrection of Jesus Christ; Christian tradition including the Hebrew and Christian Scriptures; scholarly reason; spirituality; and experience. It is a model of action and reflection, with the aim of generating transformed action. The framework indicates reflection on the Christian story, reflection on learning and teaching the Christian story, as well as reflection on the ethical way-of-being-in-the-world contained in the Christian story. This introduces and embraces the element of intentional formative or genuinely educative enterprise in its broadest sense.

Theological reflection of this nature will utilize resources such as those listed above, and many more. Learning, teaching and living in this way is seen to be for the very purpose of, or *in order to grasp* (understanding, figuring out, and being formed in), *Christian ethos* (identity, character, ethic, patterns of behavior, and practices). This view encompasses and espouses an overtone of dynamic purpose, which flows from the understanding that education is an intentional act, as distinct from informal and osmosis-style learning. Working from this foundation, the need for some planned, formative experiences becomes more evident, along with, and augmenting, a more general, holistic learning approach. A framework for education in Christianity should be seen through the overarching hermeneutic of worship as a way of life, that must include these concepts of an ongoing reflection on learning, teaching and living (with and in) the Christian story in order to grasp Christian ethos.

The action of God in the lives of individuals and communities invites ontological transformation, by means of God's Holy Spirit. Walter Brueggemann identifies the subversive note in this action in his *Mandate to Difference: An Invitation to the Contemporary Church,* when he says that the task of Christian worship, education, and pastoral work is "to move our lives from the dominant version of reality to the sub-version, finally that our old certitudes will have been subverted by the work of [God's] spirit."[1]

ONGOING PROCESS

An ongoing process of *learning, teaching and living the Christian story in order to grasp the Christian ethos* suggests an inquisitive, engaged lifestyle, not merely a segment of gathered worship on Sunday. It suggests an all-of-life vitality, intentionality, struggle, and open-endedness. It is not dependent upon a particular theory or method, content or process. Translated into daily action, this indicates a sense of lifelong personal commitment to the goal of living according to an ethos that aligns itself with the life, death, and resurrection of Jesus Christ.

The phrase, *ongoing process*, indicates a sense of continuousness and unfinished business, of always being on the way. This reflects the status of the Christian community generally. The concepts of God's continuous self-revelation and the sanctification of God's people contain an ongoing process quality. An ongoing process is one that exists for the remainder of the life of an individual or community, affecting the attitudes and behaviors of that individual or community. An ongoing process is not complete and does not stop at the end of a Sunday School lesson or Bible Study. An ongoing process infers a daily vocation in all aspects of daily life.

ACTION AND REFLECTION ON TEACHING

As an ongoing process that is based in *action and reflection*, this interpretive framework for Christian education incorporates a particular methodology.

---

1. Brueggemann, *Mandate to Difference*, 138.

This methodology involves theological reflection on Christian tradition as it actively relates to the culture and experience of the reflecting individual or community. James D. Whitehead and Evelyn Eaton Whitehead describe the community of faith as "the locus of theological and pastoral reflection."[2] In the past, the responsibility for theological and pastoral reflection tended to fall to the leadership of Christian communities alone. The insights of the Emerging Church movement demonstrate the inadequacy in this approach. Each member of the community is called to listen for the leading of God's Spirit, not only for themselves, but also for the life of the whole Body. This requires discernment, and is enhanced by training in methods of reflection on action.

We have already considered the practical theology approach outlined in this book, which has been adapted from Neil Darragh's model.[3] As we are looking at the particular elements of our interpretive framework, it is worth exploring another method that relates specifically to teaching. This method is strongly sympathetic toward teaching as a vocation and to teachers as imaginative, artistic beings. In our discussion here, it is pertinent to examine an action and reflection model that is so intimately related to the practice of teaching. The method of theological reflection relevant to this discussion is outlined in Maria Harris's *Teaching and Religious Imagination: An Essay in the Theology of Teaching*.[4] Harris's model is offered in the chapter entitled "Teaching," and offers a mutual critical correlation process model of theological reflection in order to create what is essentially a habitus of re-creation in Christian teachers. Harris writes from the stance of a theologian and philosopher,[5] but ultimately as an artistic teacher. She describes teaching as an essentially artistic and imaginative activity, and as such is:

> the incarnation of subject matter in ways that lead to the revelation of subject matter. At the heart of this revelation is the discovery that human beings are the primary subjects of all teaching, subjects who discover themselves as possessing the grace of power, especially the power of re-creation, not only of themselves, but of the world in which they live.

Harris situates her paradigm for teaching solidly within an overarching valuing perspective of Christian faith.[6] In this sense, Harris's work correlates in many ways with the pastoral cycle outlined in James and Evelyn

2. Whitehead and Whitehead, *Method in Ministry*, 5.

3. Darragh, "Practice of Practical Theology."

4. Harris, *Teaching and Religious Imagination*, 23–40.

5. Ibid., xii.

6. Ibid., 10, 11.

Eaton Whitehead's *Method in Ministry,* referred to above.[7] Firstly, Harris raises the question of the valuing perspectives that teachers use to reflect on their educational activity. Harris then presents her paradigm within the perspective of religion and religious imagination. Harris sets this out clearly from the beginning of her work, and her background as a Catholic Religious reinforces her perspective as a way of valuing and approaching a human activity where familiarity with the Christian story leads to certain ethical choices.[8]

Harris's process of theological reflection examines four types of imagination, as we have already seen. These are sourced from a psychological perception. Harris re-envisages them in specifically spiritual terms as *contemplative, ascetic, creative* and *sacramental.* Here, we observe the mutual correlation between disciplines—the conversation that enables each to enhance the other. Harris describes *contemplation* as "seeing what is there"[9] at the beginning of a teaching activity. The Contemplation Step brings together all elements of the teaching event: teacher, student, subject matter and environment or context. Harris suggests that this first "moment" gives mutual respect to each of the constituents, making each a "Thou" as in Martin Buber's *I and Thou.*[10] She describes the Contemplation Step as "the stopping, the taking time, the wide-awakeness necessary to 'take in' the personhoods involved."[11] In the model we are using, Harris's contemplation stage would correlate with Darragh's analysis of our own context.[12]

Engagement is the second step of Harris's process. Here, the teacher is asked, from her contemplation, to gather the elements in teaching and "catalyze"[13] them for the ultimate purpose of re-creation. Engagement brings the composite imagination into the picture. This composite imagination has the ability to blend disparate elements by bringing together the interrelatedness of the elements in harmony with something new.

In the Whiteheads' approach, they compare this to a crucible "where diverse materials are transformed into a single substance."[14] Darragh's model describes this step as the raising of an issue and the generating of a pivotal

7. Whitehead and Whitehead, *Method in Ministry.*

8. Ibid., 11.

9. Ibid., 26.

10. Buber, *I and Thou.*

11. Harris, *Teaching and Religious Imagination,* 28.

12. Darragh, "Practice of Practical Theology," 3.

13. Harris, *Teaching and Religious Imagination,* 30.

14. Whitehead and Whitehead, *Method in Ministry,* 89.

question.[15] Harris describes this single substance as the subject matter of that teaching task. This step enables the teacher and the subject matter to *engage* in order for understanding to occur. She discusses *subject matter* as far more than procedures or methods of presentation of the subject matter. Harris encourages teachers to richly appreciate subject matter, as "the world of meaning, order of nature, physical process, pattern of events, 'labyrinth of reality' toward which a system of clues has been designed to point."[16] Harris discusses obstacles to this making of meaning, and ways that engagement of subject matter with the other subjects can occur.

This leads to the next step of the process, *Form-giving*, where the teacher is asked to find the form that the teaching task will take. Harris uses the metaphor of working with clay to illustrate. The *contemplation* step is imaged in the playing with the clay and discovering what its properties included. Then, the person playing with the clay is blindfolded, which moves them into the step of *engagement*, where the clay is fully experienced. At this point, interaction between the artist and the clay can take place, and discovery of the form within it will take place. This is the performative activity of *form-giving*. Blindfolding the artist is a way of establishing underlying assumptions and absolute convictions regarding the exact nature of the form that a subject will take, and excluding those assumptions from the process. Form-giving includes direction from the teacher, especially with regard to the bringing to light of the presuppositions of students (with clay, it is often the obsession with making something that is functional—like an ashtray!). In the stage of *Form-giving*, the teacher is encouraged to expect the unexpected. Everything is open to the imagination, and this step demands the exercise of the religious imagination more than any other. The religious imagination draws into the process what Darragh describes as the re-reading of Scripture and the Christian Tradition. This is the step of conversation, experimentation, questioning and genuine creative dialogue possibilities.

For Harris, *Emergence* is the step that naturally follows form-giving. This is the point where something new is being birthed—the "Aha!" moment, when the teaching process all comes to fruition. It may take time and cannot be scheduled. The learning may take place long after the teaching event. For Darragh this is the *response* step. Emergence, says Harris,

> happens silently, and one does violence to keep pulling up the plant to see if the roots are still growing; emergence happens in divine time (in *illo tempore*) and not in ours. Emergence cannot

15. Darragh, "Practice of Practical Theology," 3.

16. Harris, *Teaching and Religious Imagination*, 34.

be guaranteed. Indeed, emergence is a reminder to any teacher that for new life to be born, the teacher will probably have to live through periods of sadness and grieving and staying in the darkness, even to live through periods of mourning and of death.[17]

Emergence leads to the next step in Harris's reflective process of teaching—*Release*. Release is the point where the artist must add no more. The work is finished and complete, ready to be displayed or used or put into action. It is a step of humility, where it is the object that is to be admired—the artifact, the learning—more so than the artist or teacher. In Harris's conception, Release gives rise to the completion and subsequent re-commencement of the cycle at the stage of Contemplation. As with all practical theological methodologies, including Neil Darragh's model, Harris describes a process designed to become a *habitus*, in that it moves towards re-creation and transformed action.

Harris's process is comprehensive and beautifully described, with many rich illustrations. Her reflection is based on many years of experience, training, study and research. It is thorough and from my own teaching experience works well as a reflection upon teaching and teaching events. However, the element that is missing in Harris's model, and many other Christian education action and reflection models of the mid to late twentieth century, is the reflection of the learner.

LEARNING

In the context of the worshipping Christian community, ongoing reflection on what one is learning means reflection on one's discipleship. The word "disciple" means learner. I contend that it is also a process of "un-learning" or revising and reshaping our interpretive frameworks. Jesus encouraged learners to be openly engaged in constantly reviewing and renewing their spiritual and theological paradigms when he repeatedly warned, "You have heard it said . . . But I say to you. . . ." This is, of course, another insight from the Emerging Church movement, where its predominant goal is the re-imagining of most of the interpretive frameworks the Western church has been accustomed to throughout Modernity.

Learning to live as a disciple of Christ and being formed in Christ's ways is frequently portrayed in the Scriptures as walking with God. This is an analogy that resonates well with the Emerging Church, given its emphasis on orthopraxy. In the Hebrew Scriptures, walking with God is

17. Ibid., 38.

often associated with keeping God's commands and remaining obedient to them.[18] In Deuteronomy alone, examples include 5:32,33; 8:6; 11:22; 19:9; 26:17; 28:9 and 30:10. As recorded in Deut 10:12–13, God's great requirement of the people of Israel was to "fear the LORD your God, to walk in all his ways, to love him, to serve the LORD your God with all your heart and with all your soul, and to keep the commandments of the LORD your God." Because God is described in the Psalms as loving "righteousness and justice,"[19] as a God of justice[20] and "known by his acts of justice,"[21] then keeping God's commands and walking with God means learning "the paths of justice."[22] The Emerging Church has declared that the Modern Protestant church has been frequently so enamoured with the importance of individual and personal faith that the plight of social justice has been neglected. A number of Emerging Church authors have discussed this, as we have seen in chapter 3. The insight to be attended to here is that Christian formation is not merely learning a personal belief system, or an individual morality, but that Christian discipleship always has a corporate element. This corporate understanding has often been subsumed in Western society as a whole by modern egocentrism. The Emerging Church calls for a regaining of this emphasis on social awareness and justice for all of creation, especially within discipleship.

LIVING THE CHRISTIAN STORY

The importance of orthopraxy or right living must be undergirded by critical reflection on theologically considered Christian doctrine. Many of the challenges for the postmodern church are seen by Emerging Church leaders and authors to have come as the result of Old Church's preoccupation with belief that often did not seem to result in belief-based action. Using the phrase "living the Christian story" is an attempt at a reinstatement of the balance between orthopraxy and orthodoxy. This wording places intentionality on the living out of beliefs, more so than on believing as concerned with merely accepting certain propositions or tenets. Reflection on doctrinal foundations is the basis for theologically informed action.

18. The following exegesis is outlined more fully in John M. Hull's chapter on discipleship entitled "Only One Way to Walk with God" in *Evaluating Fresh Expressions*, 106–7.

19. Ps 33:5.

20. Ps 50:6.

21. Ps 9:16.

22. Prov 8:20.

If we are to understand Christian formation as, in the first instance, ongoing reflectively teaching, learning and living the Christian story, we must look at what we mean by *story*, and what its tasks are. *Narrative* or *story* is an important area which correlates with, and deeply affects, vision and character. Narrative is formative to Christian education because story forms such a large part of Christian tradition. In any community, story helps to form history, ethos and identity. It is thus an essential category of theology and ecclesiology. The creative focus on story is another vital thread in the fabric of the Emerging Church's worship and preaching as well.

J. Edward Chamberlain notes that we learn to believe through listening to stories:

> They tell the different truths of religion and science, of history and the arts. They tell people where they came from, and why they are here; how to live, and sometimes how to die. They come in different forms, from creation stories to constitutions, from southern epics and northern sagas to native American tales and African praise songs, and from nursery rhymes and national anthems to myths and mathematics. . . . Whether Jew or Arab, Catholic or Protestant, farmer or hunter, black or white, man or woman, we all have stories that hold us in thrall and hold others at bay.[23]

Christian formation is the way in which a person's outlook on herself and her life, attitude towards others, vision and values are shaped by their understanding of God and of God's people. Much of this outlook is formed by the story of the community and the story of the individual within that community. Christian formation is concerned with an ongoing reflection on living the Christian story in order to grasp the Christian ethos. Formation and transformation involve the development of character as individuals and as the church community—the Body of Christ. As Paul implores in Rom 12:2, "Do not be conformed to this world, but be transformed by the renewing of your minds, so that you may discern what is the will of God—what is good and acceptable and perfect."

Christian formation and, in a sense, transformation, is a journey in growing progressively into conformity with God's will. This constitutes Christian ethics. Christian ethics takes into account a person's "beliefs, intentions and actions"[24] and comprises character and vision. A person's character and vision are formed, primarily by her life experiences—her story—and the interpretations they and others place onto that story as that

23. Chamberlain, *Where Are Your Stories*, 2.
24. Hauerwas, *Character*, 16.

person grows. The knowledge of where a person or group has come from, what they value and where they see themselves into the future has a cohesive, forming effect, creating a sense of belonging and membership. Narrative is formative to Christian education because story forms such a large part of Judeo-Christian tradition. The Christian *Story* includes, embraces and expresses the history, traditions, texts, beliefs, rituals and practices of the Christian faith community. Reflection on these builds community as people's individual stories intersect with the Story of God in Jesus Christ to continually form the Christian Story.

A culture's story also helps to form its history, ethos and identity. As we have seen, it is vital to theology and ecclesiology. *Teaching, learning and living the Christian story* means being open to becoming shaped by the tradition and challenge of Scripture, songs, liturgy, sermons, and communal midrash. It also includes discussion, dialogue, anecdotes, experiences and local theologies, along with accepted normative doctrine. The worshipping community is the teaching and learning community.

Shared stories can help form community and create a sense of belonging. As we have argued, if "the Christian community is the repository for and continual proclaimer of those stories which make the Christian message come alive for the average person,"[25] then the Christian community is also key to Christian formation.

IN ORDER TO GRASP

The phrase, *in order to grasp,* gathers in the notion of the purpose, intentionality and constant, robust, at times frail or hesitant grappling of the Christian educative enterprise that deals with understanding ourselves and God. The follower of Jesus is always on the journey, never at the destination. There may be occasional slow points or even rest stops, but openness to God's Holy Spirit means that Christian concepts, attitudes and practices have the potential to be formed and reformed, accepted, doubted, revised or even rejected along the way. Postmodern mindsets generally deal with this kind of fluid ambiguity better than Modernist ones.[26] The rigid desire for universality of thought and ethic is a commonly held Modernist stance that is undergoing re-envisagement (and often rejection) by a pluralistic postmodern world. As the pre-modern Apostle Paul puts it, "for now we see in a mirror, dimly, but then we will see face to face. Now I know only in part;

---

25. Crossan, *What Are They Saying,* 44.

26. Borg, *Heart of Christianity,* 12, 16–19.

then I will know fully, even as I have been fully known."[27] For the sake of this argument, we could re-envisage this statement as "now we grasp Christian ethos with fragile hands, carefully and openly. Now we know only in part; then we will know fully, even as we have been fully known."

CHRISTIAN ETHOS

Christ is the ethos of Christianity. Christian ethos or character is formed through relationship with God in Christ through the movement and work of the Holy Spirit. The call of the Emerging Church to *living the way of Christ,* infers growing toward behaving in ways that align with God's ways. A Christian ethos, then, potentially defines a Christian's action and orientation toward God and the world. As *the* Christian ethos, Christ reconciles people to God and calls them to be his disciples. If the argument that I have been making holds, it is vitally important for Christian education to orientate itself to the formation of Christian disciples as worshipping beings. This worship flows into all aspects of everyday life and addresses individually and communally what it means to be *called* and what it means to *walk with God* in a radical, countercultural community.

In order, then, to become part of this different community—the Christian community—and in order to be formed as a Christian, there must be a process in which certain knowledge, attitudes and practices are instilled. This is teaching, learning and living with the story in order to grasp the Christian ethos, most fully in the context of worship. The development of a Christian ethos involves the call to an understanding of who God is, and who Christians are, responding in the worship of God. Thus, the interpretative framework for Christian education offered in this discussion becomes: an ongoing process of action and reflection on learning, teaching and living the Christian story in order to grasp Christian ethos.

TRANSFORMED ACTION: THE WORSHIPPING COMMUNITY AS CHRISTIAN EDUCATORS

Flowing from our discussion of the worshipping community as the context, and Christian knowledge as incorporating both objective and subjective knowledge, the rightful theological place of Christian education becomes clearer. This posits Christian education in the theological and ecclesial life of the church as an intersection of *doxa* (praise and worship of God) and

27. 1 Cor 13:12.

dogma (normative knowledge of God). The imagery here may be depicted as a kind of infinite cyclical pattern—a Moebius band, so to speak. Worship is a gift of God and a means of God's self-revelation. It is in the worship of God—*doxa*—that we discover what God is like and how God has acted in the past—*dogma*. We need to know what God is like and how God has acted in the past—*dogma*—so that we can respond to God in praise—doxology and worship.

Christian education is a key intersection point of praise and worship (*doxology*) of God in response to God's grace, and an understanding of what we know and believe about God, humanity and creation (*dogma*). Christian education "clearly should shape the lives of people as agent-subjects in right relationship with God, self, other people, and all creation."[28]

Christians believe that God's right relationship with the cosmos is one of love. We love because God first loved us. In God's graciousness, God sent Jesus to save us from ourselves, to live in a right relationship with God, and for this reason we praise God. Twentieth-century theologian Karl Barth affirmed that God's self-revelation allowed the believer to speak of God by the "analogy of faith": the relationship of faith, in which the believer is set and maintained by grace, allowing them to speak of their divine benefactor. In Barth's words:

> He who believes in this God cannot wish to hide this God's gift, this God's love, this God's comfort and light, to hide his trust in (God's) Word and (God's) knowledge. The word and the work of the believer cannot possibly remain a neutral, uncommitted work and word. Where there is faith, God's *doxa, gloria,* (God's) brightness is necessarily made known on earth.[29]

Christian disciples are to be formed for *doxa*, praise and worship of God. Systematic theologian Geoffrey Wainwright, in his seminal writing on the subject of doxology, reiterates the chief purpose of humanity as glorifying God and enjoying God forever. This is a lifelong process. Wainwright notes that "communion with God, the transformation of the human character according to God's own character: this is experienced as the *enjoyment* of God.[30]

Christian education is about the transformation of the human character according to God's own character, and in so doing, to help learners glorify God and enjoy God forever. By engaging in worship and praise of God we learn about God and how God is to be glorified. We learn that God is

28. Groome, *Christian Religious Education*, 13.

29. Barth, *Dogmatics in Outline*, 30.

30. Wainwright, *Doxology*, 17.

love and that living the Christian story is a lifestyle of willingly aligning our lives with a life together in God. In the story of the congregation described earlier, Julie is learning to worship by worshipping. She is living her faith, and helping others to be involved in that reflecting, learning and teaching, in order to grasp the Christian ethos. This may be conscious or not, but it is happening. The enjoyment is evident. The belonging is real. A major role of Christian educators is to bring that awareness to light. Who then, are the Christian educators? The community of Christ—each of the people who worship with Julie, whether it be in a church service, or in a Bible study, or having a cup of tea and a chat. Julie is both teacher and learner, having been called as a disciple of Jesus. As part of the worldwide Christian community, she grows on the journey as she worships God and interacts as part of her local community. In her own real way she has reflected on what it means to grasp Christian ethos. As part of the worshipping community, we have also reflected on her enjoyment, contribution, belonging and participation in that ethos and *as* that ethos. Julie is learning, teaching, and living the Christian story.

Chapter 7

The Appropriate Place of Christian Education in the Life of the Church

At the Intersection of Doxa and Dogma

WE HAVE ALREADY NOTED that over a number of years, Christian education has experienced a loss of theological location within much of the Western Protestant church. Christian education has been relegated to pedagogy-based Sunday School—predominantly for children. We have also asserted that, since the eighteenth century, Sunday School, and other intentional teaching models which separate the worshipping community from the learning community, have often become the singular understanding of Christian education in the Christian community. This understanding is, of course, patently limiting. If this has been the best way of handing on our faith, why (as indicated by some of the statistics that we have already examined) do we have such a deep and widespread crisis of faith in contemporary Western Christianity? Granted, other factors feed into this crisis, but the question remains.

Over the life of the post-industrial church, learning has been institutionalized to the point that Christian education is rarely understood today other than through the medium of formalized Sunday School. This understanding denies the value of the whole Christian community, limits theological exploration, and hampers worship. If it even exists outside the theological hall, teaching and learning of Christian doctrine is commonly separated from teaching and learning about worship. We have begun to scrutinize the importance of maintaining the interconnectedness of worship

138

and doctrine. Now we will examine this a little more fully, and assert the place of Christian education within that interconnectedness.

God in Jesus Christ has the potential to reach into the innermost parts of human life. In Christ, God lives and breathes the joys and pain of being human together with others. As Christians reflect upon what they are learning and teaching, and how they are living the Christian story, they can grow in their knowledge of God and of themselves. This can be profoundly intimate and address life's grand questions like "What does it mean to have faith?" and "How do I want to live?" and "To what sort of community do I want to belong?" As Thomas Groome writes:

> In a teaching/learning event, power and knowledge combine to form how people respond to the deepest questions about what it means to be human, how to participate with others in the world, and the kind of future to create together out of their past and present.[1]

Groome's insights bring back to mind our preliminary definition of Christian education as a process ultimately guided by God's Holy Spirit, whereby persons intentionally guide the Christian development of persons. This is essentially relational, and thus a communal activity. It must incarnate itself in the human response to worship this all-generous God. The teaching Jesus referred to—"Love the Lord your God with all your heart, and with all your soul, and with all your mind" (Matt 22:37), and "Love your neighbour as yourself" (Matt 22:39) shows that this is neither a private task, nor the task of an individual alone. Emerging Church writer Brian McLaren, argues that "the church exists to form Christlike people, people of Christlike love."[2] Christian formation is the task of the whole Christian community past, present and future, guided by God's Holy Spirit.

Christian education, viewed in this way, as a type of truly holistic ontological formation, becomes the responsibility of each Christian. As recorded in Paul's letters to the young Corinthian church, every Christian is called by God to use their God-given gifts to build up the Body of Christ for the mission of God in the world.[3] The Emerging Church champions the importance of the shared leadership of the whole community or Body, with each member using her or his abilities creatively in this way. Brian McLaren's insights are helpful here in generating an image of this different learning community:

---

1. Groome, *Sharing Faith*, 12.

2. McLaren, *New Kind of Christianity*, 164.

3. See 1 Cor 12:4–31 for one example.

> The church, then, in Paul's mind, must be above all a school of love. If it's not that, it's nothing. Its goal is not just to pump knowledge into people, but to train them in the "way of love," so they may do the "work of the Lord," empowered by the Holy Spirit, as the embodiment of Christ. Perhaps school is not the best metaphor, though, unless we think of a karate school or a dance school or a language school—not simply a community where you learn or learn about, but where you learn to. Not simply a place where you hear lectures and amass information, but a community where you see living examples of Christlikeness and experience inner formation.[4]

This is a thoroughly postmodern statement, reminiscent of Polanyi's view of knowing. If we are to help people *respond to the deepest questions about what it means to be human* and learn to genuinely *participate with others*, Christian formation must take its rightful place. If the Christian community is to become a school of love, a community where one sees living examples of Christlikeness and experiences inner formation, Christian education must become transformed action that reflects robust theological consideration. Christian education is an intersection of the praise and worship of God (doxology), and the accumulated beliefs of Christianity about God, humanity and creation (doctrine). These need to be brought back into balance. As we have already noted, *traditio* and *traditium* are interdependent in Christian education. The content of the tradition should form the basis for a more intentional and informed praxis or process. Of course, praxis, in turn, should modify the theory, grounding it in the reality of each new context and giving birth to informed, transformed action.

In order, then, to become part of this different community—an authentic Christian community—and in order to be formed as a Christian, there must be an ongoing growing, worshipping and reflecting process (*traditium*) in which certain knowledge, attitudes and practices (*traditio*) are instilled.

Teaching, learning, and living the Christian story, in order to grasp the Christian ethos, is one way of looking at this formation. Ongoing action and reflection on what is being taught and learned and how that teaching and learning occurs and is lived implies an uncompleted process of experimentation in, critical thinking about, and constructive evaluation of the progress of the Christian journey. *The Christian story* gives boundaries of belief, behavior and belonging to a particular community, as well as being the narrative that gives life and power, imagination, and hope for the future.

---

4. McLaren, *New Kind of Christianity*, 170.

In order to grasp suggests intentionality, purpose and struggle. The *Christian ethos* is an identity and character built on an understanding of God's character, revealed to humanity in the divine-person of Jesus Christ, living today by the power of God's Holy Spirit. In practice this Christian ethos has many forms.

DOCTRINE

In the last chapter we discussed Christian education as being most appropriately situated in the context of the worshipping—doxological—community. Doxology is a means and a ground for Christian formation, encompassing its own *traditio* and *traditium*. A wider Christian *traditium* embraces other kinds of Christian knowledge as well.

In theological terms, the appropriate place of Christian education can be expressed as being an intersection point of doxology and doctrine. There now needs to be some clarification over what we mean by doctrine within the field of Christian education, set within a doxological context. Why has the concept of doctrine become so distasteful to many of those sitting in the pews? Can the notion of doctrine as foundational for orthopraxy be resurrected for postmodern Christians?

Christian education, in this discussion, has centered upon the formational and transformational aspects of the Christian faith in the context of the worshipping community. Christian education, thus expressed, is posited doxologically.

In the interpretive framework that has been developed from a study of the Emerging Church, *the Christian story* describes the *traditium* of Christian education. This chapter will examine doctrine as a part of the *story,* or at least the "grammar" of the story, which is set within a doxological context. Doctrine also forms the way worship is rightly enacted, and concomitantly is developed through acts of worship. As such, doctrine is a key contributor in the development of Christian ethos.

Let us recall some of our discussion on ethos, as a way in to a further examination of a postmodern understanding of doctrine. Ethos, in many ways, is formed by doctrine. As we have already noted, Christian formation is a process by which an individual's or group's identity, attitudes, vision and values is shaped by and for an understanding of God, and an understanding of themselves as God's people. Formation and transformation involve the development of character as individuals and as part of the church—the Body of Christ. The cycle follows: formation of Christians naturally takes place within the Body or Community of Faith, so that Christian ethos may be continually formed and re-formed. In this sense, doctrine is a kind of recipe or guide for discussion of and reflection on those elements that contribute to a distinctively Christian ethos. *Ethos* literally means *character* or *custom*, and refers to the characteristic values, beliefs, and practices of a social group or a culture. It corresponds to the Latin *mores*, "customs," which refers to "generally held moral beliefs and practices."[5] A particular ethos is made up of all-encompassing beliefs, actions and values that are generally accepted within the ethos. Doctrine is the underlying foundation or basis for these beliefs and values, which in turn potentially leads to informed action or praxis. The ethos or character of a community thus affects the "lifestyle" and world-view of that community. Without some form of doctrine, be it explicit or not, belief, values, and action have no real basis and lack stability and credence.

Modernist ethical reflection has sometimes been regarded as a problem-solving procedure with an imperative for a dualistic solution; in other words, ethical reflection giving rise to statements that denote one particular behavior as wrong, whilst perceiving another as right. This does not allow doctrine its full due. The assumption that moral decisions are based on purely rationally derived answers, promotes the conclusion that ethical thought based on doctrine is only necessary when a crisis arises, viz., when we do not know what we should do or how we should act. Reaction in this way has often led to the notion that, when reflecting ethically, it is preferable to deny, minimize or even do away with tacit factors that make up personal identity, labelling them as subjective. Because of this, disposition, context and character, along with doctrine as accepted beliefs, have not always been taken into account. Ethics, characterized this way, becomes a dry, impersonal social science.

> Faith, formation, and decision go together whenever we think about ethics, Christian or otherwise. Ethics can never be understood simply in terms of a set of principles that tell us what is right and wrong. Unless those principles are a consistent expression of our basic outlook on life, our faith, and dispositions, they may not make much sense to us or they may not be very important to us.[6]

It is doctrine which offers some consistency to the expression of faith in one's life. The way one thinks, acts and speaks is influenced by the generally accepted beliefs and behavior of the community context from which one comes. Language is a pertinent example. Within the language and

5. Childress and Macquarrie, *New Dictionary of Christian Ethics*, 208.

6. Childs, *Faith, Formation, and Decision*, 6.

practices of the Christian community, Christian ethics finds its truthful environment, and consequently, occasions for Christian education. Christians need to learn, teach and live *with* the Christian story so that their behavior reflects learning, teaching and living *out* the story.

In a modern secular theory of knowledge, typically it is perceived that ethical or moral reasoning should be rational and objective, once again dismissing such concepts as faith and character as subjective and private. Postmodern understandings can be more conducive to including the concept of personal knowledge as viable and even necessary. Generally, the Christian community holds values of faith and character as part of its ontological makeup and as such, is not limited to a purely rational, objective view of moral reflection.[7] This gives the church the kind of opportunity for axiological reform that has not been seen since pre-Modernity. Doctrine as part of what makes up the Christian story contributes to the formation of the Christian character. As Stanley Hauerwas, in *A Community of Character,* states:

> What is required for our moral behaviours to contribute to a coherent sense of the self is neither a single moral principle nor a harmony of the virtues but . . . the formation of character by a narrative that provides a sufficiently truthful account of our existence. . . . Understanding the story of God as found in Israel and Jesus is the necessary basis for any moral development that is Christianly significant.[8]

Christian doctrine as a key part of the Christian narrative or story can encapsulate the wisdom of accumulated Christian knowledge from the past with the lived faith of the present and the eschatological hope of the future. Emerging Church writers and practitioners, as we have seen, have roundly criticized the gap between doctrine and ethics, orthodoxy and orthopraxy in the Old Church paradigm. Moral philosopher Alasdair MacIntyre presents a critique of modernist ethics in his *After Virtue.*[9] Incidentally, this book is often quoted by Emerging Church authors as a central pillar of Emerging Church philosophy.[10] MacIntyre stresses the importance of narratives in shaping the outlook of a community, in that narrative is able to ground the particularity of that community in history. He observes that narrative

7. The obvious exception is Christian fundamentalism, where Scripture is foundationally taken as literal, historical or even scientific.

8. Hauerwas, *A Community of Character*, 136.

9. MacIntyre, *After Virtue.*

10. Some examples are Jones, *Postmodern Youth Ministry;* and Wilson-Hartgrove, *New Monasticism.*

functions as a bearer of a *tradition*, which illuminates the present and opens up options for the future. Once again, we are reminded of Polanyi's understanding of the place of tradition in personal knowledge. MacIntyre argues that "living traditions, just because they continue a not-yet completed narrative, confront a future whose determinate and determinable character, so far as it possesses any, derives from its past."[11] Much of contemporary consumerist thinking continues to uphold the idol of novelty and rejects that which is seen to be old or passé. Doctrine has a place here in maintaining critical balance within a community's thinking. Stories and ideas that have formed culture previously are sometimes viewed as "past their use-by date." On one hand, wisdom may be lost in this process. On the other hand, this can also be a positive sign that reformation continues. As society becomes more and more pluralistic, different stories and doctrines arise as influential. The challenge for the church with regard to an ongoing evaluation of doctrine is its ability to maintain openness whilst critically assessing fresh emphases needed for new contexts.

In another seminal publication in the arena of doctrine, *The Nature of Doctrine*, George Lindbeck reclaims its place as a cornerstone of community. He observes that the importance of doctrines lies in their centrality to establishing and maintaining community. Lindbeck emphasizes this importance in his definition of doctrines as

> communally authoritative teachings regarding beliefs and practices which are considered essential to the identity or welfare of the group in question. They may be formally stated or informally operative, but in any case they indicate what constitutes faithful adherence to a community.[12]

Lindbeck, as something of a narrative theologian, emphasises the foundational importance of the biblical narrative. In agreement with Hauerwas, Lindbeck notes that "to become a Christian involves learning the story of Israel and Jesus well enough to interpret and experience oneself and one's world in its terms."[13] In order to learn and teach the story, the community must continually experience, interpret and live the story in its terms. Thus, the importance of the church's rediscovery of biblical narrative cannot be more highly stressed. Lindbeck calls the people of God to return to the "classic pattern of biblical interpretation" with its

---

11. MacIntyre, *After Virtue*, 223.

12. Lindbeck, *Nature of Doctrine*, 27.

13. Ibid., 34.

"consensus-and-community-building potential."[14] Once again it is clear that the task for Christian education is one of retelling and reinterpretation of ancient texts and practices for new times and places.

It is not only the content of the stories of the faith community that interests Lindbeck, however. Doctrines for him are the "grammar that informs the way the story is told and used."[15] For, while he admits that doctrines can be understood as making various ontological truth claims[16] (or claims about reality), they are primarily statements designed to regulate the wider use of religious language, including its quality of *poiesis* in and through art, music and architecture. The expression of this language is, of course primarily in doxology. In other words, doctrines are the grammar of religion—the rules for the use of religious language and concepts.[17]

Lindbeck maintains that this understanding of doctrines as the grammar of religion provides a better explanation of the way doctrines have historically operated and been understood than the universalist dogmatism of modernity. Lindbeck pictures doctrines as planks of a floating raft—an analogy more acceptable to a postmodern audience than an immovable foundation on which to build faith understanding. He observes that statements and creeds have remained essentially unchanged throughout the various eras of Christian history and across many pluralistic cultural and ethical understandings and beliefs.[18] While the forms of doctrines have remained stable, their particular interpretation for particular times and places has varied considerably.[19] Some central Christian dogma (doctrines being a sub-set of dogma) has remained and been retained as normative, but once again has contained an assortment of related content. Lindbeck gives an example of the affirmation of God as creator, which is expressed in the Nicene Creed as "We believe in one God, the Father, the Almighty, maker of heaven and earth." This notion has been conceptually affirmed in terms of the ancient Middle Eastern myths found in the writings of the Hebrew Scriptures, in terms of Greek philosophy, and, more recently in terms of modern cosmology.[20] Thus the affirmation stays the same, but its content, interpretation and understanding has grown and changed enormously.

14. Lindbeck, "Scripture, Consensus, and Community," 74–101.
15. Ibid., 80.
16. Ibid., 67.
17. Ibid., 66.
18. Ibid., 82–84.
19. Black, "Future of Faith," 29.
20. Lindbeck, *Nature of Doctrine*, 82.

In this way, doctrine is the "recipe" or "grammar" for talking about God. Teaching and learning of doctrine gives the Christian community guideposts and boundaries for an evolving discussion of God, the universe, humanity and the like. Theologian Colin Gunton describes dogma as:

> that which delimits the garden of theology, providing a space where theologians may play freely and cultivate such plants as are cultivable in the space which is so defined.... Just as a garden is not a garden without some boundaries—or just as the created world is only what it is as a work of God because it is finite in space and time—so theology ceases to be Christian theology if it effectively ceases to remain true to its boundaries.[21]

Let us briefly pause in this discussion to clarify the distinction and relationship between doctrine and dogma. *Dogma* is being used in this argument to mean an accepted teaching of the church. McGrath notes that the Franciscan writer P. N. Chrisman (1751–1810) used the term *dogma* to designate formal ecclesiastical doctrine as opposed to theological opinion.

> By introducing the concept of "dogma," Chrisman hoped to bring an element of clarity to interdenominational dialogues, by distinguishing ecclesiastical teaching from private theological opinion, and restricting denominational debates to the former. The term "dogma" thus came to bear the meaning it possesses today within the Roman Catholic church: "dogma" specifically designates that which is declared by the church to be revealed truth either as part of the universal teaching, or through a solemn doctrinal judgement. Included in the concept of dogma are two quite distinct elements: the notion of divine revelation, or revealed truth; and the church's proposal or reception of such revelation or truth.[22]

In this sense, dogma encompasses and is comprised at least in part of doctrines; but not all doctrines will be considered dogma. The word *dogma* has gained a fairly negative connotation in much contemporary parlance. This is due in large part to the postmodern reaction against the notion of universal truth and authority. The accumulated wisdom of Christian theological knowledge seems to the postmodern mind to be unbending and unquestionable, and worse, boring.

On the other hand, the postmodern reaction to dogma has led to new possibilities to view doctrine as embracing the richness of pluralism, of the

---

21. Gunton, *Triune Creator*, 1.
22. McGrath, *Genesis of Doctrine*, 9.

spirit of excitement, learning and discovery about God's sharing of Godself with humanity and all of creation.

God's self-revelation retains the flexibility to vary in content according to the setting. Rigidity in its presentation and promotion comes primarily from human sources. It is to be hoped that, if Western Christianity can radically start back at the grass roots, the Body of Christ will be able to recapture the beauty, worth and vitality of an understanding of normative Christian doctrine. God's revelation in Jesus Christ is the beginning of Christian doctrine. Learning about this God-Man comes through stories of his life, death and resurrection recorded in the Scriptures. God acted in history in a personal and dynamic way by becoming human and living a human life.

The writers of the Gospels, along with Paul in his letters to the infant church, were in a sense the first recorders of doctrine. As Paul writes in 1 Cor 15:3–8:

> For I handed on to you as of first importance what I in turn had received: that Christ died for our sins in accordance with the scriptures, and that he was buried, and that he was raised on the third day in accordance with the scriptures, and that he appeared to Cephas, then to the twelve. Then he appeared to more than five hundred brothers and sisters at one time, most of whom are still alive, though some have died. Then he appeared to James, then to all the apostles. Last of all, as to one untimely born, he appeared also to me.

The earliest confessional statement is thought to be *Kurios Jesous*—"Jesus is Lord"—as recorded in both Rom 10:9 and 1 Cor 12:3. This confession stood to oppose the rival Roman oath "Caesar is Lord." This is one indication that dogma and doctrines are not restricted to the Christian faith. Systematic theologian Geoffrey Wainwright notes that "Pliny's test for alleged Christians upon arrest comprised of 'reciting a prayer to the gods,' 'making supplications with incense and wine before the emperor's statue' and 'cursing Christ.'"[23] Thus, the Roman political and religious dogma was set in fierce opposition to the basic core of the earliest Christians' belief. Many of these early Christian believers upheld fledgling Christian doctrine, making their affirmations of faith not only to God but also as a public witness to the world around them. This stands to illustrate some aspects of doctrine. Most contemporary Christians would agree that the same could still be said as a confession of Christ or witnessing to the power of Christ, two thousand years later: Christ is Lord not only of the church, but also of the world. In this sense, doctrine has a public and somewhat timeless

23. Wainwright, *Doxology*, 157.

or overarching quality, but as we have seen, emphases change according to the context. Our contemporary understanding of the notion of "Lord" is an example in point. "Lord" and "Lordship" have very different connotations today from the understandings that might have been held by a first century citizen of Rome.

Through its doctrine the Christian community declares what it sees as its truth claims in its constituent times and places. Wainwright quotes New Testament scholar Hans Conzelmann:

> The Christian community declares publicly who is its Lord. The confession not only demands a decision but has the power to produce one. . . . Christ's rule is confessed before the world because his domain is not only the Church but the world. This the Church knows, whereas it is hidden from the unbelieving world. Therefore the Church must go on disclosing to the world the truth about itself.[24]

The declaration and teaching of doctrine was important to the writers of the Gospels. As we have already observed, doctrinal or credal statements are present in the Scriptures of the Old and the New Testament. For ease of teaching, learning and living these understandings, they are often found occurring in the form of hymns, for example 1 Tim 3:16:

> Without any doubt, the mystery of our religion is great:
>   He was revealed in flesh,
>   vindicated in spirit,
>   seen by angels,
>   proclaimed among Gentiles,
>   believed in throughout the world,
>   taken up in glory.

About New Testament hymns, Wainwright notes that the apologists of the New Testament found it valuable to draw on the known hymns of the Christian community when they themselves were establishing and instructing in points of doctrine.[25] This indicates the liturgical context for the teaching of such doctrine. As the earliest theologians, Paul and the evangelists established a doxological precedent for doctrine that was to influence later ecclesiastical thinkers, authorities and theologians, as well as musicians, poets and artists.

Dogmatic statements are expressed in many of the prayers of the New Testament. Examples include the Lord's Prayer, 2 Cor 1:3, Eph 1:3 and 1

24. Ibid., 158.
25. Ibid., 159.

Peter 1:3. In the Lord's Prayer recorded in Matt 6:9 and Luke 11:1, several clear doctrinal statements are made including the nature of God as provider, preserver and redeemer of humankind. Wainwright observes that when the New Testament writers hand over at times to doxology, "the link becomes even more apparent between 'doing theology' and 'teaching ethics,' on the one hand, and worship of God on the other."[26] Wainwright cites Rom 11:33–36; 16:25–27; Eph 3:20; 1 Tim 1:17; 6:16; and Jude 24 as examples that provide models for later practices.

It is clear then, that from the earliest thinking about Christianity, doxology and doctrine are inextricably linked. The development of dogma and doctrines coincides closely with the development of Christian liturgy. The synergy of the two is conspicuous. Conversely, doctrine can be learned and taught from the liturgy of the worshipping community. Debra Dean Murphy stresses this in her book, *Teaching That Transforms: Worship as the Heart of Christian Education*. She argues for the reconnection between Christian worship and Christian learning or catechesis, noting that "it is in corporate worship that the lives of Christians are most acutely formed and shaped."[27]

The particular need for confessional statements, doctrine and creeds has been important at various stages of the church's life. There are several main reasons for this.[28] Firstly, as we have already seen, there was the need for some kind of teaching or instruction in the faith—*catechesis*. This was especially the case for Christian converts preparing for baptism, and it is still a pressing need of the church today. Statistics concerning biblical, liturgical and ecclesial illiteracy have already been discussed.

Secondly, the call for doctrinal statements has been influenced by the desire for orthodoxy in worship practices. In the early church, liturgy and hymnody were needed to teach and bring to remembrance the basics of the faith. Examples include 1 Tim 3:16—an early Christological hymn, previously noted—as well as Phil 2:6–11 and 1 Cor 15:3–7, where Paul's reference to "delivering" what he had "received" points to an interlinking of liturgical and confessional tradition. The Jewish liturgical tradition of the Shema would have influenced the confession. In 1 Cor 8:6 Paul writes, "yet for us there is one God, the Father, from whom are all things and for whom we exist, and one Lord, Jesus Christ, through whom are all things and through whom we exist." Ephesians 4:4–6 is reminiscent: "There is one body and one Spirit, just as you were called to the one hope of your calling, one Lord, one

---

26. Ibid., 160.

27. Murphy, *Teaching That Transforms*, 10.

28. Quanbeck in Buttrick, *Interpreter's Dictionary of the Bible*, 668.

faith, one baptism, one God and Father of all, who is above all and through all and in all."

A third reason for the development of doctrine has been persecution. Persecution because of one's faith presented the need to maintain an unambiguous focus of faith, so that in the hour of martyrdom one could stand up for that faith, clearly and concisely. Jesus himself made confession before Pontius Pilate, and the earliest Christians were obliged to confess Christ's name before Roman authorities also. Out of this experience, a close connection developed between confession of Christ and the concept of the witness of martyrdom.

Fourthly, heresy grew as the gospel spread throughout the known world of the early church; so, in order to counteract various heresies that sprang up, credal statements were developed, often flowing from gatherings of church officials in the form of Councils. This factor, in particular, came to influence the entire development of Christian thought, teaching and education. The catechisms and confessions of the Reformation are one example. This reflects possibly the most pressing need for the contemporary church, including much of the Emerging Church. In a postmodern world, where diverse beliefs and attitudes are often held with similar credence, there is a need to understand the boundaries of the Christian faith so that people are not misled, abused or exploited. Other factors that caused a need for doctrine included simple encouragement and the ordering of the growing church.

As we saw in chapter 4, as new converts to Christianity, catechumens were given instruction in preparation for baptism. Two examples of worship forms reflecting this instruction are found in 1 John 2:12–14 and 1 Peter 3:10–12. The catechumen had to affirm the simplest creed, "Jesus is Lord," recorded in Rom 10:9, and other confessional statements about the nature and purpose of Jesus Christ, as in the words of the Ethiopian eunuch, recorded in Acts 8:37: "I believe that Jesus Christ is the Son of God."

Examples of more formal creeds, stating belief in the three persons of the Trinity, which hearkens back to the baptismal commission of Matt 28:19, occur in descriptions of baptismal liturgies recorded by Irenaeus and Hippolytus of Rome. The Apostles' Creed probably derives from the late second century baptismal creed used in Rome.[29]

The Apostles' Creed is widely used in the contemporary Western church as a succinct summary of the major themes of the Christian faith. Its development is complex, with its origins lying in the early baptismal confessions we have already mentioned. It stemmed from Matt 28:19, where Jesus

29. McGrath, *Christian Theology Reader*, 391.

instructs his disciples to "Go therefore and make disciples of all nations, baptizing them in the name of the Father and of the Son and of the Holy Spirit."

Thus, a pattern of Trinitarian credal confession emerged. The Apostles' Creed assumed its final form in the eighth century and consists of twelve individual statements traditionally ascribed to each of the apostles (there is, in fact, no historical justification for this belief).[30]

1. I believe in God, the Father Almighty, creator of heaven and earth;

2. I believe in Jesus Christ, God's only Son, our Lord;

3. who was conceived by the Holy Spirit, born of the Virgin Mary;

4. suffered under Pontius Pilate, was crucified, dead and buried; [he descended to the dead];

5. on the third day he rose again;

6. he ascended into heaven, and is seated at the right hand of the Father;

7. and he will come to judge the living and the dead.

8. I believe in the Holy Spirit;

9. the holy catholic church; [the communion of saints];

10. the forgiveness of sins;

11. the resurrection of the body;

12. and the life everlasting.

In contemporary times, the Apostles' and Nicene Creeds have been widely accepted by mainline Christian churches as normative statements of Christian belief. The statements regarding "descent to the dead" and "communion of saints" (printed above in brackets) are not recorded in the Eastern version of the document.

The Nicene Creed in its final form was developed at the Council of Constantinople in 381, and sets out the orthodox position on the human and divine natures of Jesus Christ, as a reaction against Arian heresy. In comparing the Apostles' Creed and the Creed of Nicaea, there are similarities in structure. The Creed of Nicaea adds a number of distinctly anti-Arian phrases. These include "of one substance with the Father" in order to exclude the Arian notion that Jesus Christ was created by the Father out of

30. Ibid., 8.

nothing, and "God from God" (referring to Jesus), to argue that the Father is not alone God. Jesus Christ is named clearly as *homoousios* with the Father.

Thus, doctrines have an essential delineating purpose in the *traditium* of Christian knowledge. We originally began our discussion of Christian knowledge with the equivalent statements of Augustine and Calvin concerning knowledge of God and of ourselves. So it is fitting that we return very briefly to Calvin as he describes the limits upon attaining knowledge of God and of ourselves. The Reformer notes that, "it is evident that man never attains to a true self-knowledge until he has previously contemplated the face of God and come down after such contemplation to look into himself. . ."[31] For Calvin, contemplating God meant the examination of God's Word, Scripture, and an understanding of the church. Humanity can only know God if God chooses to be known. Forgiveness and salvation are possible through the untainted and unhelped grace of God. For Calvin, the church was of utmost importance, because it was the means to knowledge about God. Interpreted in the postmodern context as it was in pre-Modern times, the church as worshipping community is the fertile ground for learning, teaching and living the Christian story. Again in his *Institutes*, Calvin defines the two essential "marks" of the church to be the preaching of God's Word and the administration of the sacraments:

> Wherever we see the Word of God purely preached and listened to, and the sacraments administered according to Christ's institution, it is in no way to be doubted that a church of God exists. For his promise cannot fail: "Wherever two or three are gathered in my name, there I am in the midst of them" (Matt 18:20).[32]

Calvin devised a church structure that included four offices within the order of ministry, one of which was the minister as teacher. In 1541, Calvin summarized the faith in a catechism that was translated into Latin, and that led to the production of other catechisms by later Calvinists. These catechisms became the way the Reformed Christian faith was disseminated from this time on. Catechisms were also used as basic theological texts for candidates for the ministry.

Doctrine has continued to form, be formed, and grow over the centuries. It has developed in a variety of different situations for diverse reasons. It has created, and has been transformed by, countless controversies and arguments, as well as civil, political and religious events. There is not enough

---

31. Calvin, *Institutes of the Christian Religion*, I:1:1–2, 37.
32. Ibid., IV:1:9, 289.

space here for a detailed history of doctrine, but we have considered some key examples of how and why doctrine has evolved.

In *A Community of Character*, Stanley Hauerwas writes that Christians are to be a community of people "capable of hearing the story of God we find in the scripture and living in a manner that is faithful to that story."[33] Without the story and contextual interpretation of the story, there is no ability to *live* the story. Christian education as ongoing learning, teaching and living the Christian story, in order to grasp Christian ethos, is bound by doctrine. Doctrine is an extensive element of the Christian story. The Christian story involves both the *traditium* and the *traditio*. The *traditium* helps form the grammar, or recipe, or *doctrine* of the faith. Intertwined with the *traditium*, the *traditio* is the way we learn, live and express the story, *doxologically*. Intersecting these two, Christian education is a tool helping people to worship God, and in doing so delivering knowledge of God's nature and actions throughout salvation history, to enable the people of God to continue to worship God in the world.

DOXOLOGY

We have argued that there is an indissoluble link between dogma and doxology. This principal link will be further explored in this section. In his book *Worship as Theology*, Don Saliers quotes theologian Joseph Sittler regarding this connection:

> Dogma and Doxa—what we believe and what we pray, constitute a single music in contrapuntal form; the sombre remembrances and fresh probings of faith as Doxa always illuminates the freshly unfolding intelligibility and power of the faith as Dogma, as truths believed. . . . The songs of praise the church sings are a lyrical way of disclosing what the faith knows and how we know.[34]

In order to grasp the ethos or identity of their faith, Christians must live with the Christian story. A vitally important part of living as a Christian is a lifelong praising of God, so in order to examine how we learn, teach and live the Christian story, we must examine doxology—praise and worship of God. We have also argued that the worship of God becomes the encompassing context through which worshippers know about God. In fact, the communal worship of God nurtures growth, not only in knowing about God,

---

33. Hauerwas, *Community of Character*, 1.

34. Saliers, *Worship as Theology*, 39–40.

but in coming to a sense of Polanyi's personal knowledge of the God who is Father, Son and Holy Spirit. This knowledge develops through a tradition of ways of knowing that embraces *theoria, praxis,* and *poiesis.* If each of these ways of knowing are activated and nurtured, they are able to assist in the forming, in the sustaining and in the ongoing reforming of the Christian community's ethos. Doctrinal knowledge is not to be thought of separately as *theoria* alone. Doctrine informs the practices of the Christian church as it is embodied in creative production of praise and glory for God, and in turn, as it is informed by practice and worship. The Christian story is never fully formed because God is never fully known. There are different expressions of God's grace in each new setting. Doctrine cannot be rigid or stationary, but open to God's Spirit moving in fresh ways. With regard to doctrine's kinetic role in manifesting itself doxologically, Don Saliers' caution is apt: "The indicative of theology will always be diminished when it ceases to be formed in the authentic praise of God."

Doxology, from the Greek *doxologia,* literally means "words of glory." Doxology refers not only to human action in ascribing praise, but also to "something intrinsic to God: doxa as the divine glory."[35] It is inclusive of the glorious actions of God. In Catherine LaCugna's 1988 article with Kilian McDonnell, "Returning from 'The Far Country': Theses for a Contemporary Trinitarian Theology,"[36] doxology is described as "praise offered to God, because of what God has done on our behalf." The article goes on to discuss the history of creation and redemption as "the history of praise lost and regained." This history is seen in terms of stories of events within God's economy of salvation such as creation and the disobedience of humanity in the Garden of Eden; the election of Israel as covenant-partner; the prophetic warnings against idolatry; Christ's life, teaching, death and resurrection into new life; and the sending of the Holy Spirit. LaCugna and McDonnell give a logical, systematic summation of the profound relationship between doxology and soteriology. The discussion is consistent in its Trinitarian focus on the solid tangibility of God's personal presence in Jesus Christ, and the "power of the glory of God who moves our hearts to praise and who also enables our praise to reach God" as God's Holy Spirit. In humanity, created by God, "a new possibility for praise was created, a new possibility for doxology." Sin is seen as the absence of praise, and salvation as the restoration of praise. LaCugna's model of emanation and return is linked to the path of glory God personally takes *out* and *back* through history. The dual emphasis here is on *our* return (our praise): in the Spirit through Christ to God.

---

35. Ibid.

36. LaCugna and McDonnell, "Returning from 'The Far Country,'" 191–215.

The authors also discuss the relational aspects of worship. These aspects pertain firstly to relationship with God, but also to the participation in the Trinitarian *koinonia* through which the community of Christ is brought into right relationship with God, and its members with each other. LaCugna and McDonnell view worship as the remembrance and recounting of God's gracious redemption and transformation of the world through Christ in the power of the Spirit. Credal and doctrinal statements are included in the structure of doxology, as opening up the living reality of God.

This places doxology as critical to the life of the church. Praise of God is the right response to what God has done. In the sacramental worshipping life of the Christian community, people are welcomed into the very life of God, and as a part of this invitation, they are challenged to act in ways that are compassionate, reconciling and lifegiving, just as God acts. In her 1991 monograph, *God for Us*, Catherine LaCugna speaks of the welding of soteriology and doxology:

> Even if we cannot see the face of God directly, we are invited to enter into the saving act, to accompany God in history, to see and hear and recount the wonderful works of God (magnalia Dei) and in this way to offer praise and thanksgiving to God. Although we cannot name God, we can pray the name of God given to us, thereby activating relationship with the God who names Godself. Soteriology culminates in doxology.[37]

The ultimate reality of God is as Triune, personal, self-giving and existing as the mystery of persons in communion, or *perichoresis*. The communion amongst the three persons of the Trinity is shared with the worshipping community in a special way in the sharing of the Eucharist. This is the self-giving of God known throughout the economy of salvation. As Paul writes in his letter to the Romans, "in Christ we live and move and have our being" and God's Spirit is given to us as love. Trinitarian theology is a way of knowing God by means of and within the economy of salvation.[38] The mystery of God is unveiled in the person and ministry of Jesus Christ and in the power and presence of the Holy Spirit. God's self-revelation and entire self-giving for the whole of creation is proper cause for praise and worship.

This is orthodoxy in its true meaning. Orthodoxy is the practice of correct and true ascription of honour, praise and glory to God, who ultimately deserves it because of God's saving acts. Orthodoxy, maintains Saliers,

---

37. LaCugna, *God for Us*, 334–35.
38. Ibid.

is not a rational system by which we can differentiate ourselves from all others who are faithless; rather, ortho-doxy is being lured and drawn by the ethos of the liturgy to know God's glory. Orthodoxy is learning in the long, hard, joyous way to ascribe unto God the doxa due to God's name.[39]

The place of doctrine as accumulated knowledge of the ways of God is essentially tied in as a means of ultimately facilitating right worship of God. As previously discussed, Emerging Church writers have generally championed the place of orthopraxy or right action above the place of doctrine in a postmodern understanding of a life of Christian faith. Some have even advocated "replacing explicit creeds and doctrines with implicit norms devised by the group."[40] I see this as problematic for the Emerging Church, and an issue for caution in the church as a whole. It is appropriate to say that Christian ethical action demonstrates the identity, character and ethos of the Christian community in accordance with its call to be Christ's Body on earth. But so-called missional action is not to be advocated for its own sake, nor to bring kudos to the church. Orthopraxy is not generated merely out of a sense of altruism, philanthropy or even good citizenship. As part of the *missio Dei* (God's sending), Christian ethical behavior and right action in mission must be grounded in Christian doctrine and be expressed as orthodoxy, or right praise of God in the world.

This imbalance of orthopraxy over orthodoxy is predominantly a problem of post-Christendom biblical ignorance. In many Modernist Sunday School-based Christian education programs, doctrine has not been sufficiently valued or explicitly shared as underpinning Christian ethos. A Sunday School-based Christian ethos, in turn, has not always incorporated worship, liturgy, or the sacraments, and the worshipping community has been kept separate from the Sunday School. The Christian ethos that has developed in some young people's minds is along the lines of membership rules. These rules often describe behaviors that designate one as part of the group. In my informal questioning of a number of young adults about what makes a person a Christian, I have found that these "rules" include not consuming alcohol or illicit substances, and not gambling or using "bad" language. These "implicit norms" have replaced doctrine as a language of doxology in the life of these young Christians.

The separation of Christian worship and Christian learning by the relegation of the latter to the business of Sunday School has been a major contributor to this ignorance. Scripture has commonly been taught in

39. Saliers, *Worship*, 40–41.
40. Wuthnow, *Sharing the Journey*, 18, 345.

Sunday School without reference to the whole community of faith and the worshipping life of the church. In Sunday School settings, Scripture tends to be relegated to a few over-used cautionary tales and fantastic heroic legends, delivered usually in a separate location, while the parents are at worship. This is an erosion of Christian community and poor Christian education.

The Scriptures incorporate doctrine and, as the clearest form of God's self-revelation, are therefore central to the grasping of knowledge of God and humanity. As we shall discuss further in a moment, the Scriptures also teach styles and forms of worship. The Christian community (children, young people and adults) is fragmented and impoverished if it does not worship God together. The whole Christian community learns from one another and teaches one another as they experience God's word and respond to God's grace in a double doxological movement. In 1544, Martin Luther's description of this occurrence in worship was "that nothing else should happen there but that our dear Lord speak with us Himself through his holy word and we in turn speak with Him in prayer and praise."[41]

This two-way movement of doxology in the worship of God is both God's action in love for God's people as the gathered congregation and the response of the congregation to God's loving acts that have been recorded in Scripture and are demonstrated in the lives of the people. In order to make this response to God's action in Christ through the Holy Spirit over the course of salvation history, we must also pay attention to what Scripture teaches us about doxology.

The Scriptural text provides the source of the imagery and, often, the very form and style of language in prayers, chants, hymn lyrics and sermons. In similar ways to their usage in the Hebrew cult of the Old Testament, Psalms are often used in contemporary worship. Gordon Lathrop, in his liturgical theology, *Holy Things*, notes:

> To people who know the biblical stories, the very actions of the gathering (for worship) may seem like the Bible alive: an assembly gathers, as the people gathered at the foot of Mount Sinai, the holy convocation of the Lord; arms are upraised in prayer or blessing, as Moses raised his arms; the holy books are read, as Ezra read to the listening people; the people hold a meal, as the disciples did, gathered after the death of Jesus.[42]

So, in divine worship there takes place the recognition and remembrance of God's great deeds and the promises that God has given to

---

41. Luther, *Works,* Vol. 69, 1:15, quoted in Edmund Schlink, *The Coming Christ and the Coming Church*, 134.

42. Lathrop, *Holy Things*, 15.

humankind, as well as the means for the congregation to give God glory for that. The substance, and to a great extent even the form of worship, is offered as God's ever changing gift, given and received. Worship of God relates God's action throughout salvation history: the initiation and care of the cosmos, the choice and direction of Israel and the Christian church. God's ultimate act of salvation is the life, death and resurrection of God's Son, Jesus Christ. Worship also relates the eschatological promises of God for the future, to the promise of the parousia of Jesus Christ.[43]

One only has to read the words of Psalm 78 or Psalm 105 to gain a succinct summary of Old Testament salvation history. The educative element of living within and passing on the story is particularly evident in the opening verses of Psalm 78:

> Give ear, O my people, to my teaching;
> incline your ears to the words of my mouth.
> I will open my mouth in a parable;
> I will utter dark sayings from of old,
> things that we have heard and known,
> that our ancestors have told us.
> We will not hide them from their children;
> we will tell to the coming generation
> the glorious deeds of the LORD, and his might,
> and the wonders that he has done.

The Psalm continues then, to outline Israel's connection with God throughout Old Testament history. It also gives form to a response for this connection. Listening, telling parables, sharing wisdom and experience, being honest about failures, abiding in the awe of the greatness of God: these are all elements of the liturgy as the true work of the people. In worship the activity of the living God is learned, taught, celebrated and facilitated.

It is not, however, only the actions of God that doxa focuses upon, but the character and very nature of God. Worship becomes the means by which God reveals what God is like and this becomes how God is perceived. Don Saliers observes that "doxa begins as the intrinsic character of God, the shared glory in the blessed community that is God from before all time and in all time."[44] As the community of faith together contemplates the stories of Jesus' life and teaching and participates in what he does in word and sacrament, the glory of God, which inspires awe and brings hope, may begin to be incarnated in them. The actual physical acts of standing, kneeling, passing

---

43. Schlink, *Coming Christ*, 134.
44. Saliers, *Worship*, 41.

the peace are, in some ways, rehearsals of that incarnation in the world.[45] These worshipful acts embody the ways that the Christian community is to worship God in their everyday lives. For example, standing at certain times within the liturgy can be used to indicate a rejection of passivity and apathy, as in, "We will not take this sitting down!" Standing can also demonstrate honour and indicate respect for what is being shared, as in courteous rising for a special guest. In addition, standing can be a way of showing thanks or adulation, as in a standing ovation. In this physical movement, the Christian story is practiced. In the physical act of standing, as one small example, the people of God demonstrate that they are called to be active in their love and service, just and respectful in their treatment of others and grateful for the grace of God. This incarnation can form the community for service in the world in response to and as worship of that same God.[46] When this is made explicit, the Christian community better understands its role in the world. It is not just the stories that teach and form Christian ethos. The Christian story involves liturgical traditions, ritual and gestures as ways of knowing as well.

In ongoing formation as Christian followers, the Christian community is learning, teaching and living with the Christian story by experiencing it, being immersed in it and reflecting on it, in order to grasp and embody Christian ethos or Christian behavior and action in life. In the Scriptures, the glory of God revealed, incarnated and embodied in Jesus Christ is repeatedly recorded and demonstrated. In John 1:14, for example, the writer of this Gospel notes, "the Word became flesh and lived among us, and we have seen his glory, the glory as of a father's only son, full of grace and truth." The Emerging Church has reminded the whole Christian community that the ways of Jesus cannot remain as words on a page, they must become flesh, being brought to life. This means actively living out the Christian story by Jesus' Body on earth, the church.

As growth and familiarity with the Christian story is formed in an individual's or community's character, Christ the Word can be further revealed, and awareness of a need to respond to this Word also may grow. The nature and actions of a self-revealing God initiate worship as the first doxological movement. Human response is the second movement of doxology, where the liturgy, as the work of the people, can be praise, thanks, contrition, lament, or offering, to name but a few of the doxological options. "We have seen his glory," John proclaims. What does that mean? The source of goodness and love in the cosmos is being explicitly recognized and

---

45. Murphy, *Worship That Transforms*, 105.

46. See also Anderson, *Worship and Christian Identity*, 58–59.

acknowledged. This is truth for followers of Christ. In Christian worship there is a participation in the glory of God by ascribing glory and honour and power to the triune God. By doing this, learning of the language of doxology takes place.[47]

Learning the language of doxology means participating in doxology as people who have been invited to be partakers with God, in communion within Godself. As God's people, the church has been invited to celebrate with God in the Eucharistic feast. Jesus Christ is present with his people. Jesus Christ, the risen Lord of the church, invites his people to communion with him giving his very identity, his own self in his words, "This is my body that is for you. Do this in remembrance of me. . . . This cup is the new covenant in my blood. Do this, as often as you drink it, in remembrance of me."[48] For Christians, Jesus Christ is present as both giver and gift, for the forgiveness of sins and life in union with him. In giving himself in this way, the people of God are reminded of Christ's self-giving act on the cross. As the great High Priest, Jesus shares in this communion the sin offering that he presented to God on the cross. And by doing this, Jesus brings the people of God into the new covenant that God enacted in Christ's blood.[49]

God comes, reconciling the world to Godself as the first doxological movement toward humanity in all of creation, and the creaturely response is to be praise and adoration, as the upward movement of doxology and liturgy. In gathered divine worship, this takes the form of confessions of faith or credal statements, hymns and prayers.

Liturgically, Christians confess their faith, announcing what they believe or assent to, both before God and before each other. This means that confession or affirmation of faith in the form of credal statements is both doxological and doctrinal. In worship, Christians praise God and tell of God's great deeds, addressing both God and fellow human beings. In confessing the faith encompassed in its doctrine, the Christian community gives boundaries to the story. This is what the worshipping community says it believes, what has been learned, taught and lived of God.

In common liturgical practice, the people of God affirm their faith as a response to the Scriptures read and proclaimed in the preaching of the word. In his letter to the Romans, Paul teaches:

> The word is near you, on your lips and in your heart (that is, the
> word of faith that we proclaim); because if you confess with your

47. Saliers, *Worship*, 139–53.

48. 1 Cor 11:24, 25.

49. For a fuller discussion on this, see also Torrance, *Worship, Community and the Triune God*, 36–40.

lips that Jesus is Lord and believe in your heart that God raised him from the dead, you will be saved. For one believes with the heart and so is justified, and one confesses with the mouth and so is saved.[50]

In confessing faith not only to God but also to the worshipping community there is a sharing of the story, a learning, a teaching and a living of the story. In living out the ethics of the Christian story, there can be an "owning" of the story as ours, and our community's, with God. By genuinely confessing faith one is invited to enter into engagement with it and to live it out. Engagement involves amongst other things, observing, inquiring, questioning, even doubting about God, faith and about oneself. By confessing the faithfulness of God, the worshipping community is called to assist in the extending of God's grace to others, so that an attitude of thanksgiving towards God may begin to be formed. As Paul writes in 2 Cor 4:13–15:

> But just as we have the same spirit of faith that is in accordance with scripture—"I believed, and so I spoke"—we also believe, and so we speak, because we know that the one who raised the Lord Jesus will raise us also with Jesus, and will bring us with you into his presence. Yes, everything is for your sake, so that grace, as it extends to more and more people, may increase thanksgiving, to the glory of God.

We have already discussed some reasons for the development of the Apostles' and the Nicene Creed, used as early initiation rituals, summarising the content of the gospel, and as a safeguard against heresy and controversy. There is also an obvious affinity between the creeds and some New Testament texts designated as "hymns."[51] In the singing of hymns, the people of God are affirming their faith in God, that is, telling the Christian story, praising God and ascribing worth and majesty to God. St Augustine defined hymns as having the following three characteristics: a hymn is praise; it is praise of God; it is the sung praise of God.[52]

In this discussion of doxology, what do we mean by praise? Firstly, praise is acclamation. The most popular acclamation of the Old Testament Temple cult was "Hallelujah."[53] This was often used as a refrain. The psalms are filled with acclamations. In Psalms 93, 97, and 99 we find the words, "The Lord reigns." Psalms 105, 106, 107, 118, and 136 contain the phrase,

---

50. Rom 10:8–10.

51. Wainwright, *Doxology*, 183.

52. Augustine, quoted in Wainwright, *Doxology*, 198.

53. Old, *Themes and Variations*, 41.

"O give thanks to the LORD for he is good; for his steadfast love endures forever" as a kind of chorus or antiphon. The song of the seraphim in Isa 6:3, "Holy, holy, holy is the Lord of hosts; the whole earth is full of his glory!" resounds as a greeting of the true sovereign of the cosmos. In acclamation, there is recognition and acknowledgment.

Acclamation of God's presence also includes the naming of God's attributes. The writer of Exodus describes God as "The LORD, a God merciful and gracious, slow to anger, and abounding in steadfast love and faithfulness."[54] The Psalmist gives similar attributes in Psalm 117's song of praise:

> Praise the LORD, all you nations!
> Extol him, all you peoples!
> For great is his steadfast love toward us,
> and the faithfulness of the LORD endures forever.
> Praise the LORD!

God's grace and faithfulness are seen to extend eternally. God is an infinite being whose praise is also to continue to be maintained ad infinitum. The God who is acclaimed forever is identified as worthy to be praised by all peoples. Here we see a movement, in the praise of God, towards telling the stories of God. There is the element of proclamation, *kerygma*, even within praise.

So, praise is acclamation and, to some extent, proclamation. Praise is also to be thought of as prophetic, in the sense that it must be constantly calling the people of God to transformation and reformation. Hymns of praise include this element of calling the Christian community back to its source, so that it is able to look forward, eschatologically. Jesus, in the line of the Old Testament prophets, was critical of the Temple worship of his day, calling the liturgical leaders "hypocrites" (Matt 6:2, 5, 16). In this passage, Jesus outlines true worship as including teaching on the place of piety (6:1), stewardship (6:2–4), prayer (6:5–13), forgiveness (6:14–15) and fasting (6:16–18). He stresses that these outward forms of doxology are not, however, the sacrifice of praise that God requires, rather, God seeks the inward, unseen devotion of the heart. In John 4:23 and 24, Jesus is recorded as stating:

> But the hour is coming, and is now here, when the true worshippers will worship the Father in spirit and truth, for the Father seeks such as these to worship him. God is spirit, and those who worship him must worship in spirit and truth.

54. Exod 36:4.

In this statement, Jesus is calling worship an act of faith. Praise of God incorporates human faith in God as well as, and more importantly, God's faithfulness to humanity. The worshipper who believes that God is faithful and merciful, consequently is able to turn confidently to God in times of need. Here, Jesus affirms that it is God's Holy Spirit who enables the praise given by God's people, guiding, refining and perfecting their worship. Doxology is a gift of God's graciousness. It is Jesus mediating God's love to humanity in and through the power of the Holy Spirit.

Truthful praise has a prophetic quality, in that it forms and reforms individuals and worshipping communities in God's image. By God's initiation, such prophetic praise offers encouragement towards repentance, the turning away from past brokenness, back towards a reconciling God. This repentance involves the placing of oneself or one's community at the mercy of God and being willing to align again with God's ways. As Paul appeals to the Romans:

> by the mercies of God, to present your bodies as a living sacrifice, holy and acceptable to God, which is your spiritual worship. Do not be conformed to this world, but be transformed by the renewing of your minds, so that you may discern what is the will of God—what is good and acceptable and perfect.[55]

Another attribute of praise, then, is the attitude of turning from evil and appealing for God's mercy and forgiveness. Many of the psalms reflect this human struggle with sin as conflict, brokenness and separation from God, and God's graciousness in removing those transgressions "as far as the east is from the west."[56]

In addition, praise is *epicletic*, calling upon God for help. This is commonly known as invocation. The very act of calling on God is worship, and God is glorified. Calling on the name of the Lord can include the cries of lamentation so common throughout the Psalms. Praise is not always celebratory or "happy." Praise reflects the journey of life with God who walks beside the worshipper as immanent, and yet, sometimes seeming a long way off, as transcendent. The Psalmist cries out to God, lamenting:

> Hear my prayer, O LORD; let my cry come to you. Do not hide your face from me in the day of my distress. Incline your ear to me; answer me speedily in the day when I call.[57]

---

55. Rom 12:1, 2.

56. Ps 103:12.

57. Ps 102.

For Jesus, epicletic praise was vital to the way he spoke to God. A good example is found in the opening lines of the Lord's Prayer recorded in Matt 6:9, 10, and again in Luke 11:2—

> Our Father in heaven,
> hallowed be your name.
> Your kingdom come.
> Your will be done,
> on earth as it is in heaven.

Here, Jesus, in his divinity and humanity, demonstrates an understanding of his own need to cry out to his Father, God. Jesus understood the purely human need to do the same, and taught his disciples to pray in a way that reflects this.

So praise encapsulates many moods, attitudes and concepts in worship, including acclamation, proclamation, prophetic exhortation, and invocation. Music in worship is not purely entertainment. The consumerist element of Western culture often views "good" worship as associated with the type of music used within that worship. In this shopping mall mentality, if people like the music, they will invariably like the worship. Christian education, as an intersection of doctrine and doxology, has a major role in helping worshippers understand more deeply what praise and worship can be. Learning about praise, as well as learning the ways to praise, are integral parts of the formation of the Christian community. Consequently, sung praise of God in the gathered Christian community should reflect this. For example, sung praise should not focus essentially on the individual and the individual's personal experience. Knowledge of God is embodied corporately, communally, and shared together in the gathered people of God. Certainly, individual worship is valid, and appropriate, but it is in worshipping as part of the one holy catholic and apostolic church that the Christian community ensures, through an ongoing reflection on teaching, learning and living the Christian story in Scripture and Tradition, that understanding of God remains orthodox. In gathered worship, individual stories and the Christian community stories are offered the opportunity to connect and are given the boundaries of doctrine.

Doxology in this way encompasses doctrine and enhances Christian formation. In his preface to the *Collection of Hymns for the Use of the People Called Methodists* written in 1780, John Wesley places a strong emphasis on the teaching of doctrine through hymnody:

> [The Collection of Hymns] is large enough to contain all the important truths of our most holy religion, whether speculative

or practical; yea, to illustrate them all, and to prove them both by Scripture and reason: and this is done in a regular order. The hymns are not carelessly jumbled together, but carefully ranged under proper heads, according to the experience of real Christians. . . . In what other publication of the kind have you so distinct and full an account of scriptural Christianity: such a declaration of the heights and depths of religion, speculative and practical: so strong cautions against the most plausible errors; particularly those that are now most prevalent? and so clear directions for making your calling and election sure; for perfecting holiness in the fear of God?[58]

The writer to the Colossians instructs the early Christians to use hymns and songs as a means of sharing, learning, teaching and living the Christian story in order to grasp the Christian ethos:

> Let the word of Christ dwell in you richly, as you teach and admonish one another in all wisdom, and as you sing psalms and hymns and spiritual songs with thankfulness in your hearts to God.[59]

Doxology and doctrine are, thus, inseparable. Orthodoxy, as *right* praise of God, must include some knowledge of what makes such praise *right*, viz., doctrine. Doctrine, as a framework of belief, is by its very nature doxological. The nature of doctrine is to offer the "recipe" for relationship with God, which in turn points to human existence as freed, forgiven worshippers of God through Jesus Christ, in the power of the Holy Spirit. The church cannot afford to lose this formative aspect of its life. Christian education as formation finds its place as an intersection of doxology and doctrine.

Prayer is another of the liturgical elements that form part of the upward movement of doxology to God. The people of God pray in the name of Jesus for the church and the world. Thanks and praise is offered to God for the historical act of salvation, along with prayer that God will continue to act in creation and in the whole cosmos eternally. This reinforces the eschatological aspect of doxology, praising God for the hope offered in Christ in the past, in the present and into the future. If God is to be thought of as eternal, and outside of time and space, it follows that God is to be praised as such, for what has been, what is now and what will be. The writer of 1 Thess 5:17, 18, and 19 entreats Christians to "Pray without ceasing, give thanks in all circumstances."

---

58. Wesley, quoted in Wainwright, *Doxology*, 201–2.
59. Col 3:16.

We have already touched on a number of aspects of prayer as doxology, including epiclesis, confession, adoration and intercession, along with thanksgiving for the great actions of God throughout salvation history. Prayer is communication, and in this sense it is more than merely the upward or God-ward movement. Prayer is relating to God through the mediation of Jesus Christ by the power of the Holy Spirit. Importantly, God is also at work in prayer. Thus, prayer includes an element of silence, of waiting on God, of listening for God.

The language of doxology, then, must also include not speaking at all. Catherine LaCugna cites Augustine's notion of silence as the only true way of doing justice to the mystery of God: "Augustine, like every seminal Christian thinker, perceived the inherent incongruity entailed in the doing of theology. Only a fool would be so bold as to presume to speak authoritatively about God's ineffable mystery."[60]

The eternal God has continued to reveal Godself to humanity throughout salvation history, and yet even the accumulated knowledge of God is, at best, partial and imperfect. Even though God's self-revelation in Christ is grounded in and corresponds to the very essence of God, it is incomprehensible as it is in itself. The essence of God is unknowable, but over the centuries Christians have nonetheless attempted to advance different theoretical understandings. The Eastern church tended towards the method of *apophasis*, whilst the Western church has favoured the method of *kataphasis* or *analogy*.

Apophasis, which is literally *denial of speech*, is also known as negative theology. Apophasis is the acute consciousness of God's transcendence of all created conceptions. This style of theology, reflecting Augustine's stance, asks, *How can humankind even begin to talk about God and what God is like in Godself?* It therefore limits itself to statements about what God is *not*, rather than making any claims to know God in Godself. Apophasis goes beyond human categories and notions, and often leads fundamentally to silence. There are no words that can possibly do God justice.[61] On the other hand, kataphasis, from the Greek for *affirmation*, or positive theology, founds itself on the acknowledgement that God, as the origin of a physical cosmos can be physically named, even if only inadequately, by the cosmos.[62] Nevertheless, apophasis is sometimes the only appropriate response to the glory of God. Participation in prayed words and liturgical actions give the worshipping community a way into communion with God, but there, words

---

60. LaCugna, *God for Us*, 324.

61. Ibid.

62. Ibid., 325.

and actions are not always relevant, useful or ever enough. Silence becomes the only worship that is appropriate. Augustine declared, "Let human voices be still and mortal thinking be silent. They should strive toward what is incomprehensible not as if they were going to comprehend, but as if they were going to participate."[63]

Another way of gaining some understanding of God and God's relationship with the cosmos is through the use of analogy, or what God is like. The notion of analogy was developed by Thomas Aquinas from earlier work done by Aristotle. Basically, Aquinas worked on a system of arguments, adopting the mathematical scheme of proportion. An analogy is a comparison or a proportion, for example, duck is to bird as apple is to fruit. The analogy works because of both a similarity (the comparison) and a dissimilarity (an apple is not a bird). God and God's creation are distinct ontologically, but creation in some way resembles God. Within the perichoresis of the Trinity, God is not fully knowable but theology may nevertheless describe the unknowable God from God's outward action in salvation history and most supremely in Jesus Christ.[64] From his study of Aristotle and the neo-Platonists' work around the concept of analogy, Aquinas was able to determine useful ways of moving from creation to creator, while acknowledging the infinite difference between the two.[65]

Observing theologian W. Pannenberg's comments about analogy, with regard to doxology, Geoffrey Wainwright notes:

> In religious language, the transfer is not from human language to the being of God, but from everyday statements to liturgical and theological statements. Pannenberg understands the 'sacrifice of praise' in a strong sense: we surrender our words to God and so open them to be filled by [God].[66]

God is beyond human comprehension and simply because we can use human language to depict God does not mean that we are rationally able to comprehend God. Human language used as doxology is necessarily limited, waiting for God's perfection of it. Again quoting Pannenberg, Wainwright concludes:

> "The humility of adoration protects it against becoming the overweening pride of having comprehended the eternal truth of

---

63. Augustine, quoted in Schaff and Wace, *Select Library*, 1:8:667.

64. LaCugna, *God for Us*, 330.

65. Burrell, in *New Dictionary of Theology*, 16.

66. Wainwright, *Doxology*, 282.

God by means of human words." The very fact that we use "personal" language of God is a tribute to his "non-manipulability."

Poiesis, as a way of knowledge of God, is often expressed through the visual arts. Art and architecture in their many forms can be immanently doxological, and excellent expressions of that which cannot be expressed in words. The analogous and the symbolic can richly enhance knowledge and understanding of God, and can be a powerful and stimulating response to God's saving grace. Used in worship, the arts have the ability to inspire the worshipper and teach more profoundly than mere words or theological statements. We have seen the importance of the arts in the worship of the Emerging Church. In a postmodern world, Western society is saturated with imagery of all kinds, from television, magazines and movies to computer games, the internet and social media. It stands to reason that as people are exposed to numerous forms of daily communication that are so commonly graphic representations, the expectation for such visual enhancement becomes the norm in communicating worship. If a community's "everyday statements" hold greater visual awareness in both form and substance, this is likely to be reflected in its liturgical statements that may or may not include words. It is crucial that, in the same way the spoken and written language of worship must reflect doctrinal boundaries of analogy, so must artistic language and forms of communication.

Christ himself used analogy in teaching with parables. Many of these narratives begin with the words, "The Kingdom of God is like . . ." However, there can be no better image or analogy for God than Christ himself. Christ is one with God and mediates for us on God's behalf. All praise for God, doxology, is limited by human boundedness and a finite world. God, however, is not limited and Christians believe that God's transforming love is eternal. In reflecting on learning, teaching and living the Christian story, the ultimate goal is the transformation that God brings in the life of God's people. As Catherine LaCugna aptly concludes:

> The face of God whom we seek is already turned toward us. Kataphatic theology is necessary because the record of God's self revelation is replete with images, metaphors, and narratives about God and God's relationship to us. At the same time, all images, concepts and doctrines of God must be forthrightly modest, not to fulfill a technical requirement but as an act of doxology that places us in the presence of the living God. The glory of God outshines all images and concepts. . . . Apophasis

teaches the correct attitude of all theologians: one does not speculate about God but is transformed by God.[67]

CONCLUSION

In our discussion thus far, we have dialogued aspects of theology including epistemology, doxology, doctrine and dogma with related areas in the fields of education, philosophy, history, and sociology in attempting to posit Christian education in its appropriate place for the life of the church now and into the future. The outcome, at every instance, has been an intersection by Christian education, as formation in the worshipping community, of the dovetailed doxology and dogma. The image of weaving may help to illustrate. In this image, the entwined doxa and doctrine become the warp of the fabric and Christian formation becomes the weft. The resulting cloth is both strong and beautiful. The weaver is God, carefully and creatively blending patterns and colors. The weaver's loom is like the Christian community, holding the forming fabric in place so it is strong and can be used out in the world. The developing fabric is the lived worship of God, or Christians in action in partnership with God.

Christian education has been given a new interpretive framework, set within the dual doxological and doctrinal context of Christian community. This reflects its formative place in "giving glory to God and enjoyment of God" as the chief goal of Christian life. As the people of God celebrate God's life in the world, there is sharing and learning of God and of the actions of God in the salvation story of God.

God's self-revelation is expressed by the power of the Holy Spirit, in Jesus Christ the living Word, in Scripture, Tradition and in the church's proclamation of this Story. This is celebrated in the Christian worshipping community. So, to learn, teach and live the Christian story in order to grasp what it means to be in relationship with the wholly transcendent, yet intimately immanent God, we must sense and experience the Story through a life of doxa—praise of God.

This living is to be intentional as well as implicit. Christian education as formation finds its place as never separate from the worshipping church. What the Body of Christ does in its worship, and the statements that it makes about what it believes, are tantamount to Christian education. As we have seen, God, as source and perfector of human worship actively facilitates forms and transforms Christian ethos.

67. LaCugna, God for Us, 331.

Therefore, an individual's story is embraced in the life of the corporate Story. Christianity is not a private, individualised spirituality. It is the community of the people of God reflectively living the Christian story in order to grasp and learn and contribute and participate in the Christian ethos. The *living* is doxa and dogma and doctrine. The *story* is dogma and doctrine and doxa as well. Christian education intersects them, winding its way through them, strengthening and nurturing and growing them. This is the appropriate place of Christian education.

Chapter 8

Transformed Action in Christian Education

A Teaching and Learning Matrix

THE DISCUSSION THUS FAR, following a practical theology methodology, has led to the point of transformed action in Christian education. This transformed action stems from examining some of the practices of the Emerging Church and critically reflecting upon them in the light of the church's ministry in a postmodern context. This has facilitated the development of a new interpretive framework, locating Christian education in the context of the worshipping Christian community, as an intersection of doxology and doctrine. In many senses, this is the transformed action that has arisen from this discussion. But as praxis, it cries out to be used, to be put into practice. It demands to be outlined and critiqued, reflected upon, learnt, taught and lived in order to grasp a Christian ethos in a postmodern world. The way I propose to share this transformed action is by offering some options for making more explicit some learnings that could take place in the liturgical worship of God, as well as offering some which occur in the worship of God in all of life. This will take the form of the matrix which will be described shortly. First, however, let us bring back to mind some of what has led us to this point.

We have seen how the separation of worship from Christian education has been detrimental to the development of transformed Christian action. I have argued that the most appropriate context for Christian education is the Christian worshipping community.[1] In this study, the church has been described as the community that tells the story of Jesus today. As we have also seen, the worshipping community of the church is the living memory of Jesus, the same anamnesis inherent in the Eucharist, in that it is a recalling of the past, active in the present and anticipating the future. The postmodern milieu of Christian worshipping communities is broad and varied. This is especially so within the Emerging Church movement. The Western Protestant church consists of a number of different forms of worshipping communities. Sometimes this has been as a consequence of evangelical concerns, sometimes because of declining attendances and resources. New paradigms continue to emerge, often without the theological and educational resources to sustain them for longterm existence. Pragmatic concerns have often outweighed a clear understanding of doctrinal aspects in the formation of Christians. The consequence of this move away from the intentional teaching of theology and doctrine has often been a rearrangement of ministry priorities, towards a purely evangelical numbers game.[2] Worship suffers when pragmatic concern for numbers dictates its style and substance. The preferences of the potential "market" or "clientele" determine every aspect, from how the attendee parks her car as she comes onto the church property, to the theology presented in worship. This kind of consumerist attitude to worship is often accepted without question. The argument based on insights gained from observing the Emerging Church, and the resulting interpretive framework presented here, is offered as something of an attempt to balance to this attitude.

In many ways the Emerging Church movement is both a result of this consumerist attitude to faith and worship, and a reaction against it. There has been, in the Emerging Church, a reflection of the pendulum swing towards an emphasis on daily orthopraxy as the key to orthodoxy, in response to a heavy focus on an evangelical saving of souls for heaven, some time in the future. So, at the same time as promoting a strong missiological approach, Emerging Church writers have, in some of the more recent literature, started to see that this approach must be backed by a sound theological foundation. One pertinent example is British Emerging Church leader, Steve Chalke, who rightly cautions that "our theology . . . must unpack itself through our missiology . . . which must shape our ecclesiology."[3] This has been the impetus for my theological argument that Christian education can be viewed

1. See also Murphy, *Teaching That Transforms*, Anderson, *Worship and Christian Identity*, Parrett and Kang, *Teaching the Faith*, 335–43.

2. See Edgar, "Worship in All of Life," 339–57, especially 340–45 regarding some "Misguided Strategies" for worship.

3. Chalke and Watkis, *Intelligent Church*, 13.

as an intersection of doxology and doctrine. Without a doctrinally sound doxological base, mission can become idolatrous and purely self-serving. A balance of orthopraxy with orthodoxy is needed, and will act to help form Christians who consciously try to live what they proclaim. The interpretive framework (for Christian education set in the worshipping community and seen as an intersection of doxa and doctrine) can be used in this way. The framework undergirds the matrix and its key questions, and the examples of learning experiences will illustrate this.

This understanding of Christian education's rightful theological place opens up possibilities for fresh approaches to teaching and learning across the whole worshipping community. Each person in the community who tells Jesus' story can be thought of as a teacher as well as a learner. This is an essential part of the process being described. All are involved in the forming of others in the worshipping community. It has always been the case that each worshipper teaches and learns from others as the community worships together. Outwardly, the gestures of worship, such as standing, sitting, kneeling or raising one's hands, are taught and learned by observing others. As well, attitudes, both positive and negative, can be communicated and learned through the body language of other community members. Ultimately, it is also the actual action of worshipping that teaches and forms Christian identity.[4]

As a major contributor to the formation of Christian ethos, ongoing theological reflection on this action of worshipping is vital. This reflection has to be made explicit and taught explicitly. Reflection leads to the imbibing of, indwelling and consciously joining oneself (communing) with the action of worship. This is the embodying of the story of Jesus by those who are frail and broken, and yet who are also redeemed, forgiven and loved by God, able to participate in this *work of the people*. People learn to worship by worshipping. People can also learn about God and themselves by giving honour and glory to God, gathered together with others who are motivated to do the same. People not only learn how to worship in a church service on a Sunday, but also how to worship God in their daily lives from Monday to Saturday. The purpose of worship is to give God glory; the nature of worship is thus not explicitly formative, yet the very giving of glory to God has the potential to transform the worshipper spiritually. The formative elements that occur naturally within worship have often been neglected, and they need to be intentionally brought to the fore. This is reinforced by the "In Life" section of the matrix, as we shall see.

4. Anderson, *Worship and Christian Identity*, 29.

In the discussion about the rise of monasticism and its revival in the form of New Monasticism, I suggested that intentional theological teaching has had a strong and substantial place in the life of the church, but that generally across the Western church, there has been a loss of authority of the teaching ministry. In the process described here, with the application of a new interpretive framework in a worship setting, the concept of the minister or priest as a key theological teacher of the whole community takes on new importance. Formal qualifications in theology and doctrine should indicate that one has reached a certain level of competence in those areas. Theological knowledge, skills and attitudes are to be valued, proclaimed and energetically shared amongst the community of faith. The teaching role of the clergy needs to be reflectively recaptured. In this, the forming and equipping of lay people to serve God in many and varied ways, including preaching and leading worship, is imperative. Of course, the minister or priest is by no means to be seen as the only teacher, as we have already discussed. It is the whole Christian community who are teaching, learning and living the Christian story in order to grasp Christian ethos. The role of the clergy as theological teachers, however, cannot be underestimated. This is also a critical matter for theological education and ministerial formation programs. There should be an expectation that the minister, pastor or priest, as leader of the worshipping community, displays some ability to teach and share theological concepts as part of living a Christian ethos. It seems that this expectation has been seriously eroded in recent times, with ordained persons being expected to undertake myriad other roles in the life of the church, along with the consumerist pressure of giving worshippers purely what they want.

Through the insights gained by our examination of the Emerging Church, we have come to reconsider the ways that Christian education is approached. It needs to be experiential, sensory, creative, and participatory, but taken seriously as a vehicle into and leading out from, right praise of God. Noting that the theological place of Christian education can be viewed as an intersection of doxology and doctrine, it must be solidly theologically based and set within the worshipping Christian community.

THE MATRIX

With the theological place of Christian education so viewed, in this chapter I will be outlining a matrix of possible strategies for undertaking Christian education in ways appropriate to current and possible future "worshipping community" contexts. These strategies are designed to be suitable for use with Emerging Churches of all descriptions.

The term *matrix* is defined in the Macquarie Dictionary as that which gives origin or form to a thing.[5] This matrix is designed to give body and life to the approach to Christian formation that has been outlined throughout this book. It enables the birth of transformed action for worship and Christian formation.

The worship elements used in the matrix are based on those of common liturgical patterns, namely: gathering; praise and thanksgiving; confession; hearing God's word; Eucharist and Baptism; and responding, which includes being sent out to worship in the world. The particular worship elements have been chosen because they represent a fairly common general order for mainline Protestant worship.

These worship elements are intersected by two learning continuums, in order to form the matrix. The continuums are titled "In Liturgy," referring to the customary hour of community worship, and "In Life," referring to worship as a whole-of-life experience. The concept of continuum has been used in order to avoid a definitive sense of linear progression, and to make it clear that anyone at any stage may participate anywhere in the continuum. "In Liturgy" will contain rubrics that can be used for teaching and learning about each worship element. Physically, these rubrics are sentences printed so that they could be inserted into an order of worship, or used with a worship folder or in a news sheet.

The "In Life" continuum will contain discussion starters and other learning experiences designed to relate the learning which may occur from that worship element to the everyday lives of Christians. This is designed as a small group discussion that could occur as part of a more formal worship celebration, or, if possible, before worship as a pre-worship learning and teaching group.

The "In Life" discussions are designed to take about an hour to an hour and a half, but can be started in one session and continued in the next session. They should not be rushed and are intended to be carried out in a hospitable, friendly, interactive environment. They have been shaped to be used with older teenagers and adults, but the material could be adapted for younger members of the worshipping community. The insights that have been gained from participation in the discussions should be shared in worship with children and young people as part of the whole community's learning and teaching experience.

5. *Macquarie Dictionary*, 1099.

Many of the learning experiences will relate to typically key practices of the Christian faith. Christian practices convey knowledge through action.[6] The practices that have been selected are based on the work of Craig Dykstra, Dorothy C. Bass, Don Richter and the Valparaiso Project.[7] They are: hospitality; honoring the body; forgiveness; saying yes and saying no; keeping the Sabbath; testimony; discernment; shaping communities; household economics; healing; dying well and singing our lives.

Grasping these new approaches to Christian formation may constitute a substantial paradigm shift for many. Firstly the interpretative framework for Christian education as a process of ongoing reflection on teaching, learning and living the Christian story in order to grasp the Christian ethos, may present a very different starting point for some Christian educators. The interpretative framework for Christian education developed in this thesis is utilised and gives boundaries to the discussion, reflection, learning experiences and strategies in the "In Life" continuum.

The setting of the worshipping community as the catechetical context often presents a clash with the understanding that education means schooling or babysitting. On one hand, particular practices within worship can be thought of as sacred, not to be tampered with. On the other hand, worship has often been thought of as a commodity which can be taken or left, depending on personal preferences. Based on the studies we have examined, there may be a lack of confidence in the worshipping community, when it comes to their perceived knowledge or ability to explain biblical or theological concepts. These issues will be dealt with by the actual process of reflection. This process moves from non-threatening stories arising out of our own experience, to deeper dialogue with normative texts, to new insights and understandings. A participant is not expected to know the theological answers, but contributes to the community's generating of them.

The "In Life" process is undertaken predominantly through the use of questions as small group discussion starters. This is a typically catechetical approach. In the present process, however, participants are encouraged to communally create and produce the theologically transformed responses. Each topic should continually refer back to the element of worship to which it relates. The focus of this process is always to be the active worship of God. The "In Life" sessions are educationally planned to include various learning styles and Gardner's multiple intelligences.[8] The sessions contain various modes of learning to balance the discussion component. These include

6. McDannell, *Religions of the United States*, introduction.

7. Dykstra, "What Are Christian Practices?"

8. Gardner, *Multiple Intelligences*.

music, visuals, stories, and hands-on learning. The "In Life" sessions are meant to be fun and to encourage inquisitiveness, curiosity, experimentation, discovery and mutual sharing. Each Key Question may have a number of sessions.

The sessions are designed to be added to and adapted for local settings. It is essential that local worshipping communities are involved in creating new teaching and learning experiences that relate to their own contexts, based on this reflective process. Engaging with the patterns and process of reflection on the action of teaching, learning and living the Christian story is the most important aspect of the matrix's design.

There is benefit in understanding some of the flow of worship, why certain aspects are included and what can be learned from each. The first worship element to be considered is the gathering of the people of God.

GATHERING

In gathering there is a coming together of this different community. Its difference is in its motivation and purpose. It is countercultural in that it does not come together for itself alone, but to bear witness to Christ as its head, and to give glory to God, with the help of God's Holy Spirit. The Christian community embodies difference in gathering to praise and worship God in Jesus Christ. The difference is that this community does not exist for itself, but to worship God in thought, word and deed. The gathering may be virtual or online, but the purpose is still to be the same.

In his letter to the Corinthians, Paul encourages Christians to gather as a group. He is recorded as using the phrase, "When you come together" repeatedly.[9] Paul discusses worship gatherings extensively in 1 Cor 11–14. He gives instructions about what should constitute the Corinthians' Christian worship, including participation in the Eucharist, the use of charismata or spiritual gifts, the sharing of scripture, and the singing of hymns.

The purpose of worship is to respond to God's goodness by thanking God and giving God "God's worth" or the "worth" that God is due. This "worth-ship" is where the word "worship" originated. Christians gather to share together in worship of God. Concomitantly, worship helps form Christians and Christian ethos, but that is not its primary role or value. The gathered worshipping community is the context and hermeneutic for formation processes whether that happens liturgically, in small groups or in everyday life.

9. See 1 Cor 11:18, 20, 33; 14:23.

Christian worship is service and praise of God in and through Jesus Christ. This is given explanation and definition by the writer to the Hebrews where the sacrifices made by the high priest in the Jewish worship of the time, are contrasted with Jesus' sacrificial death on the cross, and consequently with the different sacrifice of worship for followers of Jesus:

> For the bodies of those animals whose blood is brought into the sanctuary by the high priest as a sacrifice for sin are burned outside the camp. Therefore Jesus also suffered outside the city gate in order to sanctify the people by his own blood. Let us then go to him outside the camp and bear the abuse he endured. For here we have no lasting city, but we are looking for the city that is to come. Through him, then, let us continually offer a sacrifice of praise to God, that is, the fruit of lips that confess his name. Do not neglect to do good and to share what you have, for such sacrifices are pleasing to God.[10]

Eugene Peterson's *The Message* interprets the same instruction in his version, which uses contemporary language:

> The altar from which God gives us the gift of himself is not for exploitation by insiders who grab and loot. In the old system, the animals are killed and the bodies disposed outside the camp. The blood is then brought inside to the altar as a sacrifice for sin. It's the same way with Jesus. He was crucified outside the city gates—*that* is where he poured out the sacrificial blood that was brought to God's altar to cleanse his people.
>
> So let's go outside, where Jesus is, where the action is—not trying to be privileged insiders, but taking our share in the abuse of Jesus. This "insider world" is not our home. We have our eyes peeled for the City about to come. Let's take our place outside with Jesus, no longer pouring out the sacrificial blood of animals but pouring out sacrificial praises from our lips to God in Jesus' name.
>
> Make sure you don't take things for granted and go slack in working for the common good; share what you have with others. God takes particular pleasure in acts of worship—a different kind of "sacrifice"—that takes place in kitchen and workplace and on the streets.[11]

This highlights the active nature of Christian worship in the world. Christians are to serve the world for which Christ died, and to spend time

10. Heb 13:11–16.
11. Peterson, *Message*, 476–77 (his emphasis).

together in fellowship with God and each other enjoying God and glorifying God.

In gathering to worship, people may learn and teach: relationship (which includes dealing with elements of exclusion and grief as well as positive inclusion); belonging; cooperation; welcoming; hospitality; generosity; purpose; the knowledge that we are not alone, we are not all the same, we have a commonality in Jesus Christ; and that learning and teaching happen as we meet together.

Table 1: Gathering, with Key Questions for Reflection—In Liturgy and In Life

WORSHIP OF GOD	REFLECTION: IN LITURGY Key Questions	REFLECTION: IN LIFE Key Questions
Gathering	What is the "Call to Worship"?	What is the practice of worship? What is the worship environment? How do we enter into worship? What is the "Call to Worship"? What do we bring to worship? What is hospitality and why is it important? What is the church? What is Christian Community?

The next worship element to be considered is that of Praise and Thanksgiving.

PRAISE AND THANKSGIVING

Praise and thanks to God is the human response to God's graciousness to all of creation. At this early point in worship, adoration is expressed to remind worshippers of the holiness and greatness of God, and that this is the reason for their worship. Praise in the form of prayer and song is directed to God for God's goodness, power and love. The words recorded in Deut 32:3–4 give one example of an imperative for praise of God: "Ascribe greatness to our God! The Rock, his work is perfect and all his ways are just. A faithful God, without deceit, just and upright is he."

Thankfulness is the attitude of appreciation and gratitude for God's past, present and future actions in creation. Acts of thanksgiving confer recognition and credit. Acts of thanksgiving can include prayer, song, graphic art and other visuals, signing, dance, and drama. Examples of biblical calls to thank God include: 1 Chron 29:12, 13; 2 Chron 20:21; Ps 50:14; Ps 92:1; Ps 111:1–3.

In praising and giving thanks, people may learn and teach: graciousness; gratitude; relief that they are not alone; appreciation; enjoyment; relationship; admiration of the beauty and greatness of the cosmos; experiences of awe, wonder, and God's self-revelation.

Table 2: Praise and Thanksgiving, with Key Questions for Reflection
—In Liturgy and In Life

WORSHIP OF GOD	REFLECTION: IN LITURGY Key Questions	REFLECTION: IN LIFE Key Questions
Praise and Thanksgiving	What is praise? What is thanksgiving?	Who is the triune God? What is the nature of the cosmos? What is the nature of humanity? What is God's grace? Why is gratitude important? How can we incorporate praise and thanks into everyday life? What is prayer?

The third worship element is the prayer of confession and the declaration of forgiveness and assurance.

PRAYER OF CONFESSION AND DECLARATION OF FORGIVENESS AND ASSURANCE

The practice of shared or corporate confession reminds the worshipping Christian community that they are human beings who fail and need forgiveness over and over. As William Dyrness notes, "they do not claim any special exemption from sin and selfishness, but rather, amazingly, recognize exactly the kind of people they are."[12]

Christians believe that God's Holy Spirit works in the Christian community and in the lives of all who follow Jesus. The reality of human brokenness, guilt and sin gives expression to the way that God allows humans freedom to choose whether to follow or not. Individuals and whole communities sometimes choose to align themselves with God's Spirit, letting love interpret and inform their actions. Sometimes these same individuals and whole communities, through fear, perceived inadequacy, ignorance or by deliberate means, do not live the gospel of Christ. Christian transformation in and by the Holy Spirit is a lifelong process.

12. Dyrness, *Primer on Christian Worship*, 128.

Therefore, Christians believe that they need God's forgiveness, pardon and a fresh start, again and again. The Scriptures are full of stories describing the ways that God's people sometimes choose to follow God, and more often than not, how they do not. Scripture also portrays a God who calls people to repentance, graciously forgives them and assures them of God's presence, peace and comfort, again and again. This is celebrated liturgically in corporate prayers of confession and the assurance of pardon.

In Protestant corporate worship the confession that is called for is corporate confession. This should be noted in the wording of communal prayers. Each one may have their own personal confession, but this is the worship of the community and the confession of the community. The psalms were often used in Jewish corporate worship to express God's forgiveness for communal sin. In Psalm 103 there is one such expression:

> The Lord is merciful and gracious,
> slow to anger and abounding in steadfast love.
> He will not always accuse,
> nor will he keep his anger for ever.
> He does not deal with us according to our sins,
> nor repay us according to our iniquities.
> For as the heavens are high above the earth,
> so great is his steadfast love towards those who fear him;
> as far as the east is from the west,
> so far he removes our transgressions from us.[13]

Paul, in his letter to the Romans, recorded in Rom 3:21–24, makes the point that there are no exemptions in this. He describes how God is perfect or righteous, and accordingly provides, in Jesus, redemption and freedom from sin.

> But now, irrespective of law, the righteousness of God has been disclosed, and is attested by the law and the prophets, the righteousness of God through faith in Jesus Christ for all who believe. For there is no distinction, since all have sinned and fall short of the glory of God; they are now justified by his grace as a gift, through the redemption that is in Christ Jesus.

The word "confession" is used both for confessing faith and for confessing sin. This is because confession is an acknowledgment of God's grace and faithfulness. God's love is the matter to be emphasized, not individual sins.[14] Christians confess that it is God's eternal graciousness in Jesus that al-

---

13. Ps 103:8–12.

14. Gribben, *Guide to Uniting in Worship*, 48.

lows pardon or absolution from sin. Prayers of forgiveness are thus followed by the assurance that the gospel (good news) of Christ is that, in Jesus, God does forgive, that God continues to show mercy, and that God continues to desire to be in loving relationship with all of creation. The Christian response to the gospel is to be one of praise and thanksgiving, but it is concomitantly a response of action in, moreover, forgiving others. Jesus' words are recorded in Mark's Gospel, "Whenever you stand praying, forgive, if you have anything against anyone; so that your Father in heaven may also forgive you your trespasses."[15]

In confession and assurance, people may learn and teach: about admission and acknowledgement of culpability, wrongdoing, sin; consequences of actions; that sin is a fracturing of our relationship with God and others, not a list of do's and don'ts; God's forgiveness can free us from the guilt and pain that sin can cause in our lives; what saying, "Sorry" means; repentance; a fresh start is available in Jesus, free from fear and apathy; reconciliation; and assurance of an ongoing relationship with God.

Table 3: Prayer of Confession and Declaration of Forgiveness and Assurance, with Key Questions for Reflection—In Liturgy and In Life

WORSHIP OF GOD	REFLECTION: IN LITURGY Key Questions	REFLECTION: IN LIFE Key Questions
Confession and Assurance	What is sin? What is confession? Why do we confess our sin? What is repentance? What is forgiveness? What is assurance?	What is sin? What do we mean by reconciliation, salvation, redemption and justification? What is repentance? What is forgiveness? What is assurance?

The next element for reflection is Hearing God's Word.

HEARING GOD'S WORD

Hearing God's word in Scripture, the creeds, and in the proclamation of the word in preaching, are all acts of worship offered to the glory of God. The church, as the community of people who are to tell the story of Jesus and live the Christian story, has a responsibility to do so in ways that help worshippers to grasp Christian ethos. Living *out* the Christian story may come as a result of learning, teaching, and living *with* the Christian story.

15. Mark 11:25.

The Scriptures of the Old and New Testament have historically been understood by the church as the word of God. In this sense, much like Jesus Christ, the Scriptures could be described as being both divine and human at the same time.[16] The Bible is God's word given to various human writers at various times and places in history. It is a library of different books of numerous genres, which needs to be interpreted on a number of levels. To discover the original meaning intended for middle-eastern hearers in the first century and before, one must exercise the tools of exegesis. To interpret the word of God to engender meaning for contemporary listeners, one must turn to hermeneutics. We do not have the space to deal with these issues to any degree here, except to raise their importance. There is much information available to anyone who would take the study of the Scriptures seriously.

The skill in proclaiming God's word in preaching, is bringing the meaning of the story in its original context into engagement with what meaning that story has for a contemporary context. As theologian Colin Gunton notes in the preface of his *Theology through Preaching*, "the theologian who preaches becomes a different kind of theologian, for the activities in which we engage shape the kind of people that we are."[17] Theology or "God words" is not only words about God, or about the meaning of words about God, but God's words in self-revelation—God's words about Godself. "Preaching is what God says."[18] So the theologian who preaches, also learns and teaches what God says about God, and is a part of an incarnation of God's word as *the Word*, Jesus Christ. Preaching God's word in the power of the Holy Spirit can give an awareness of God in Christ.

The Nicene and Apostles' Creeds are historic statements of the catholic faith of the Christian church. Based in Scripture, they help to tell a large part of the Christian story and offer worshippers a way of showing allegiance to the triune God. They are also used when a confession of faith is required at points in the sacramental life of the church.[19] The Apostles' Creed was first used as a statement of faith recited by Christian converts as they were about to be baptized.[20] The Nicene Creed was collectively developed later over many years, in order to counter heresies about the substance of God. In the historic creeds we have much of the normative doctrine of Christianity.

16. Fee and Stuart, *How to Read the Bible*, 21.

17. Gunton, *Theology Through Preaching*, vii–viii.

18. Willimon, *Proclamation and Theology*, 8.

19. Gribben, *Guide*, 54.

20. Walsh, et al., *Apostles' Creed*, 5.

Proclamation of the Christian story can help to realize the incarnation of a living, breathing baby born in a stable to refugees, an itinerant middle-eastern teacher, a leper cleansing healer of souls or a scandalous Savior nailed to a cross. Proclamation of the Christian story in this way also has the potential to challenge, confront, and as Augustine stated: teach, edify and convert.[21]

For Augustine, the lived faith of the preacher and the message preached must be in accord. "Someone who speaks wisely and eloquently, but leads a wicked life, does indeed teach many . . ., yet, as it is written, has 'not won the favor of the Lord' (Eccl 3:21)."[22] The result of this dissonance, according to Augustine's timeless wisdom, is that listeners learn to distrust the word of God as well as the preacher.

In hearing God's word, people may learn and teach: the Christian story; identification of our stories with the Christian story; listening with all senses, as well as intuitively, creatively, emotionally and thoughtfully; enjoyment; theological reflection; to question and critique; awareness of differences in interpretation; boundaries; how others have acted and lived as God's people; meaning in sacred texts, stories, proclamation, tradition; and acknowledgement of the church's history and God's salvation history.

**Table 4: Hearing God's Word, with Key Questions for Reflection
—In Liturgy and In Life**

WORSHIP OF GOD	REFLECTION: IN LITURGY Key Questions	REFLECTION: IN LIFE Key Questions
Hearing God's Word	What is Scripture? What is preaching? What are Creeds?	What is Scripture? What is hermeneutics? Why are stories important? What is "the Word"? How did Scripture come to be? What are Creeds?

The sacraments, Eucharist and Baptism, make up the fifth worship element suggested for inclusion in the matrix.

21. Augustine, *Sermon 17*. http://augnet.org/default.asp?ipageid=398.

22. Augustine, *De Doctrina Christiana* IV 27, 59–60. http://augnet.org/default. asp?ipageid=398.

EUCHARIST AND BAPTISM

The sacraments of Baptism and Eucharist are central to the Christian church's life and purpose. They are signs of God's desire for communion with humanity just as God is in communion *in se* (within Godself, amongst the three persons of the Trinity). The triune God is concerned with community because the one God is communal—Father, Son and Holy Spirit.

Christ is the center of Christian worship, who as the Great High Priest, has made the atoning sacrifice on our behalf, to redeem us and to restore communion friendship between creation and God. Jesus' sacrifice allows humankind free entrance into the very life of God. Through Baptism and Eucharist, Christians are able to participate in what Christ has done for the world, once and for all. Christ continues to work in Christians when the visible elements of water, bread and wine are used as God has commanded, in the sacraments.

In Christian Baptism, it is Christ who baptizes people by God's Spirit, so that each one might participate in God's renewing of his/her humanity and each one is thus adopted into Christ's Body, the church. At the Eucharist, Christ brings to remembrance or anamnesis his life, death and resurrection and invites participants to join in Holy Communion shared with one another at God's table. This is a kind of prolepsis or anticipation of God's reign, a taste of heaven, so to speak. So much more needs to be said about the Christian Sacraments, but once again, the questions are raised to invite further exploration of this huge and vital area.

In celebrating the Sacraments, people may learn and teach: God's grace in giving God's very self to each participant; community; God's triune nature; sharing; God's hospitality and generosity; Jesus' role in God's salvation history; the meaning of Jesus' life, death and resurrection; what intimacy with God can mean; belonging; acceptance; adoption and the joining with the family of God; and testimony, the sharing of how individual stories and God's Story coincide and intersect.

Table 5: Eucharist and Baptism, with Key Questions for Reflection
—In Liturgy and In Life

WORSHIP OF GOD	REFLECTION: IN LITURGY Key Questions	REFLECTION: IN LIFE Key Questions
Eucharist and Baptism	What is a Sacrament? What is Baptism? What is Eucharist?	What is a Sacrament? What is Baptism? What is Eucharist? What are some of the key historical issues surrounding the sacraments?

The sixth worship element is responding to the graciousness of God.

RESPONDING

The response of worshippers to all that God has done, as we have observed, flows from active, to reflective, to renewed active worship of God. When Christians offer prayer for others, give financially to the work of the church, share in the notices concerning the everyday worship activities of the community, and are sent out to share the good news of Jesus Christ with those they meet, they are responding to all that has gone before in the worship service, and in their lives. God's grace is the undeserved love God has for humankind. It is a free gift, in Christ. No response that we could make will impel God to love humankind any more perfectly. Christians respond to God's love, because God loved us first. There should be no sense of being virtuous or doing good deeds, or being conscientious, so that we can win God's favor. We already have it. Let our orthopraxy be orthodoxy.

In responding, people may learn and teach: love for one another in service and mission; consideration of the needs of others; giving of oneself and the world back to God; how to pray; kinds of prayer; what prayer is for; what prayer is not; what is meant by "answers" to prayer; being the "answers" to prayer ourselves; creating responses to God's graciousness; celebrating God's provision; generosity; reinforcement that all we have is already God's; community building; and opportunities to continue to actively worship God.

Table 6: Responding, with Key Questions for Reflection—In Liturgy and In Life

WORSHIP OF GOD	REFLECTION: IN LITURGY Key Questions	REFLECTION: IN LIFE Key Questions
Responding	Why do we respond to God's grace?	Why do we respond to God's grace? How do we respond to God's grace? What is stewardship? What is giving? What is meant by Christian service? What does it mean to pray for others and ourselves?

The second part of responding to God's graciousness incorporates the benediction, the blessing, and being sent out to worship in the world.

Table 7: Benediction, Blessing, Being Sent Out to Worship in the World, with Key Questions for Reflection—In Liturgy and In Life

WORSHIP OF GOD	REFLECTION: IN LITURGY Key Questions	REFLECTION: IN LIFE Key Questions
Benediction, Blessing, Being Sent Out to Worship in the World	What is a Benediction? What is a Blessing? What is the mission of the church? How can we participate in God's mission?	What is the mission of the church? How can we participate in the God's mission? How do we go on actively worshipping God?

MATRIX SMALL GROUP SESSION FORMAT EXAMPLES

The following are some examples of the format for "Reflection in Life" small group sessions relating to the Key Questions set out in Tables 17 from the Matrix above. Sessions like these make up the ongoing learning and teaching experiences. The matrix is left unfinished so that local Christian communities can take responsibility for their own learning and teaching, researching and developing new sessions once they have been introduced to the reflective approach, interpretive framework and format. In this format, the particular worship element forms the overarching content, with one Key Question discussed in each session. The reflective process outlined in Table 8 below guides the session, relating the learning about that part of liturgical worship to learning about worship in everyday life. While the examples outlined below should all be considered as encompassed by the title "Table 8," the treatment of each Key Question has been set out as Table 8A, Table 8B etc., as it is envisaged that only one Key Question will be discussed in each teaching and learning session.

TABLE 8: SMALL GROUP SESSION FORMAT EXAMPLES

Table 8A: Key Question—What Is the Practice of Worship?

Gathering KEY QUESTION: WHAT IS THE PRACTICE OF WORSHIP?	
Reflective Process	**Strategies**
Start with your context.	Discuss: What is worship? Why do Christians worship? What are some worship practices you know? (Check this again after you've looked at one of the definitions that are recorded below).
What is the issue for you?	Environment, surroundings, context, ecosystems, gathering for worship, entering worship, the language of the worship environment
What is the pivotal question for you?	

Gathering	
KEY QUESTION: WHAT IS THE PRACTICE OF WORSHIP?	
Reflective Process	**Strategies**
What Bible texts, stories or verses might relate to this issue and question? What Christian Traditions might relate to this issue and question?	Read this definition of practice, written by moral philosopher, Alisdair MacIntyre: "any coherent and complex form of socially established cooperative human activity through which goods internal to that form of activity are realized in the course of trying to achieve those standards of excellence which are appropriate to, and particularly definitive of, that form of activity, with the result that human powers to achieve human excellence and human conceptions of the ends and goods involved, are systematically extended." —Alisdair MacIntyre, *After Virtue*, 187. As Byron Anderson, in discussing this definition, points out: the "goods" internal to a game are realized only by playing. When asked what an event "means," we could only repeat the event; when asked what a particular piece of music means, we can only play the music. When asked what baptism means, while we may have many words of explanation, in the end we can only baptize. —E. Byron Anderson, *Worship and Christian Identity: Practicing Ourselves*, 103–104. There are different ways of knowing. As we practice worship, we are growing in knowledge of God, of ourselves, of our Christian community. The "goods" from participating in worship come from the actual participation itself.
How do you respond?	Where can worship of God take place? How does worship take place in church/in life?
What will you do about that today and tomorrow?	
Related Topics: Worship in life	

Table 8B: Key Question—What Is the Worship Environment?

Gathering	
KEY QUESTION: WHAT IS THE WORSHIP ENVIRONMENT?	
Reflective Process	**Strategies**
Start with your context.	Walk around your worship environment if possible. Have some photos prepared if necessary. What is the first thing you see when you enter your worship environment? How does that help you to worship? What dominates the environment? What does this say to you? How does that help you to worship? How can the worship environment be enhanced to reflect a particular theme of the liturgy?
What is the issue for you?	Environment, surroundings, context, ecosystems, gathering for worship, entering worship, the language of the worship environment
What is the pivotal question for you?	
What Bible texts, stories or verses might relate to this issue and question? What Christian Traditions might relate to this issue and question?	Read: Riddell, et al., "New Approaches to Worship," 136–46. If it is not possible to access the entire chapter, this is a section from the above (138): Worship preparation is primarily about providing a context rather than a content. The context being an environment in which heart, soul, mind and strength have opportunity to respond to God. This is not to deny content (although the gospel is primarily about a relationship rather than propositions), but to emphasize that the content can be understood in a variety of ways according to the context it's placed in. As an example, the re-enactment of Jesus' last meal with his disciples could emphasize forgiveness, community transformation, relationship or salvation, depending on the context it is presented in. Worship has generally majored in content, with little or no appreciation of what the context is doing to that content. For example, what does it mean to talk about loving one another in a building where we sit and look at the back of each other's heads, or listen to teaching on the priesthood of all believers and "body ministry" when the service is led entirely from the front by elderly white males?

Gathering	
KEY QUESTION: WHAT IS THE WORSHIP ENVIRONMENT?	
Reflective Process	**Strategies**
What Bible texts, stories or verses might relate to this issue and question? What Christian Traditions might relate to this issue and question?	If the worship producer sees herself as a curator or artist, then context becomes very important. The curator of an art or museum exhibition will arrange the elements of the exhibition in a carefully thought-through context, designing for a particular effect or response, and aware that juxtaposition, distance, light, shade, color, texture, proximity, background, temperature, space, interaction, and words will all affect how people respond. So the worship curator needs to consider all these elements of context (and more) in preparing worship for others. She is providing a frame for the existing elements, a frame that conveys a particular message; a message beyond that of the individual elements. This provides a boundary within which a certain worship content or experience is provided. The same elements arranged in a different way would provide a different context and be capable of conveying a different message. Discuss with relation to your worship environment. How do you respond to the worship leader being called a curator or artist? What does this mean for worship?
How do you respond?	Where can worship of God take place? How does worship take place in church/in life?
What will you do about that today and tomorrow?	
Related Topics: Sacred space, sacred place; art as a language of worship; environment; context; interpretation.	

Table 8C: Key Question—How Do We Enter into Worship?

Gathering	
KEY QUESTION: HOW DO WE ENTER INTO WORSHIP?	
Reflective Process	**Strategies**
Start with your context.	Have you ever been in a courtroom, or seen one on TV? How are people expected to act as they enter a courtroom? How do you enter an art gallery? How do you enter into worship? What is the first thing you do when you worship?
What is the issue for you?	Entering worship. Our attitude, our posture, our senses.

Gathering KEY QUESTION: HOW DO WE ENTER INTO WORSHIP?	
Reflective Process	**Strategies**
What is the pivotal question for you?	
What Bible texts, stories or verses might relate to this issue and question? What Christian Traditions might relate to this issue and question?	Psalm 100; Psalm 118: All (especially verses 21–29). Sing this song of praise: I will enter His gates with thanksgiving in my heart, I will enter His courts with praise, I will say this is the day that the Lord has made I will rejoice for He has made me glad. He has made me glad, He has made me glad, I will rejoice for He has made me glad. He has made me glad, He has made me glad, I will rejoice for He has made me glad. #139 *Scripture in Song* Fifth Edition. Public Domain. What do these texts suggest about worship? How are we encouraged to enter into worship? Consider Marva Dawn's comments: "George Lindbeck has emphasized that Christianity is a language. . .a way of speaking about, and living in response to God. . .We need to be like Shakespeare or Martin Luther, who virtually created modern and German languages, respectively. In a culture that is no longer Christian, we need to create a new bridging language that is both faithful to the biblical vocabulary about God and understandable to the people around us. In evangelism, I think, we should veer a bit closer to the culture; in worship, on the other hand, we bend (and bow) closer to God to hear his language more faithfully (while still retaining accessibility). What we must take extra pains to avoid is translating the splendor of God into commercialized language, since that is the primary idiom of our milieu. The ancient formula "In the Name of the Father and of the Son and of the Holy Spirit," which traditionally began worship services, positively demonstrates this. . .and clearly reminds us that worship is for the Trinity—and that worship is possible only because God has called us there. One congregation . . .underscored this perspective by inviting congregants to meditation before worship with these lines at the top of the worship folder: "We speak to God before the service. God speaks to us in the service. We speak to each other after the service. As you are seated, please bow in silent prayer." —Marva J. Dawn, *A Royal Waste of Time*, 302, 303.

Gathering	
KEY QUESTION: HOW DO WE ENTER INTO WORSHIP?	
Reflective Process	**Strategies**
	Discuss. A.W. Tozer wrote: "Is it not a beautiful thing for a business man to enter his office on Monday morning with an inner call to worship; 'The Lord is in my office—let all the world be silent before Him." —A.W. Tozer in Dan Kimball, *Emerging Worship*, 205. Discuss.
How do you respond?	Where can worship of God take place? How does worship take place in church/in life?
What will you do about that today and tomorrow?	
Related Topics: Sacred space, sacred place; art as a language of worship	

Table 8D: Key Question—What Do We Bring to Worship? 1. Our Culture of Consumerism

Gathering	
KEY QUESTION: WHAT DO WE BRING TO WORSHIP? 1. OUR CULTURE OF CONSUMERISM	
Reflective Process	**Strategies**
Start with your context.	What are you usually doing just before you enter your worship environment? What do you think are the biggest threats to worshipping God in spirit and in truth? (John 4:23,24) Spiritually, what do you bring with you, into worship? How does that help you to worship? What else could you do in the time before worship, to enhance your gift to God in worship? What particular cultural elements do you observe in your worship?
What is the issue for you?	Time management; gathering for worship, entering worship, culture and faith, who is worship for?
What is the pivotal question for you?	

Gathering KEY QUESTION: WHAT DO WE BRING TO WORSHIP? 1. OUR CULTURE OF CONSUMERISM	
Reflective Process	**Strategies**
What Bible texts, stories or verses might relate to this issue and question? What Christian Traditions might relate to this issue and question?	Ezekiel 37:1–14; John 4:23,24: 23But the hour is coming, and is now here, when the true worshippers will worship the Father in spirit and truth, for the Father seeks such as these to worship him. 24God is spirit, and those who worship him must worship in spirit and truth. What does it mean to worship God in spirit and truth? biblical scholar, Walter Brueggemann has said: "The contemporary American church is so largely enculturated to the American ethos of consumerism that it has little power to believe or to act." —Walter Brueggemann, *The Prophetic Imagination*, second edition, 1. How do you react to this statement?
How do you respond?	One response: *A Litany of Lament:* Leader: In mercy, O God, you confront us and expose our sin. **People: May we respond in spirit and in truth,** **confessing our failure,** **reclaiming our hope.** Even as we lift up your name, we offer allegiance to the patterns of this world. **In passive and in active ways,** **we yield our souls to what is false.** In our lust for lifeless objects and our relentless pursuit for more, we cross the line between innocent desire and masked idolatry. **We dismiss our inner protests** **and slowly displace our faith with commercial philosophy** **and promises.** We begin to seek salvation in spiritless things, to worship you for our own gratification, to see ourselves and each other as mere consumers and commodities.

Gathering KEY QUESTION: WHAT DO WE BRING TO WORSHIP? 1. OUR CULTURE OF CONSUMERISM	
Reflective Process	**Strategies**
How do you respond?	**We treat people as expendable products and place ultimate significance in manufactured objects. In our avoidance of human vulnerability, we deny our creation in your image.** We, your people, have swallowed a subtle poison. We have invested ourselves in the religion of our culture, and our substance has wasted away. **We have become a valley of dry bones.** Forgive us, O God, for we have sinned. **In your mercy, raise us from the dead.** Breathe new life into your people. Empower us to be a prophetic community, living the gospel of Jesus. **All: Create in us a consuming passion to love and serve you in Jesus' name, Amen.** Adapted from E. Ann Bell, *Practicing Our Faith* website.
What will you do about that today and tomorrow?	
Related Topics: Idolatry, money,	

Table 8E: Key Question—What Is Hospitality and Why Is It So Important?

Gathering KEY QUESTION: WHAT IS HOSPITALITY AND WHY IS IT SO IMPORTANT?	
Reflective Process	**Strategies**
Start with your context.	What do you think of when you hear the word, hospitality? When have you experienced hospitality? How did you feel about that?
What is the issue for you?	Gathering, welcome and relationship in worship. Who is worship for?
What is the pivotal question for you?	What is hospitality in worship?

Gathering
KEY QUESTION: WHAT IS HOSPITALITY AND WHY IS IT SO IMPORTANT?

Reflective Process	Strategies
What Bible texts, stories or verses might relate to this issue and question? What Christian Traditions might relate to this issue and question?	Matthew 5:1–12 (The sermon on the mount); Matthew 5:38–42 (retaliation); Matthew 5: 43–48 (love your enemy); John 8:1–11. Read "Scribbling in the Sand" in Bob Hartman, *Telling the Bible* 2, 121–22.
How do you respond?	Why are we called to show hospitality? How do we show hospitality?
What will you do about that today and tomorrow?	
Related Topics: Generosity, forgiveness.	

Table 8F: Key Question—What Is Forgiveness?

Confession and Assurance
KEY QUESTION: WHAT IS FORGIVENESS?

Reflective Process	Strategies
Start with your context.	What do you think of when you hear the word, forgive? When have you experienced forgiveness? How did you feel about that? When have you experienced God's forgiveness? What was that like?
What is the issue for you?	Forgiveness, being forgiven, forgiving.
What is the pivotal question for you?	Why are Christians to forgive?

Confession and Assurance KEY QUESTION: WHAT IS FORGIVENESS?	
Reflective Process	**Strategies**
	John 8:1–11. Read "Scribbling in the Sand" in Bob Hartman, *Telling the Bible 2*, 121–22:
	At dawn Jesus appeared again in the temple courts, where all the people gathered around him, and he sat down to teach them. The teachers of the law and the Pharisees brought in a woman caught in adultery. They made her stand before the group and said to Jesus:
'Teacher, this woman was caught in the act of adultery. In the Law Moses commanded us to stone such women. Now what do you say?' They were asking this question as a trap, in order to have a basis for accusing him. But Jesus bent down and started to write on the ground with his finger.
'Forsaken.' That's what he wrote. And much more besides. 'Forsaken. Abandoned. Just a plaything, if you're honest. You told her that you loved her, that you would leave your wife for her, that no one in this world meant more than her. But when push came to shove, when your unfaithfulness was exposed, you ran away and left her to her fate. If you were the man you said you were, the man she thought you were, you would be here now, beside her. But you weren't and you aren't. Because she was just a bit of rough, and this is just a lucky escape.'
What Bible texts, stories or verses might relate to this issue and question? What Christian Traditions might relate to this issue and question?	At the sight of these words, a man, hiding behind a pillar, slipped away from the crowd and out of the temple courts. But the teachers of the law and the Pharisees refused to let up.
When they kept on questioning him, Jesus straightened up and said to them, 'If any of you is without sin, let him be the first to throw a stone at her.' Again he stooped down and wrote on the ground.
And what he wrote was 'Forgotten.' 'Forgotten' and so much more. 'You're old, now, I know—respectable religious leaders. But have you forgotten? Forgotten your past? One of you was a stallion, once—spreading yourself all over town. One of you has a mistress, still. One of you is wealthy only because of a shady deal that ruined the business of another of you! One of you knows and is seeking revenge. One of you spends far too much time with little boys. One of you. . .'
At this, those who heard began to go away one at a time, the older ones first, until only Jesus was left, with the woman still standing there. Jesus straightened up and asked her, 'Woman, where are they? Has no one condemned you?
'No one, sir,' she said.
'Then neither do I condemn you,' Jesus declared. 'Go now and leave your life of sin.'
So the woman went. But before she did, she looked again at the ground. And now, somehow, there was only one word. One word and nothing more.
Not 'Forsaken.'
Not 'Forgotten.'
Just 'Forgiven.'
	Why are Christians called to show forgiveness? How do we do this?

Confession and Assurance KEY QUESTION: WHAT IS FORGIVENESS?	
Reflective Process	**Strategies**
How do you respond?	
What will you do about that today and tomorrow?	
Related Topics: Hospitality; generosity, confession.	

Table 8G: Key Question—What Is Hermeneutics?

Hearing God's Word KEY QUESTION: WHAT IS HERMENEUTICS?	
Reflective Process	**Strategies**
Start with your context.	Needs: Sheets of cellophane of various colors. Take a piece of cellophane and look through it at your surroundings. How do you see when you look through the cellophane? Try combining the sheets for some color mixing. We all have ways of viewing the world that tint (or color) the way we see things. Read the picture book, *Voices in the Park* by Anthony Browne. The same events are truthfully told from four different perspectives or voices, and yet they seem to portray quite different situations. How does our perspective color our telling of a situation? In what ways is our perspective formed? This is our interpretation. Hermeneutics looks at the way a text is interpreted.
What is the issue for you?	Perspectives, hermeneutics.
What is the pivotal question for you?	What hermeneutics do I use? What hermeneutics do others use?

Hearing God's Word KEY QUESTION: WHAT IS HERMENEUTICS?	
Reflective Process	**Strategies**
What Bible texts, stories or verses might relate to this issue and question? What Christian Traditions might relate to this issue and question?	Read: Hermeneutics is the theory of interpreting or giving meaning to texts of various kinds, including literary works, artistic expressions and sacred writings such as the Bible. Hermeneutics is concerned with the development of criteria that assist in gathering interpretive understanding of texts—whatever their particular genre. What are examples of texts that we interpret in everyday life? The term hermeneutics comes from the Greek *hermeneuein*, which means to interpret, or expound. In Greek mythology, Hermes was the messenger of the gods, with the role of explaining to humans what the gods had decided or planned. Hermes was particularly quick and athletic, wearing winged sandals, which meant he was able to travel between the divine and human realms. Show slides with depictions of Hermes. Hermes was the communication link or translator of the heavenly mysteries which were beyond human intelligence. Hermeneutics relates especially to the interpretation of sacred texts, which are viewed by believers as divinely inspired or "the word of God." In hermeneutics we are interested in the relationship between the expression of the ideas, thoughts and emotions that a text portrays, and how a reader interprets or finds meaning in them. In hermeneutics we are faced with the ongoing project of the interpretation of God's self-revelation to humankind. This revelation is mediated to us via various "texts," often named as Scripture, Tradition, Reason, and Experience. Discuss as necessary. Scripture presents the fullest "text" we have of God's self-definition—the person of Jesus Christ. In Christ we are shown who God is and what comprises God's relationship with humanity. The Bible provides us with the primary source of Christian doctrine and the text from which we draw our knowledge of Jesus as God and human being. Other "texts" for hermeneutics could include Christian liturgy, doxology, art and even architecture. The project of hermeneutics is paramount in any study of theology. As Werner Jeanrond surmises: the crucial question is not whether or not (theology) need(s) hermeneutics, but which hermeneutics may be considered to be adequate for a particular kind of theological thinking. —Werner Jeanrond, *Theological Hermeneutics*, 159.

Hearing God's Word KEY QUESTION: WHAT IS HERMENEUTICS?	
Reflective Process	Strategies
	Biblical hermeneutic approaches have attempted to devise contemporary methods of reading the Bible, in response to the question asked of all interpreters: How do we make sense of ancient texts whose worldview we no longer share? In answer to this question, there are a number of exegetical "tools" available to the reader of Scripture. Diachronic methods are concerned with the historical antecedents of the text and the context of the author, and include historical source, redaction and form criticism. Synchronic methods are concerned with the text as it stands as well as interaction between the text and its interpreters, and includes literary, narrative, feminist, reader-response and postmodern techniques. —Anna L. Grant-Henderson, *Handbook for Practical Use of Exegetical Tools*, 6. Discuss. View and discuss the PowerPoint presentation, "What is Hermeneutics?"
How do you respond?	
What will you do about that today and tomorrow?	
Related Topics: Scripture, the arts in worship, worldviews.	

REFLECTION IN LITURGY

The second continuum in the teaching and learning matrix is Reflection in Liturgy. "In Liturgy" indicates that these reflections are designed to take place in the gathered worship of the congregation. These reflections would be suited to short rubric style comments made by the worship leader as liturgical worship progresses. They could also be displayed in other ways, for example in a printed service order, on a screen, or on cards left in the seats. The comments would explain the nature and meaning of various actions performed in liturgical worship. A particular explanation would be given and repeated over a number of worship services, and then another would be introduced and would take its place. This would be initiated not as a formal teaching and learning time, but almost as a brief aside, so that worshippers grow to understand why certain actions occur and that this understanding can be enriching to the practice of worship in the liturgy and in life. This is a form of "in-service" training! One example is a brief explanation of the reason for standing for particular elements of worship. So, for example, the worship leader would simply say that we stand as the offering is brought forward because in standing we are indicating that we give our whole selves to God, and not only money. This would have to be done at the worship leaders' discretion and in accordance with the congregation's knowledge and needs. Any denominational doctrinal or local requirements would have to be considered as well. The worship leader has a vital and complex role to play in raising awareness of and developing the formative aspects in worship.

Worship helps Christians to grasp, embrace and embody Christian ethos together. Some key insights that the Emerging Church has re-discovered for the whole contemporary church are critical theological reflection on what worship is and why it must become more participatory. These are precious gifts that require urgent attention if the church is to be effective in its loving witness to a postmodern world.

Conclusion

THE EMERGING CHURCH'S LEADERS and writers have much they can share with the Western mainline Church. An emphasis on hospitality, participation, shared leadership and the arts can surely benefit the worshipping life of the whole church. There is much more to be learned about how to continue to pass on the Christian faith to present and future generations.

This book has been an attempt to offer practical theological reflection on of Christian education facing a third millennium. A practical theology methodology has been utilized throughout the work, including the process for employing the teaching and learning matrix outlined in the final chapter. It has been important to demonstrate the flow of this process throughout the chapters, leading to the renewed theology and practice. This is, of course, not the end of the process. Renewed and informed practice is opportunity for the birth of new and ongoing reflection. That, however, is a story for future generations!

In review, the process that has been followed here, however, entailed entering into a critical reflection on and analysis of contemporary issues which face the Western Christian church in a postmodern context. Initially, the focus was predominantly philosophical, looking at the transitional state of contemporary Western society. The historical development of Modernity was investigated, from the Enlightenment to the Second World War and beyond, so as to be able to conduct a meaningful analysis of the current context. The development of Western thought during the demise of Modernity was examined, along with the concomitant emergence and evolution of postmodernity.

There was an investigation of some attempts by the church to address Western postmodern issues like rapid social change, a rising interest in spirituality, increasing consumerism, and the development of new technologies. We reflected on how these issues affected the epistemology, education and ecclesiology of the Western Protestant church. The Emerging Church continues as an international response to the challenges and possibilities faced by the church in postmodernity.

Before a determining appraisal was possible, however, a further question became apparent. This became the pivotal question for that part of the discussion and needed to be dealt with before proceeding further. In Western society generally, and sadly in the church as well, there is a substantial loss of understanding of what the church is and what it is for. The theological identity of the church has also been a question for the Emerging Church. Many in the postmodern West would claim to be spiritual but not religious, or that they identify with Jesus but not with the institutional church. For the theological clarity of the rest of the analysis, it was important to enter into a discussion about the nature of the church and its relationship with Jesus Christ. Some examples of Emerging ecclesiastical efforts to address the more general issues of postmodernity were also included.

This led to the introduction and discussion of the nature, origins, themes and theology of the Emerging Church. The Emerging Church represents a genuine attempt to speak the language of the extant postmodern culture. The movement is, in many respects, a reaction against some key aspects of the church of Modernity. This is clear from the common themes observed across the movement. Some of these emphases have developed as direct counters to traits like homogeneity, self-preservation, stinginess, and introspection that Emerging Church proponents had experienced in mainline Christian denominations. The Emerging Church is intentionally outwardly focussed and missional, with a major focus on orthopraxy. There is strong emphasis on community, hospitality, generosity, and participatory worship and spirituality. This is evidenced by the high value placed on the experiential and the arts used in worship, often expressed digitally.

The integral matter of *paradosis*, however, is only beginning to be seriously considered. Even in informal, personal conversations with Emerging Church leaders and authors, it becomes clear that Christian education has not yet been thoroughly explored. This has presented a real gap in the theological and practical development of the Emerging Church. In this absence of postmodern theological reflection on the place of Christian education, the Emerging Church has displayed little essential difference to the rest of the Western church. This vacuum has been as evident in the Emerging Church as it is in the wider Western church. Overall, confusion about the nature of a broadly based Christian education and its place in the church in a changing world needed to be addressed.

Hence, in chapter 4, we entered into a discussion defining Christian education and outlining the emergence of Christian education through the influence of ancient Greek educational philosophy and the Hebrew heritage, to the earliest forms and teaching of the catechumenate. The discourse then moved to viewing these pre-Modern antecedents as possibly providing parallels for postmodern application. One example is monasticism, which has a strong parallel with the New Monasticism of the Emerging Church. Comparison was then drawn with Modernity's solution to the issue of Christian education, the development of the Sunday School movement.

Chapter 5 outlined the current crisis of Christian education, brought about in many ways by Sunday School's separation of Christian education from the Christian worshipping community. The formation of Christian ethos most appropriately occurs within the context of the worshipping Christian community, not separated from its doxological life. Following practical theology methodology, where Christian practice is then placed in dialogue with contemporary experience and understanding, to produce a transformed action or practice, some current approaches, methodologies and desired outcomes of Christian education were summarized. This served to strengthen the argument that especially in a postmodern context, as reinforced by the more participatory focus of the Emerging Church's worship practices, the worship of God in the community of faith is eminently formative.

This formation process was then pursued as postmodern epistemology was applied to the distinctive requirements of Christian knowledge and ways of knowing. From that discussion, it became apparent that in a postmodern, spiritually open climate, a unique opportunity exists to reinterpret Christian education. This new interpretive framework, centered in practical theological process, is designed to operate within the Emerging Church milieu, which does not exclude more inherited ecclesiastical settings. It is established in the heart of the active worshipping community, encompassing experience, enfolded in story and designed to enhance all-of-life worship. The framework that I have developed here interprets Christian education as an ongoing process of action and reflection on teaching, learning and living the Christian story in order to grasp the Christian ethos. Each element of the framework has been described in detail and related to the worshipping community as the teachers, learners and compelling embodiment of the Christian ethos. In other words, the members of the Christian worshipping community are the Christian educators.

This needs to be communicated explicitly to the worshipping community. Modern Western Christian worship has tended to be restricted to Sunday for an hour or so, as a prelude to the Sunday roast. The Emerging Church has raised the importance of aligning orthopraxy with orthodoxy. So, worship in a postmodern context must retain its countercultural qualities and intentionally be extended to include worship in all of life, where it always should have been. Worship needs to be re-imagined, not as a personally preferred commodity but as a gift of the community to God, to glorify God and enjoy God forever, every day.

The necessity of orthopraxy aligning with orthodoxy, together with a view of worship understood as the most appropriate context for Christian formation, posits Christian education as an intersection of doxology and doctrine. Once again, this proposal is intended to address a theological gap in the orthopraxy of the Emerging Church. Reflection on all of this undergirded the resulting invitation to transformed action.

This invitation beckons as a series of Christian learning experiences, in the form of a teaching and learning matrix. In the matrix, common worship elements are reflected upon in terms of worship in liturgy and worship in life. Worship in Liturgy offers short teaching experiences in the context of the community's regular liturgy. These are rubric style and relate to the actions, movements, gestures and rituals of liturgical worship. Worship in Life attempts to make explicit some of the learnings that participating in worship may generate. These discussion based teaching and learning experiences are designed to form an awareness of worship of God in everyday life. They are designed to show people how gathered worship is able to form their lives as Christians and how they, in turn may help in forming and enhancing the Christian faith in others.

The unfinished matrix serves as a tool to help worshipping communities to understand what worship is, as well as their role as educators within it. The matrix is unfinished because it must always be open for local communities to add their particular local flavor and unique learning opportunities for transformed action. This action can be enhanced by the process of ongoing reflection on teaching, learning and living the Christian story in order to grasp Christian ethos.

The Emerging Church embodies a rich source of innovative, challenging conversation about postmodern ecclesiology. In exploring the Emerging Church, we have been offered insights which can go some way towards the construction of a postmodern interpretation for Christian faith formation.

Bibliography

Adams, Daniel J. "Toward a Theological Understanding of Postmodernism." *Cross Currents* 47.4 (1998). http:www.crosscurrents.org/adams.htm.

Adler, Mortimer J. *Adler's Philosophical Dictionary.* New York: Scribner, 1995.

Alfino, Mark. "The First Phenomenologist." *GU Web.* 1997. http://guweb2.gonzaga.edu/faculty/alfino/cfma/courses/420/Lecture_1st_phenologist.htm.

Ammerman, Nancy T., et al., eds. *Studying Congregations: A New Handbook.* Nashville: Abingdon, 1998.

Anderson, E. Byron. *Worship and Christian Identity: Practicing Ourselves.* Collegeville, MN: Liturgical, 2003.

Anderson, Leith. *A Church for the 21st Century.* Minneapolis: Bethany House, 1992.

Anderson, Ray S. *An Emergent Theology for Emerging Churches.* Downers Grove, IL: InterVarsity, 2006.

———. *The Shape of Practical Theology: Empowering Ministry with Theological Praxis.* Downers Grove, IL: InterVarsity, 2001.

———, ed. *Theological Foundations for Ministry: Selected Readings for a Theology of the Church in Ministry.* Grand Rapids: Eerdmans, 1979.

Anthony, Michael Baker, ed. *Evangelical Dictionary of Christian Education.* Grand Rapids: Baker Academic, 2001.

Appignanesi, Richard, et al. *Postmodernism for Beginners.* Cambridge: Icon, 1995.

Augustine. *City of God,* vol. I. *Online Liberty Library.* http://oll.libertyfund.org/title/1153/87975.

———. "Confessions 2:1." In *Creeds, Councils and Controversies: Documents Illustrating the History of the Church AD 337-461,* edited by J. Stevenson. Rev. ed. London: SPCK, 1989.

———. *De Doctrina Christiana,* vol. IV. *Augnet.* http://augnet.org/default.asp?ipageid=398.

———. "On the Catechising of the Uninstructed: In One Book." In C. Marriott, *S. Augustini Opuscula quoedam,* translated by S. D. F. Salmond, chapter 1:1. Oxford: Parker, 1885.

———. *Sermon 17. Augnet.* http://augnet.org/default.asp?ipageid=398.

———. *The Soliloquies of St. Augustine.* Translated by Rose Elizabeth Cleveland. Boston: Little, 1910. http://oll.libertyfund.org/title/1153/87975.

Australian Anglican-Roman Catholic Dialogue, Why the Church?: An Agreed Statement of the Anglican-Roman Catholic Dialogue 2007. Sydney: St Paul's, 2007.

Baker, Jonny. "Emerging, Missional, Mosaic, and Monastic." In *The New Conspirators: Creating the Future One Mustard Seed at a Time*, edited by Tom Sine, 32–55. Downers Grove, IL: InterVarsity, 2008.

———. "Religion Report: Emerging Church." *ABC Radio National*, June 4, 2008. http://www.abc.net.au/rn/religionreport/stories/2008/2264940.htm.

Baker, Jonny, et al. *Alternative Worship: Resources from and for the Emerging Church*. Grand Rapids: Baker, 2004.

Ballard, Paul, and John Pritchard. *Practical Theology in Action: Christian Thinking in the Service of Church and Society*. London: SPCK, 1996.

Ballis, Peter H., and Gary D. Bouma. *Religion in an Age of Change*. Kew, Victoria: Christian Research Association, 1999.

Barna, George. *The Frog in the Kettle: What Christians Need To Know about Life in the 21st Century*. Ventura, CA: Regal, 1990.

Barth, Karl. *Church Dogmatics Volume III/3*. Edinburgh: T. & T. Clark, 1956–75.

———. *Dogmatics in Outline*. London: SCM, 1949.

———. *Protestant Theology in the Nineteenth Century: Its Background and History*. London: SCM, 1972.

Bass, Dorothy C., and Craig Dykstra, eds. *For Life Abundant: Practical Theology, Theological Education and Christian Ministry*. Grand Rapids: Eerdmans, 2008.

Bass, Dorothy C., and Susan R. Briehl, eds. *On Our Way: Christian Practices for Living a Whole Life*. Nashville: Upper Room, 2010.

Bednar, Tim. "We Know More Than Our Pastors: Why Bloggers Are the Vanguard of the Participatory Church." *Mustard Seed Associates*. 2004. http://msainfo.org/articles/the-new-conspirators-the-emerging-church-touring-the-emerging-stream.

Bell, Rob. *Velvet Elvis: Repainting the Christian Faith*. Grand Rapids: Zondervan, 2005.

Benson, Peter L., and Carolyn H. Elkin. *Effective Christian Education: A National Study of Protestant Congregations—Summary Report on Faith, Loyalty, and Congregational Life*. Minneapolis: Search Institute, 1990.

Bessey, Sarah. "Walk Like an Emergent." *The Ooze: Conversation for the Journey*. 2007. http://www.theooze.com/articles/print.cfm?id=1861.

Bettenson, H. *The Early Church Fathers*. London: Oxford University Press, 1956.

Borg, Marcus. *The Heart of Christianity: Rediscovering a Life of Faith*. San Francisco: Harper, 2003.

Bos, Rob. "The Emerging Church." *Theology and Discipleship: A National Agency of The Uniting Church in Australia*, March 18, 2003. http://nat.uca.org.au/TD/emerging.htm.

Bouma, Gary D. *Australian Soul: Religion and Spirituality in the Twenty-first Century*. Cambridge: Cambridge University Press, 2006.

———, ed. *Many Religions, All Australian: Religious Settlement, Identity and Cultural Diversity*. Melbourne: CRA, 1997.

Bourdieu, Pierre. *The Logic of Practice*. Cambridge: Polity, 1992.

———. *Outline of a Theory of Practice*. Translated by Richard Nice. Cambridge: Cambridge University Press, 1977.

Boys, Mary C. *Educating in Faith*. San Francisco: Harper and Row, 1989.

Browne, Anthony. *Voices in the Park*. London: Doubleday, 1998.

Browning, Don S. *A Fundamental Practical Theology: Descriptive and Strategic Proposals*. Minneapolis: Augsburg, 1991.

———, ed. *Practical Theology*. San Francisco: Harper and Row, 1983.

———, ed. *Religious Ethics and Pastoral Care: Theology and Pastoral Care Series,* Philadelphia: Fortress, 1983.

Brueggemann, Walter. *Mandate to Difference: An Invitation to the Contemporary Church.* Louisville: Westminster John Knox, 2007.

———. *The Prophetic Imagination.* 2nd ed. Minneapolis: Fortress, 2001.

Buber, Martin. *I and Thou: A New Translation, with a Prologue and Notes by Walter Kaufmann.* New York: Touchstone, 1970.

Burke, Spencer, and Colleen Pepper. *Making Sense of Church: Eavesdropping on Emerging Conversations about God, Community, and Culture.* Grand Rapids: Zondervan, 2003.

Burns, Stephen, and Anita Monro, eds. *Christian Worship in Australia: Inculturating the Liturgical Tradition.* Strathfield, Sydney: St Paul's, 2009.

Burt, Susan. "Christian Education and the Imaginative Spirit." In *The Emerging Christian Way: Thoughts, Stories and Wisdom for a Faith of Transformation,* edited by Michael Schwartzentruber, 201–18. Kelowna, BC: Copper House, 2006.

Buttrick, G. et al., eds. *The Interpreter's Dictionary of the Bible,* vol. 1. Nashville: Abingdon, 1962.

Calvin, John. *Institutes of the Christian Religion.* Translated by Henry Beveridge. Grand Rapids: Eerdmans, 1989.

Caputo, John D. *On Religion.* London: Routledge, 2001.

Carson, D. A. *Becoming Conversant with the Emerging Church: Understanding a Movement and Its Implications.* Grand Rapids: Zondervan, 2005.

Chadwick, Henry. *The Early Church.* Rev. ed. London: Penguin, 1993.

Chalke, Steve, and Anthony Watkis. *Intelligent Church: A Journey Towards Christ-Centred Community.* Grand Rapids: Zondervan, 2006.

Chamberlain, J. Edward. *If This Is Your Land, Where Are Your Stories?: Finding Common Ground.* Toronto: Alfred A. Knopf Canada, 2003.

Cheyne, Thomas K., and John Sutherland Black, eds. *Encyclopaedia Biblica: A Critical Dictionary of the Literary, Political, and Religious History, The Archaeology, Geography, and Natural History of the Bible.* 4 vol. New York: Macmillan, 1899–1907.

Childress, J. F., and J. Macquarrie, eds. *A New Dictionary of Christian Ethics.* London: SCM, 1986.

Childs, J. M. *Faith, Formation and Decision: Ethics in the Community of Promise.* Minneapolis: Fortress, 1992.

Chrystosom, John. "On Vainglory and the Raising of Children." In *Raising Children According to Saint John Chrysostom,* 39–41. http://www.orthodoxinfo.com/praxis/raising-children-according-to-saint-john-chrysostom.aspx.

Clement of Alexandria. "Stromateis." In *A New Eusebius: Documents Illustrating the History of the Church to AD 337,* edited by J. Stevenson, 1.5.28.1–3. London: SPCK, 1987.

Corney, Peter. *Change and the Church: How To Initiate and Manage Constructive Change in the Local Church.* Sydney: Aquila, 2002.

Cowdell, Scott. *God's Next Big Thing: Discovering the Future Church.* Mulgrave, Australia: John Garratt, 2004.

Cox, Harvey. *The Future of Faith.* New York: HarperOne, 2009.

Cray, Graham. "Introduction." *Fresh Expressions.* http://www.freshexpressions.org.uk/about/introduction.

Cremin, Laurence. *Traditions of American Education*. New York: Basic Books, 1977.

Croft, Stephen. *Transforming Communities: Re-Imagining the Church in the 21st Century*. New York: Orbis, 2005.

Crossan, J. *What Are They Saying about Virtue?* New York: Paulist, 1985.

Cully, Iris V., and Kendig Brubaker Cully, eds. *Harper's Encyclopedia of Religious Education*. San Francisco: Harper and Row, 1990.

Darragh, Neil. "The Practice of Practical Theology: Key Decisions and Abiding Hazards in Doing Practical Theology." *Australian E Journal of Theology* 9 (2007). http://dlibrary.acu.edu.au/research/theology/ejournal/aejt_9/darragh.htm.

Dawn, Marva J. *A Royal Waste of Time: The Splendor of Worshiping God and Being Church for the World*. Grand Rapids: Eerdmans, 1999.

Dearborn, Tim A., and Scott Coil. *Worship at the Next Level: Insight from Contemporary Voices*. Grand Rapids: Baker, 2004.

DeVine, Mark. "The Emerging Church: One Movement—Two Streams." In *Evangelicals Engaging Emergent: A Discussion of the Emergent Church Movement*, edited by William Henard and Adam W. Greenway, 4–47. Nashville: Broadman and Holman, 2009.

DeYoung, Kevin, and Ted Kluck. *Why We're Not Emergent (By Two Guys Who Should Be)*. Chicago: Moody, 2008.

Dowley, Tim. *The Christians*. Oxford: Lion Hudson, 2007.

Driscoll, Mark. *Religion Saves: And Nine Other Misconceptions*. Wheaton, IL: Crossway, 2009.

Dykstra, Craig. *Growing in the Life of Faith: Education and Christian Practices*. Louisville: Westminster John Knox, 2005.

Dykstra, Craig, and Valparaiso Project. "What Are Christian Practices?" *Practicing Our Faith*. http://www.practicingourfaith.org/what-are-christian-practices.

Dyrness, William A. *A Primer on Christian Worship: Where We've Been, Where We Are, Where We Can Go*. Grand Rapids: Eerdmans, 2009.

Edgar, William. "Worship in All of Life." In *Give Praise to God: A Vision for Transforming Worship*, edited by Philip Graham Ryken, et al, 339–57. Phillipsburg, NY: P & R, 2003.

Eldridge, Daryl, ed. *The Teaching Ministry of the Church: Integrating Biblical Truth with Contemporary Application*. Nashville: Broadman and Holman, 1995.

Evans, Craig A., and Stanley E. Porter, eds. *Dictionary of New Testament Background*. Downers Grove, IL: InterVarsity, 2000.

Fee, Gordon D., and Douglas Stuart. *How to Read the Bible for All Its Worth*. Grand Rapids: Zondervan, 2003.

Feldman, L. H. "Josephus: Interpretive Methods and Tendencies." In *Dictionary of New Testament Background*, edited by Craig A. Evans and Stanley E. Porter, 590–96. Downers Grove, IL: InterVarsity, 2000.

Field, Anne. *From Darkness to Light: How One Became a Christian in the Early Church*. Ben Lomond, CA: Conciliar, 1997.

Forrester, Duncan B. *Truthful Action: Explorations in Practical Theology*. Edinburgh: T. & T. Clark, 2000.

Foster, Charles R. *Educating Congregations: The Future of Christian Education*. Nashville: Abingdon, 1994.

Frame, Tom. *Losing My Religion: Unbelief in Australia*. Sydney: University of New South Wales Press, 2009.

Freeman, Andy, and Pete Greig. *Punk Monk: New Monasticism and the Ancient Art of Breathing*. Ventura, CA: Regal, 2007.

Frost, Michael. *Exiles: Living Missionally in a Post-Christian Culture*. Peabody, MA: Hendrickson, 2006.

Frost, Michael, and Alan Hirsch. *The Shaping of Things To Come: Innovation and Mission for the 21st-Century Church*. Peabody, MA: Hendrickson, 2003.

Gangel, Kenneth O. "Towards a Biblical Theology of Marriage and Family." *Journal of Psychology and Theology* 5 (1977) 60.

Gangel, Kenneth O., and Warren S. Benson. *Christian Education: Its History and Philosophy*. Chicago: Moody, 1983.

Gardner, Howard. *Multiple Intelligences: New Horizons*. New York: Basic, 2006.

Ghisi, Marc Luyckx. "WCC Champion of Tolerance and Re-enchantment." Presented at the World Council of Churches Ninth Assembly, Porto Allegro, Brazil, February 18, 2006.

Gibbs, Eddie, and Ryan K. Bolger, eds. *Emerging Churches: Creating Christian Community in Postmodern Cultures*. Grand Rapids: Baker Academic, 2005.

Gibbs, Eddie, and Ian Coffey. *Church Next: Quantum Changes in Christian Ministry*. Downers Grover, IL: InterVarsity, 2001.

Goodliff, Paul. "Our Story." In *Transforming Communities: Re-Imagining the Church for the 21st Century*, edited by Steven Croft, 20–24. New York: Orbis, 2005.

Graham, Elaine. "Practical Theology as Transforming Practice." In *The Blackwell Reader in Pastoral and Practical Theology*, edited by James Woodward and Stephen Pattison, 107. Oxford: Blackwell, 2000.

Graham, Elaine, et al. *Theological Reflection: Methods*. London: SCM, 2005.

Grant-Henderson, Anna. *Handbook for Practical Use of Exegetical Tools: Ways To Help Us Get Deeper Meaning from the Text*. Adelaide, Australia: MediaCom, 2007.

Greer, Robert C. *Mapping Postmodernism: A Survey of Christian Options*. Downers Grove, IL: InterVarsity, 2003.

Gribben, Robert. *A Guide to Uniting in Worship*. Melbourne: Uniting Church, 1990.

Groome, Thomas H. *Christian Religious Education: Sharing Our Story and Vision*. San Francisco: Harper and Row, 1980.

———. *Sharing Faith*. San Francisco: Harper and Row, 1991.

Gropius, William. "Bauhaus Manifesto." In *Modern Architecture: A Critical History*, edited by Kenneth Frampton, 124. New York: Thames and Hudson, 1992.

Gunton, Colin. *Theology Through Preaching*. Edinburgh: T. & T. Clark, 2001.

———. *The Triune Creator: A Historical and Systematic Study*. Grand Rapids: Eerdmans, 1998.

Hall, Douglas John. *Remembered Voices: Reclaiming the Legacy of "Neo-Orthodoxy."* Louisville: Westminster John Knox, 1998.

Harpur, Tom. "New Creeds." In *The Emerging Christian Way: Thoughts, Stories and Wisdom for a Faith of Transformation*, edited by Michael Schwartzentruber, 51–64. Kelowna, BC: Copper House, 2006.

Harris, Maria. *Teaching and Religious Imagination: An Essay in the Theology of Teaching*. San Francisco: Harper Collins, 1991.

Hartman, Bob. *Telling the Bible 2: More Stories and Readings for Sharing Aloud*. Oxford: Lion, 2005.

Hauerwas, Stanley. *Character and the Christian Life*. San Antonio, TX: Trinity University Press, 1975.

———. *A Community of Character*. Notre Dame: University of Notre Dame, 1981.

———. "Discipleship as a Craft, Church as a Disciplined Community." *The Christian Century* (1991) 881–84.

Hegel, G. W. F. *The Phenomenology of Spirit*. Translated by A. V. Miller. Oxford: Clarendon, 1977.

Heidegger, Martin. "The Word of Nietzsche: 'God Is Dead.'" In *The Question Concerning Technology and Other Essays*, translated by W. Lovitt. New York: Harper and Row, 1977.

Henard, William, and Adam W. Greenway, eds. *Evangelicals Engaging Emergent: A Discussion of the Emergent Church Movement*. Nashville: B&H, 2009.

Heylighen, F. "Epistemology." In *Principia Cybernetica Web*, edited by F. Heylighen, et al. Brussels: Principia Cybernetica, 2000. http://cleamc11.vub.ac.be/REFERPCP. html.

Hill, Michael. *The Knowledge of God: Primitive Partial or Profound*. Edited by Ian R. Mears. Sydney: Christian Education, 1989.

Hirsch, Alan, and Darryn Altclass. *The Forgotten Ways Handbook: A Practical Guide for Developing Missional Churches*. Grand Rapids: Brazos, 2009.

Hodgson, Peter C. *God's Wisdom: Toward a Theology of Education*. Louisville: Westminster John Knox, 1999.

Howell, James C. "Fellow Students: Theological Formation in the Parish." *Christian Century* 124.4 (2007) 32–35.

Hughes, Philip. "Five Ways People Approach Christian Education." *Journal of Christian Education* 45.1 (2002) 35–43.

———. *Making Disciples: A Survey of Christian Education in UCA Congregations*. Melbourne: Uniting Education, 2000.

———. "A Maze or a System? Changes in the Worldview of Australian People." *Christian Research Association Research Paper* 2 (1994).

Hull, John M. "Only One Way to Walk with God." In *Evaluating Fresh Expressions: Explorations in Emerging Church*, edited by Louise Nelstrop and Martyn Percy, 106–7. Norwich: Canterbury, 2008.

———. "RE, Nature of." In *A Dictionary of Religious Education*, edited by John M. Sutcliffe, 284–86. London: SCM, 1984.

Illich, Ivan. *Deschooling Society*. London: University of London Press, 1970.

Inbody, Tyron. "Postmodernism: Intellectual Velcro Dragged Across Culture?" *Theology Today* 57.4 (1995) 524.

Jasper, David. *A Short Introduction to Hermeneutics*. Louisville: Westminster John Knox, 2004.

Jeanrond, Werner G. *Theological Hermeneutics: Development and Significance*. New York: Crossroad, 1991.

Johnson, Susanne. *Christian Spiritual Formation in the Church and Classroom*. Nashville: Abingdon, 1989.

Joint Commission on Church Union of The Congregational Union of Australia and New Zealand, The Methodist Church of Australasia, The Presbyterian Church of Australia. *The Basis of Union*. Melbourne: Aldersgate, 1971.

Jones, Tony. *Postmodern Youth Ministry: Exploring Cultural Shift, Cultivating Authentic Community, Creating Holistic Connections*. Grand Rapids: Zondervan, 2001.

———. *The New Christians: Dispatches from the Emergent Frontier*. San Francisco: Jossey–Bass, 2008.

Josephus, Flavius, Against Apian 2:6 quoted in Emil Schurer, *A History of the Jewish People in the Time of Jesus Christ: Die Schriftgelehrsamkeit Schule und Synagogue*, 4th–5th edition, Volume 2. Leipzig, 1907.

Kant, Immanuel. *An Answer to the Question: "What is Enlightenment?"* Translated by H. B. Nisbet. London: Penguin, 2009.

Kennedy, Philip. *A Modern Introduction to Theology: New Questions for Old Beliefs.* London: I.B. Tauris, 2006.

Kennet Millar, Craig. *Next Church Now: Creating New Faith Communities.* Nashville: Discipleship Resources, 2000.

———. *Postmoderns: The Beliefs, Hopes and Fears of Young Americans (1965–1981).* Nashville: Discipleship Resources, 1996.

Killen, Patricia O'Connell and John de Beer. *The Art of Theological Reflection.* New York: Crossroad, 1994.

Kimball, Dan. *The Emerging Church: Vintage Christianity for New Generations.* Grand Rapids: Zondervan, 2003.

———. *Emerging Worship: Creating Worship Gatherings for New Generations.* Grand Rapids: Zondervan, 2004.

———. *They Like Jesus but Not the Church: Insights from Emerging Generations.* Grand Rapids: Zondervan, 2007.

Kirby, Peter. "Galen." *Early Christian Writings.* 2006. http://www.earlychristianwritings.com/galen.html.

Knight, George A. *Christ the Center.* Grand Rapids: Eerdmans, 1999.

Knoff, G. E. *The World Sunday School Movement.* New York: Seabury, 1979.

Komonchak, Joseph, et al., eds. *The New Dictionary of Theology.* Dublin: Gill and Macmillan, 1990.

Labberton, Mark. *The Dangerous Act of Worship: Living God's Call to Justice.* Downers Grove, IL: InterVarsity, 2009.

LaCugna, Catherine Mowry. *God for Us: The Trinity and Christian Life.* San Francisco: Harper Collins, 1991.

LaCugna, Catherine Mowry, and Kilian McDonnell. "Returning from 'The Far Country': Theses for a Contemporary Trinitarian Theology." *Scottish Journal of Theology* 41.2 (1988) 191–215.

Lane, Tony. *The Lion Concise Book of Christian Thought.* Sydney: Lion and Albatross, 1984.

Lathrop, Gordon. *Holy Things: A Liturgical Theology.* Minneapolis, Fortress, 1993.

Lehmann, Daniel J. "Whatever Happened to Sunday School?" *Christian Century* 106.13 (1989) 404–5.

Lindbeck, George A. *The Nature of Doctrine: Religion and Theology in a Postliberal Age.* Philadelphia: Westminster, 1984.

———. "Scripture, Consensus, and Community." In *Biblical Interpretation in Crisis,* edited by R. Neuhaus, 74–101. Grand Rapids: Eerdmans, 1989.

Lings, George. "What is 'Emerging Church'?" *EmergingChurch.Info.* 2003. http://emergingchurch.info/reflection/georgelings/index.htm.

Long, Jimmy. *Emerging Hope: A Strategy for Reaching Postmodern Generations.* 2nd ed. Downers Grove, IL: InterVarsity, 2004.

Lundin, Roger, et al. *The Responsibility of Hermeneutics.* Grand Rapids: Eerdmans, 1985.

Lyotard, Jean-François. "It's Not About the Old Ways—It's About the Much Older Ways." In *Reclaiming God's Original Intent for the Church,* edited by Wes Roberts and Glenn Marshall, 17–30. Colorado Springs: NavPress, 2004.

———. *The Postmodern Condition: A Report on Knowledge.* Translated by Geoff Bennington and Brian Massumi. Minneapolis: University of Minnesota Press, 1979.

MacIntyre, Alasdair. *After Virtue: A Study in Moral Theory.* Notre Dame: University of Notre Dame Press, 1981.

Mackay, Hugh. *Advance Australia . . . Where? How We've Changed, Why We've Changed, and What Will Happen Next?* Sydney: Hachette Australia, 2007.

———. *Re-Inventing Australia.* Sydney: Angus and Robertson, 1993.

Maddock, S., and G. Maddock. "An Ever-Renewed Adventure of Faith: Notes from a Community." In *An Emergent Manifesto of Hope,* edited by Doug Pagitt and Tony Jones, 80–88. Grand Rapids: Baker, 2007.

Maeda, John. *Art is Everything.* 2006. https://www.ted.com/talks/john_maeda_how_art_technology_and_design_inform_creative_leaders?language=en.

Manson, T. W. *The Teaching of Jesus: Studies in Its Form and Content.* London: Cambridge University Press, 1967.

Marriott, C. S. *Augustini Opuscula quoedam.* Translated by S. D. F. Salmond. Oxford: Parker, 1885.

Martin, J. E. Harvey. "Catechumenate." In *Evangelical Dictionary of Christian Education,* edited by Michael Baker Anthony, 113–14. Grand Rapids: Baker, 2001.

Martin, Ralph P., and Peter H. Davids, eds. *Dictionary of the Later New Testament and Its Developments.* Downers Grove, IL: InterVarsity, 1997.

Martyr, Justin. In *After the Gospels: Readings from Great Christians of the Early Church,* edited by David Winter, 73. Oxford: BRF, 2001.

———. In *A New Eusebius: Documents Illustrating the History of the Church to AD 337,* edited by J. Stevenson, 61–62. London: SPCK, 1987.

McDannell, Colleen. *Religions of the United States in Practice,* Volume One. Princeton: Princeton University Press, 2001.

McGrath, Alister E., ed. *The Christian Theology Reader.* Oxford: Blackwell, 1995.

———. *The Future of Christianity.* Oxford: Blackwell, 2002.

———. *The Genesis of Doctrine: A Study in the Foundation of Doctrinal Criticism.* Grand Rapids: Eerdmans, 1990.

McKnight, Scot. "Five Streams of the Emerging Church." *Christianity Today,* February, 2007. http://www.christianitytoday.com/ct/2007february/11.35.html.

McLaren, Brian. *The Church on the Other Side: Doing Ministry in the Postmodern Matrix.* Grand Rapids: Zondervan, 1998.

———. *Everything Must Change.* Nashville: Thomas Nelson, 2007.

———. *Finding Our Way Again: The Return of the Ancient Practices.* Nashville: Thomas Nelson, 2008.

———. *A Generous Orthodoxy: Why I Am a Missional, Evangelical, Post/Protestant, Liberal/Conservative, Mystical/Poetic, Biblical, Charismatic/Contemplative, Fundamentalist/Calvinist, Anabaptist/Anglican, Methodist, Catholic, Green, Incarnational, Depressed-yet-hopeful, Emergent, Unfinished Christian.* Grand Rapids: Zondervan, 2004.

———. *A New Kind of Christianity: Ten Questions that Are Transforming the Faith.* London: Hodder and Stoughton, 2010.

Mead, Loren B. *The Once and Future Church: Reinventing the Congregation for a New Mission Frontier.* New York: Alban, 1994.

Mears, Ian R., ed. *The Knowledge of God: Primitive Partial or Profound.* Sydney: Christian Education, 1989.

Mobsby, Ian J. *Emerging and Fresh Expressions of Church: How Are They Authentically Church and Anglican?* London: Moot Community, 2008.

Mommsen, Peter. *Homage to a Broken Man.* Farmlands, PA: Plough, 2007.

Moore, Lucy. *Messy Church.* Abingdon: Bible Reading Fellowship, 2006.

Moynagh, Michael. *EmergingChurch.intro: Fresh Expressions of Church, Examples That Work, The Big Picture, What You Can Do.* Oxford: Monarch, 2005.

Mudge, Lewis and James N. Poling, eds. *Formation and Reflection: The Promise of Practical Theology.* Philadelphia: Fortress, 1987.

Murphy, Debra Dean. *Teaching That Transforms: Worship as the Heart of Christian Education.* Grand Rapids: Brazos, 2004.

Nelson, C. Ellis, ed. *How Faith Matures.* Louisville: Westminster John Knox, 1989.

Neuhaus, R., ed. *Biblical Interpretation in Crisis.* Grand Rapids: Eerdmans, 1989.

Newbigin, Lesslie. *The Gospel in a Pluralist Society.* Grand Rapids: Eerdmans, 1989.

Niebuhr, H. Richard. *Christ and Culture.* New York: Harper and Row, 1951.

Nietzsche, Friedrich. *Twilight of the Idols and the Anti-Christ* (1889). Translated by R. J. Hollingdale. London: Penguin, 1990.

"Now Ready for Prime Time Players: Reinventing Christianity for Our Day." *Let Us Reason Ministries.* 2008. http://www.letusreason.org/current73.htm.

Oden, Thomas C. *Turning around the Mainline: How Renewal Movements Are Changing the Church.* Grand Rapids: Baker, 2006.

Old, H. *Themes and Variations for a Christian Doxology: Some Thoughts on the Theology of Worship.* Grand Rapids: Eerdmans, 1992.

Olsen, Roger E. and Adam C. English. *Pocket History of Theology.* Downers Grove, IL: InterVarsity, 2005.

Osmer, Richard R. *A Teachable Spirit: Recovering the Teaching Office in the Church.* Louisville: Westminster John Knox, 1990.

———. "A New Clue for Religious Education?" In *Forging a Better Religious Education in the Third Millennium,* edited by James M. Lee, 188. Birmingham, AL: Religious Education, 2000.

Pagitt, Doug. *Church Re-imagined: The Spiritual Formation of People in Communities of Faith.* Grand Rapids: Zondervan, 2005.

Pagitt, Doug, and Tony Jones, eds. *An Emergent Manifesto of Hope.* Grand Rapids: Baker, 2007.

Paine, Thomas. *The Age of Reason* (Luxembourg, 1794). *World Union of Deists.* http://www.deism.com/theageofreason.htm.

Palmer, Parker J. *To Know as We Are Known: Education as a Spiritual Journey.* San Francisco: Harper, 1993.

Parrett, Gary A. and S. Steven Kang. *Teaching the Faith, Forming the Faithful: A Biblical Vision for Education in the Church.* Downers Grove, IL: InterVarsity, 2009.

Pazmiño, Robert W. *Foundational Issues in Christian Education: An Introduction in Evangelical Perspective.* Grand Rapids: Baker, 1988.

———. *God Our Teacher: Theological Basics in Christian Education.* Grand Rapids: Baker Academic, 2001.

Pence, Gregory. *A Dictionary of Common Philosophical Terms.* New York: McGraw-Hill, 2000.

Peterson, Eugene H. *The Message: The New Testament in Contemporary Language,* Colorado Springs: Navpress, 1994.

Phenix, P. H. *Philosophy of Education.* New York: Holt, Rinehart and Winston, 1961.

Plato. *The Republic.* Translated by Jowett. http://plato.evansville.edu/texts/Jowett/republic17.htm.

Polanyi, Michael. *Personal Knowledge: Towards a Post-Critical Philosophy.* London: Routledge, 1958.

Poling, James N., and Donald Miller. *Foundations for a Practical Theology of Ministry.* Nashville: Abingdon, 1985.

Porter, Muriel. *The New Puritanism: The Rise of Fundamentalism in the Anglican Church.* Melbourne: Melbourne University Press, 2006.

"Postmodernism." *Economic Expert.* http://www.economicsexpert.com/a/Postmodernism.htm.

Power, Edward J. *Evolution of Educational Doctrine: Major Theorists of the Western World.* New York: Appleton-Century-Crofts Educational Division, 1969.

Raeper, W., and L. Smith. *A Beginner's Guide to Ideas: Religion and Theology Past and Present.* Oxford: Lion, 1991.

Rauche, G. A. *A Student's Key to Ancient Greek Thought.* Pretoria: Sigma, 1994.

Reno, R. R. *In the Ruins of the Church: Sustaining Faith in an Age of Diminished Christianity.* Grand Rapids: Brazos, 2002.

Richardson, Alan, ed. *A Dictionary of Christian Theology.* London: SCM, 1969.

Riddell, Michael, et al. "New Approaches to Worship." In *Worship at the Next Level; Insight From Contemporary Voices,* edited by Tim A. Dearborn and Scott Coil, 136–46. Grand Rapids: Baker, 2004.

———. *The Prodigal Project.* London: SPCK, 2000.

Rieger, Joerg. *God and the Excluded: Visions and Blindspots in Contemporary Theology.* Minneapolis: Fortress, 2001.

Ritzer, George. *The McDonaldization of Society: An Investigation into the Changing Character of Contemporary Social Life.* Newbury Park, CA: Pine Forge, 1993.

Roberts, Paul. *Alternative Worship in the Church of England.* Cambridge: Grove, 1999.

Robinson, D., and J. Groves. *Introducing Philosophy.* Cambridge: Icon, 1999.

Rodrigues, Chris, and Chris Garratt. *Introducing Modernism.* Sydney: Allen and Unwin, 2004.

Roehlkepartain, Eugene C. *The Teaching Church: Moving Christian Education to Center Stage.* Nashville: Abingdon, 1993.

Rogers, M. Scott. "Coming out of the Cocoon." *Next-Wave ezine: Church and Culture.* 2008. http://www.the-next-wave-ezine.info/bin/_print.cfm?id=40and=ARTICLES_CHURCH.

Rowse, Darren. "What Is the Emerging Church?" *Living Room.* 2003. http://www.livingroom.org.au/blog/archives/what_is_the_emerging_church.php.

Russinger, Greg, and Alex Field, eds. *Practitioners: Voices within the Emerging Church.* Ventura, CA: Regal, 2005.

Rutba House. *Schools for Conversion: 12 Marks of a New Monasticism.* Eugene, OR: Cascade, 2005.

Sajjadi, Seyed Mahdi. "Religious Education and Information Technology: Challenges and Problems." *Teaching Theology and Religion* 11.4 (2008) 185.

Saliers, Don E. *Worship as Theology.* Nashville: Abingdon, 1994.

Schaff, Philip, and Henry Wace. *A Select Library of Nicene and Post Nicene Fathers of the Christian Church.* Grand Rapids: Eerdmans, 1956.

Schleiermacher, Friedrich. *The Christian Faith.* Edited by H. R. Mackintosh and J. S. Stewart. Philadelphia: Fortress, 1928.

Schlink, Edmund. *The Coming Christ and the Coming Church.* Edinburgh: Oliver & Boyd, 1967.

Schurer, Emil. *A History of the Jewish People in the Time of Jesus Christ: Die Schriftgelehrsamkeit Schule und Synagogue.* 4th–5th ed. Volume 2. Peabody, MA: Hendrickson, 1994.

Schwartzentruber, Michael, ed. *The Emerging Christian Way: Thoughts, Stories and Wisdom for a Faith of Transformation.* Kelowna, BC: Copper House, 2006.

Scorer, Tim. "Experience: The Heart of Transformation." In *The Emerging Christian Way: Thoughts, Stories, and Wisdom for a Faith of Transformation,* edited by Michael Schwartzentruber, 33–47. Kelowna, BC: Copper House, 2006.

Seymour, Jack L., ed. *Mapping Christian Education: Approaches to Congregational Learning.* Nashville: Abingdon, 1997.

Seymour, Jack L., and Donald E. Miller, eds. *Contemporary Approaches to Christian Education.* Nashville: Abingdon, 1982.

———, eds. *Theological Approaches to Christian Education.* Nashville: Abingdon, 1990.

Simpson, D. P., ed. *Cassell's Latin and English Dictionary.* Hoboken, NJ: Wiley, 2002.

Sine, Tom. "Brave New Worldview." *Leadership Journal* 21.4 (2000) 53.

———, ed. *The New Conspirators: Creating the Future One Mustard Seed at a Time.* Downers Grove, IL: InterVarsity, 2008.

"Slight Decrease Seen in Sunday School Classes." *Christian Century* 122.16 (2005) 15.

Smith, Adrian B. *Tomorrow's Faith: A New Framework of Christian Belief.* Ropley, UK: John Hunt, 2005.

Stafford, Tim. "This Little Light of Mine: Will Sunday School Survive the 'Me Generation'?" *Christianity Today* 34.14 (1990) 29–32.

Stassen, Glen Harold, et al. *Authentic Transformation: A New Vision of Christ and Culture.* Nashville: Abingdon, 1996.

Staub, Dick. *The Culturally Savvy Christian: A Manifesto for Deepening Faith and Enriching Popular Culture in an Age of Christianity-Lite.* San Francisco: John Wiley and Sons, 2007.

Stevenson, J., ed. *Creeds, Councils and Controversies: Documents Illustrating the History of the Church AD 337–461.* Rev. ed. London: SPCK, 1989.

———. *A New Eusebius: Documents Illustrating the History of the Church to AD 337.* Rev. ed. London: SPCK, 1993.

Stokes, Philip. *Philosophy: 100 Essential Thinkers.* London: Arcturus, 2002.

Strauss, William, and Neil Howe. *Generations: The History of America's Future, 1584–2069.* New York: Quill, 1991.

Sutcliffe, J., ed. *A Dictionary of Religious Education.* London: SCM, 1984.

Swanson, Karen. "Move Over Baby Boomers." In *Next-Wave Church and Culture E-Zine.* www.the-next-wave-ezine.info/bin/_print.cfm?id=40&ref=ARTICLES_CULTURE.

Sweet, Leonard, ed. *The Church of the Perfect Storm.* Nashville: Abingdon, 2008.

Sweet, Leonard, et al. *A is for Abductive: The Language of the Emerging Church.* Grand Rapids: Zondervan, 2003.

Swinton, John, and Harriet Mowat. *Practical Theology: Descriptive and Qualitative Research*. London: SCM, 2006.

Taylor, Steve. *The Out of Bounds Church? Learning to Create a Community of Faith in a Culture of Change*. Grand Rapids: Zondervan, 2005.

Thiselton, Anthony C. *New Horizons in Hermeneutics*. Grand Rapids: Zondervan, 1992.

Tickle, Phyllis. *The Great Emergence: How Christianity Is Changing and Why*. Grand Rapids: Baker, 2008.

Torrance, James B. *Worship, Community and the Triune God of Grace*. Carlisle: Paternoster Press, 1996.

Torrance, Thomas. "Foundation of the Church." In *Theological Foundations for Ministry*, edited by Ray S. Anderson, 201. Edinburgh: T. & T. Clark, 1979.

Tozer, A. W. In Dan Kimball, *Emerging Worship: Creating Worship Gatherings for New Generations*. Grand Rapids: Zondervan, 2004.

Tracy, David. *The Analogical Imagination*. New York: Crossroad, 1981.

———. *Blessed Rage for Order: The New Pluralism in Theology*. Minneapolis: Seabury, 1975.

———. "Foundations of Practical Theology." In *Practical Theology*, edited by Don S. Browning, 61–82. San Francisco: Harper and Row, 1983.

Treier, Daniel J. *Virtue and the Voice of God: Toward Theology as Wisdom*. Grand Rapids: Eerdmans, 2006.

Turnbull, Neil. *Get a Grip on Philosophy*. London: Weidenfeld and Nicolson, 1999.

Turner, Paul. "The Role of the Catechist: Augustine's Catechizing Beginners." *Living Light* 39.1 (2002) 17.

Veling, Terry A., ed. *Practical Theology: 'On Earth as It Is in Heaven.'* New York: Orbis, 2005.

Vesey, G., and P. Foulkes, eds. *Collins Dictionary of Philosophy*. London: Collins, 1990.

Viola, Frank, and George Barna. *Pagan Christianity? Exploring the Roots of Our Christian Practices*. Carol Stream, IL: Barna, 2008.

Volf, Miroslav, and Dorothy C. Bass, eds. *Practicing Theology: Beliefs and Practices in Christian Life*. Grand Rapids: Eerdmans, 2002.

Wainwright, Geoffrey. *Doxology: The Praise of God in Worship, Doctrine and Life, A Systematic Theology*. New York: Oxford University Press, 1980.

Walsh, Chad, et al. *The Apostles' Creed: An Introduction*. Cincinnati, OH: Forward Movement, 1966.

Walzer, Richard R. *Galen on Jews and Christians*. Oxford: Oxford University Press, 1949.

Ward, Graham. "Barth, Modernity, and Postmodernity." In *The Cambridge Companion to Karl Barth*, edited by John Webster, 274–95. Cambridge: Cambridge University Press, 2000.

Ward, Karen. "What Is the Emerging Church?" In *Emerging Churches: Creating Christian Community in Postmodern Cultures*, edited by Eddie Gibbs and Ryan K. Bolger, 27. Grand Rapids: Baker Academic, 2005.

———. "Welcoming the Stranger." In *The New Christians: Dispatches from the Emergent Frontier*, edited by Tony Jones, 120. San Francisco: Jossey-Bass, 2008.

Watson, D. F. "Education: Jewish and Greco-Roman." In *Dictionary of New Testament Background*, edited by Craig A. Evans and Stanley E. Porter, 308–13. Downers Grove, IL: InterVarsity, 2000.

Weate, J., ed. *A Young Person's Guide to Philosophy: I Think Therefore I Am.* London: Dorling Kindersley, 1998.

Webber, Robert E. *Ancient-Future Faith: Rethinking Evangelicalism for a Postmodern World.* Grand Rapids: Baker, 1999.

———, ed. *Listening to the Beliefs of Emerging Churches: Five Perspectives.* Grand Rapids: Zondervan, 2007.

Webster, John, and George P. Schner, eds. *Theology after Liberalism: A Reader.* Oxford: Blackwell, 2000.

"What Are Christian Practices?" *Practicing Our Faith.* http://www.practicingourfaith. org/what-are-christian-practices.

Whitehead, James D., and Evelyn Eaton Whitehead. *Method in Ministry: Theological Reflection and Christian Ministry.* New York: Seabury, 1983.

Wilds, Elmer H., and Kenneth V. Lottich. *A History of Educational Thought.* Columbus, OH: Merrill, 1960.

Willimon, William H. *Proclamation and Theology.* Nashville: Abingdon, 2005.

Wilson, Jonathan R. *Living Faithfully in a Fragmented World: Lessons for the Church from MacIntyre's 'After Virtue.'* Harrisburg, PA: Trinity, 1998.

Wilson, Ken. *Jesus Brand Spirituality: He Wants His Religion Back.* Nashville: Thomas Nelson, 2008.

Wilson-Hartgrove, Jonathan. *New Monasticism: What It Has To Say to Today's Church.* Grand Rapids: Brazos, 2008.

Wood, Donald. "The Place of Theology in Theological Hermeneutics." *International Journal of Systematic Theology* 4.2 (2002) 156–71.

Woodward, James, and Stephen Pattison, eds. *The Blackwell Reader in Pastoral and Practical Theology.* Oxford: Blackwell, 2000.

Wright, Tim. *The Prodigal Hugging Church: A Scandalous Approach to Mission for the 21st Century.* Minneapolis: Joy Resources, 2001.

Wuthnow, Robert. *Sharing the Journey: Support Groups and America's New Quest for Community.* New York: Free, 1994.

Wyckoff, D. C. "Education: Theories of." In *Harper's Encyclopedia of Religious Education,* edited by Iris V. Cully and K. B. Cully, 207–14. San Francisco: Harper and Row, 1990.

Yaconelli, M., ed. *Stories of Emergence: Moving from Absolute to Authentic.* Grand Rapids: Zondervan, 2003.

Yoder, John Howard. "How H. Richard Niebuhr Reasoned: A Critique of Christ and Culture." In *Authentic Transformation: A New Vision of Christ and Culture,* edited by Glen H. Stassen, et al., 41–42. Nashville: Abingdon, 1996.

Zdziarski, Jonathan A., trans. *The Didache: The Lord's Teaching through the Twelve Apostles to the Nations.* 2006. http://www.zdziarski.com/papers/Didache-Zdziarski.pdf.

Zizioulas, John D. *Being As Communion: Studies in Personhood and the Church.* New York: St Vladimir's Seminary, 1985.

Zimmerman, Jens. *Recovering Theological Hermeneutics: An Incarnational-Trinitarian Theory of Interpretation.* Grand Rapids: Baker Academic, 2004.

Index

action, and reflection, xii, 126, 127–31
analogy, 131, 136, 145, 166–69
apologists, 81–86
apophasis, 166, 168–69
Aristotle, 71–72, 113, 114, 115, 116,
  167
Augustine, 80–81, 84–85, 161,
  166–67, 184

Baker, Jonny, 32, 55, 57, 59
baptism, 20, 79–80, 81, 106, 149, 150,
  185–86
Barth, Karl, 38, 136
Bell, Rob, 49
Borg, Marcus, 21, 23, 25–26, 30–31,
  35, 46
Bouma, Gary, 14
Browning, Don S., 1, 2, 3–4, 5, 43

Calvin, Jean, 20, 111, 152
catechumenate, 69, 78–86, 91, 92
Chalke, Steve, 47–48, 53–54, 172
Christian
  education, definitions, ix, xi, 67–68
  ethos, 126–27, 133–34, 135, 137,
    141–43
  formation, ix, xii, 54, 63–64, 90,
    96–99, 100, 103, 104–5, 107–9,
    112, 115, 117, 120, 124, 126,
    132–35, 141–43, 169
  story, 126–27, 129, 132–34, 139,
    140, 141, 143, 153, 154, 159, 161,
    164, 182–84
  church, definition, 16–22
    see Fresh Expressions of Church

see also Uniting Church in
  Australia
creed, 145, 147–48, 149–53, 156,
  160–61, 183, 184

Darragh, Neil, 1, 128–31
Didache, 78–80
doctrine, 61–62, 75, 80, 82, 84–86,
  92, 93, 109, 113, 114, 132, 138,
  141–53, 154, 156, 157, 160, 164,
  165, 169–70, 183, 199
dogma, 85, 113–14, 135–36, 145,
  146–53
doxology, xi, 114, 115–16, 136, 141,
  149, 153–68, 199

Enlightenment, 6–9, 11, 12, 20, 35, 38
epistemology, 9, 43, 84–85, 112–24
Eucharist, 20, 21, 52–53, 65, 78, 106,
  155, 172, 177, 185–86
evangelism, 49, 65, 99, 102–4, 105,
  192

foundationalism, 7, 11
Fresh Expressions of Church, 26–28,
  68
fundamentalism, 15, 35, 37, 44–46

Groome, Thomas H., 85, 112, 139

habitus, 120–21, 128, 131
Harris, Maria, 64, 115, 128–31
Hauerwas, Stanley, 108–9, 143, 153
Hegel, Georg, 117
Heidegger, Martin, 12

hermeneutical spiral, 1, 5
Holy Communion, see Eucharist
hospitality, 52–53, 59, 89, 176, 179,
    185, 195–96

Jones, Tony, 11–12, 29, 33, 59, 60
Justin Martyr, 19, 82

Kant, Immanuel, 6–7, 9, 11
knowledge, 9, 11, 52, 56, 64–65, 67,
    68, 70, 71, 78, 80, 84, 85, 104,
    109, 110–24, 134, 135, 139, 141,
    143–44, 146, 152–54, 156, 157,
    164, 166, 168, 176, 189, 199

Lyotard, Jean-François, 8–9, 10, 21

McLaren, Brian, 33, 47–48, 49–50,
    58–59, 60, 70–71, 139–40
Murphy, Debra Dean, 55, 64–65, 149
mutual critical correlation, xii, 1, 2,
    128

Neo-Orthodoxy, 38, 41
New Monasticism, 56, 87–90, 174
Nietzsche, Friedrich, 12

orthopraxy, 46, 48–52, 62, 65, 131–32,
    141, 143, 156, 172–73, 186, 204,
    205–6

paradosis, 63, 68, 204
phronesis, 16
Plato, 69–75, 76, 82, 84, 113
poiesis, 113, 115–16, 145, 154, 168
Polanyi, Michael, 118–24, 144,
    153–54
Porter, Muriel, 44–45
Positivism, 7, 11, 118
Post-Impressionism, 8–9

postmodernism, ix, 6, 8, 10–13, 30,
    32–33, 42, 44, 63
practice, 1–5, 21, 31, 34, 46–57, 60,
    61, 65, 68–69, 75, 78, 80–81, 90,
    94, 96–99, 108–10, 116, 119, 121,
    126, 134–35, 140, 142–43, 145,
    149, 154, 155, 171, 176, 177–201,
    203, 205
praxis, 5, 115, 126, 135–37, 140, 171

reflection, theological, 1–5, 39, 52, 60,
    89–90, 126, 127–31, 173, 184,
    201, 204
Religious Education, 68, 87, 101–2
Roehlkepartain, Eugene C., 95–99

Schleiermacher, Friedrich, 36–37
Sine, Tom, 32–33, 35, 43
story, 12, 21, 35, 42, 63–64, 115,
    133–34
Sunday School, 90–94, 97, 109, 138,
    156–57

Taylor, Steve, x, 55–56, 57,
theology, practical, x–xi, 1–5, 16, 17,
    22, 61, 124, 127–31, 205
Tickle, Phyllis, 31–32, 35
traditio, traditium, 67, 68, 69, 85, 86,
    90–91, 109–10, 117, 119, 121,
    140, 141, 153
transmodernity, ix, 22–23

Uniting Church in Australia, xi,
    22–25, 58, 97–99

Wainwright, Geoffrey, 109, 136, 147,
    148, 149, 167–68
Wesley, John, 164–65
worshipping community, as Christian
    educators, 105–10, 135–37, 149,
    169–70, 171–74, 176, 177